This book is dedicated to my dear husband Jacob and to our future daughter Haven (arriving soon after this book goes off to print). First off, thank you Jacob for inviting me to move to the country with you. Thank you for keeping me fed, our business going, the grass mowed and the garden weeded while I wrote this book. Thank you Haven for giving me the courage to take this project on and reminding me (with your kicking) to take breaks and take good care of myself. I can't wait to meet you. I love you both so much.

PAGE STREET
PUBLISHING CO.

First published in 2017 by
Page Street Publishing Co.
27 Congress Street, Suite 105
Salem, MA 01970
www.pagestreetpublishing.com

Distributed by Macmillan, sales in Canada by The Canadian Manda Group.

20   19   18   17   1   2   3   4

ISBN-13: 9781624143915
ISBN-10: 1624143911

Library of Congress Control Number: 2016916446

Cover and book design by Page Street Publishing Co.
Photography by Alissa Hessler

Printed and bound in China

As a member of 1% for the Planet, Page Street Publishing protects our planet by donating to nonprofits like The Trustees, which focuses on local land conservation. Learn more at onepercentfortheplanet.org.

DITCH THE CITY
and GO COUNTRY

How to Master
the Art of Rural Life From
a Former City Dweller

ALISSA HESSLER
Creator of Urban Exodus

PAGE STREET
PUBLISHING CO.

MEETING YOUR MATES

Making friends and dating / 117

EMBRACING THE SEASONS

Finding your rhythm in winter, spring, summer and fall / 135

STAYING ALIVE

Preparing for natural disasters, animal attacks and the unexpected / 161

MAKING THAT MONEY

Earning a living in the country / 177

THE LONG GAME

Enjoying the good life / 193

INTRODUCTION

Welcome! This is the book I wish I had five years ago, in the winter of 2012, when I left my corporate existence, packed a car with all my worldly belongings and drove 3,230 miles from the bustling metropolis of techie Seattle to a new life in a small seaside summer community in Maine. It is the book I wish I had several years later, as I continued to struggle to learn the myriad of new skills, survival techniques and social morays that had never occurred to me in my previous urban existence.

If I'm being entirely honest, my first year in Maine was incredibly difficult. When I wasn't busy working, I mostly stayed at home. Standing at over six feet tall, wearing impractical clothes, my partner and I stood out like sore thumbs. Or more accurately, like urbanites from a foreign metropolis. People would drive by our farmhouse a little too slowly, lingering a little too long, creeping to a near stop to take in the newcomers: young, weak, pallid and dressed all in black. Every store I visited people would say, "You're not from around here, huh?" Initially I thought, how nice to be acknowledged, to be noticed, but I realized after a few months that this was more ridicule than a friendly greeting.

News of our arrival spread like wildfire, and the anonymity I had become so accustomed to in the city was gone. My mother-in-law, thrilled to have us living across the street, broadcast our arrival to the entire town. Strangers approached me on the street, in the grocery store, in the post office, having recognized me from the photos on my mother-in-law's Facebook page. I had been an extrovert in the city, but with all eyes focused on me, my social awkwardness intensified and all I wanted to do was hide out at home.

It wasn't that I thought the city or my previous life was any better, because it wasn't. In Seattle, I lived in a tiny room in an apartment that I shared with a roommate. I was constantly on the road for work and, because of my schedule, I had fallen out of touch with many of my friends. When I would get home from a business trip I would just dump my suitcase into the washer, transfer it to the dryer and then put everything immediately back in my bag. Although some of the places I traveled to were places I'd always wanted to visit, I spent nearly all of my time there working in a windowless room or cubicle. I ate many meals alone at airport sports bars, and I was trying to learn to cope with years-off-your-life levels of stress. I was dreaming of leaving the rat race and building a life in the country. This was my first, albeit common, rookie mistake. I thought that by escaping the city, I would be escaping my depression and stress. I didn't comprehend that my problems would follow me and that changing my surroundings wouldn't magically simplify my life and allow everything to finally fall into place.

During my first few months living in Maine, I found immense satisfaction in menial tasks like painting walls, pruning fruit trees and making our farmhouse feel like home, but I still felt without purpose and direction. I couldn't find a rhythm to my days and was still working at the same frantic pace I had in the city—all hours—day and night. For every item crossed off our 'to do' list, several more things would be added in its place. I felt like I could literally work forever and still not get everything done.

I was incapable of relaxing without the structured observance of a weekend. I didn't know how to create boundaries for myself to ensure that I actually made time to walk in the woods, sit by the ocean, connect with my new community and enjoy all of the wonderful things my small town had to offer.

I made so many missteps that first year. I didn't wave at people driving by when I was out working in the yard—something that I now know is an imperative gesture. I wore ridiculous clothes. Ridiculous. Think ballet flats in the snow and a bikini in the vegetable garden. I didn't sign up for classes, I didn't go to talks, I didn't make friends with our neighbors. I thought I was succeeding with the move: our house was painted, our bags were unpacked, we were settling in. And yet, I was terribly unhappy. I realized I was failing at the transition to country life.

I felt like giving up, throwing in the towel and finding a job in the city that I would commute back and forth from on the weekends. And then this voice in my head said, "Are you freaking crazy? You are living in Vacationland (Maine's nickname). You have everything right at your fingertips, you just need to shake off all of these insane city snobberies and conformities. Find your way here, because this place, and the life you could have here, is worth it." I had dug myself into a hole in the sand and getting out of it was going to take effort and guidance from others who'd made this transition. I was a city-idiot, fumbling along, and it was time to be proactive; I needed to change my ways. I wanted to learn how to thrive in the country.

I yearned to find a community of others who had made this move so I could learn from their experiences. I began scouring the Internet for stories of other people who had moved from city to country life and could only find beautiful and idyllic stories that were devoid of any actual, honest advice. The articles I found online were overly romantic and didn't address any hardships or heartaches. Couple moves to country. Couple buys chickens and goats. Couple grows amazing garden. Couple lives happily ever after. They would never say anything about their struggles, how they found work or about how they learned to assimilate in their new community.

I came up with the idea for Urban Exodus in the spring of 2013. I would create a website with stories, photographs and interviews with ex-urbanites who moved to greener pastures. Urban Exodus would give me the opportunity to build what I was looking for, and what I imagined others might be seeking as well. A place where the solidly rooted, newly transplanted and city folk dreaming of leaving could learn from one another's triumphs and missteps. A place where you could both be inspired and gain useful information. A myriad of stories with the common underlying theme of urban to rural migration and transition.

I shared the idea of Urban Exodus on a walk with some girlfriends who had also moved to our small community in recent years from various cities. They loved the idea and said they also had Googled "city to country move" when they were looking for advice and help from others who'd transitioned. Each offered me the opportunity to photograph and interview them to get the project started. I initially found my Urban Exodus subjects via word of mouth, and each new person I met and photographed for the project fanned the flames of an ever-growing fire inside. For the first time since making the move, my path felt entirely right. I learned more in three months photographing and working on Urban Exodus than I had in my first year living in the country. I felt honored to be able to share the wisdom and stories of others—some who were struggling and some who had found their stride.

My husband came with me on most of my visits with ex-urbanites, acting as my camera assistant. He too was inspired and motivated by the stories we heard, the advice we were given and the things we were taught. Farm animal behavior, animal husbandry, beekeeping, creative ways of inexpensively building or renovating your home, how to live off-grid, how to homestead, how to become a member of your new community, the evolution of homeschooling, the catastrophe of losing a job and struggling to find a new one, crop blights, the importance of choosing the right small town for you, the struggles of first-time farmers, the evolution of an artist's work when their environment changes. Many of the things we learned were things that we were already familiar with, but hearing first-hand accounts added a whole new dimension to these valuable lessons and pieces of advice.

I took what I learned from every person I met and applied it to my own experience. I began waving at everyone driving by, putting myself out there more, taking workshops, attending talks and offering a hand to friends and neighbors. I created a designated work space and work hours to structure my day. I made an effort to learn to cook more things and created copycats of cuisine that I was desperate for and couldn't find locally. I made time to be outside and enjoy nature—beyond laboring in the garden and doing yard work. I started canning foods from our garden to make the produce-lean winter months more bearable. We worked with farmers and small businesses, trading web design for produce and services. We began teaching at the local photography school and were welcomed into our town's creative community.

Fast-forward four years to today and I couldn't imagine living anywhere else. There are still hard days and dark times but the rewards are deep. I have learned to wear lots of hats (literally and figuratively), work hard, complain little and always lend a hand. I have become a technical-clothes-wearing, mountain-climbing, snowshoeing, chain-sawing, brush-clearing, off-roading, garden-growing, small business owner. I am part of a community that looks out for one another. I am no longer a nameless face in the crowd or a cog in the corporate machine. I can see the stars shine bright at night and hear the birds singing and the coyotes howling.

To some, knowing how to adapt and thrive in the country might seem obvious, but after interviewing hundreds of people who've made the transition, it is impossible to ignore the reccurring themes of social blunders, financial hardships and steep learning curves associated with urban to rural migration.

And so here I am today to offer you a fast track, a shortcut, an outsider's guide to a rewarding life in the country. I will share the tips, tools, hacks and advice I have learned along the way—both on my own journey and on the journeys of others I've met through Urban Exodus. If you haven't made the leap yet, spare yourself the discomfort of making the move blindly. If you're already living in the country but feeling overwhelmed, depressed or like an outsider, do yourself a countrified favor: keep reading. Country life isn't easy, but as Helen and Scott Nearing famously said, it is a "Good Life." Come join us.

Alissa Hessler

LOCATION, LOCATION, LOCATION

How to choose the right place for you

"Know that you will be intimately connected to and dependent on your new community,
so pick one whose values you respect."
— Cooper Funk, Farmer

Country living is everything it is cracked up to be, and much much more. It is important to leave the city for the right reasons, with a willingness to accept that your lifestyle and daily rhythms will change. If you're escaping the city just to own your own house and still want to keep everything else in your life the same, you won't be happy in a rural environment. Stores, bars and restaurants close earlier, delivery and takeout food is hard to come by and you will drive around considerably more than you ever did before. Ask yourself your top reasons for wanting to leave the city. Is it for more space? Cleaner air? To become more self-sufficient? To be able to afford a house? To find community? These are all good reasons, but most people find it helps to have a bigger mission in mind to keep committed to their new rural locale when times get tough. An ancestral history in the area, a solid job, children in school or owning a home will strengthen your resolve to stay when difficulties arise, as well as a "mission" call to farm, homeschool, ideals directing you to live off-grid, etc.

First, let's take a moment, take a deep breath and get your ducks in a row (literally). The most common mistake people make when moving out of the city is not doing enough research to set themselves up for success. Once you leave the city, it is hard to return if your country life doesn't end up how you envisioned. It is also difficult to adapt to your new community and rural life if the location you selected isn't a good fit. There are hundreds of things to consider before moving, and deciding on a location is at the very top of the list. Realtors have been chanting "location, location, location" forever, but it's surprising how many people really don't take the time to intimately get to know the area that they are considering before uprooting their life.

ONE VISIT IS NOT ENOUGH

Just because you spent a lovely weekend in a small town doesn't mean that it is the town for you. It's easy to fall head over heels for a quaint country village on a first visit, but before making the leap, try to visit your potential new community at least a handful of times. Stay a week, observe the weekday and weekend patterns, attend a town council meeting, go to the farmer's market and meet the people growing the town's food. If you're religious (or even if you're not) attend a service at the community church and sign up for a class with a local artist or craftsman. Showing interest in the place you are thinking of moving will not only help break the ice with the locals, but it will also provide you with lots of valuable information from the people who know the place inside and out.

EXPERIENCE ALL THE SEASONS

Maybe your family has had a lake house or cabin in a small town for decades and you spent every summer tromping through the woods and drinking root beer floats at the local diner. Just because you have a working knowledge of an area during one season does not mean you are prepared for, or will enjoy, living in that location the rest of the year. If you can, try to spend some time in your prospective locale in each season to make sure it will be a good fit for you long term. In popular summer towns, a lot of businesses close in the winter and don't open until the late spring when the crowds return. Are you prepared for only a handful of stores and restaurants open, depressing Soviet-era root vegetables at the grocery store and the realities of making it through severe weather? You never know unless you try. Experience these things before you move to better inform your decision on the right rural location for you.

RENT FIRST

So many new country transplants I've interviewed said their biggest mistake was not renting first. Heady with the comparably low price of listings, they jumped in headfirst and bought a place. They knew what they wanted in a house but they didn't consider the location and community they were moving into: the repairs and maintenance, access to services, zoning and building code laws, the time it would take them to drive to the market/post office/bank/hospital, access to water, weather and so on. When you are living in a city and can't afford to own your own place, looking at land and homes well within your reach in the country can be a recipe for disaster. If you know you want to live in an old farmhouse, rent a farmhouse for a year and learn the quirks (I can tell you from experience, farmhouses have A LOT of quirks).

Try to find a rental within 20 miles of your desired area. It doesn't have to be everything you've dreamed of, it just has to be livable for a year while you acclimatize to this new life you're building. If the rental doesn't have access to land or a green space and you want to eventually farm or grow your own food, research community garden spaces or intern part-time on a farm so you can start to learn about the soils, water table, pests, blights and the like before investing in your own property. It is important to note that some small communities don't have many, if any, monthly or yearly rentals available. Touristy towns might have weekly rentals at exorbitant rates in the prime season, but those same rentals are available monthly in the off-season for a bargain. Calling a local real estate agency and inquiring about rental availability is a good way to start. Real estate agencies will know of available rentals and if potential homes on the market might have a motivated seller that's open to a respectful renter while waiting for a buyer. It's also a good idea to check local newspapers and community bulletin boards.

VIRTUAL PARTICIPATION

A lot of research can be done from your current home in the city. Read local newspapers and Facebook community pages for towns that interest you. Reading the paper can help give you a sense of what that particular community values: the arts, sports, outdoor activities, etc. Newspapers can also give you plenty of information on jobs available and the police blotter can give insight on crime rates and drug abuse. Sign up for newsletter blasts from local non-profits and businesses and add Google Alerts for all of the villages you are thinking about to stay in the know. If you are interested in relocating a home business, reach out to potential local clients and do some research on competitors in your area to figure out if there is a need for your services and if customers will be prepared to pay your current rate. You can also browse job boards and postings to determine if they have a healthy job market and decent salaries available.

ACCESSIBILITY

One of the most important things to research when it comes to a potential location is access to services: medical care, ambulatory transport, firefighters, law enforcement, veterinary care, construction companies, electricians, plumbers and even the more trivial services like a decent hairstylist, a marriage counselor or a place where you can get a massage or a facial. Sure, not all of these things are important to everyone, but even things that you don't feel like you want or need now may become more important later in life and so you should do your due diligence and know what's available. Medical care is highest on the list, as you never know when you might need a good doctor or surgeon to put you back together or deliver your baby into the world. Living in a rural location means that you don't have many options when it comes to medical care. In smaller communities you might only have one town doctor that everyone sees and if you don't like them, tough luck. Before deciding on a location, look up the medical options available, including both Western and holistic medicine.

If the area is populated enough to have a hospital close by, look up the hospital rating online and see what services they offer. How many primary care doctors are practicing in the area and, more importantly, how many are accepting new patients? I learned the hard way that just because there were several options for OB/GYN doctors in our area, that didn't mean that I could have my pick, as only one of them was accepting new patients. Look up reviews on available doctors and call their offices to see if they are accepting patients—it can save you a lot of frustration later. The same goes for dentists, optometrists, dermatologists, acupuncturists, physical therapists, cancer treatment facilities and the like. It is important that you know if the area you are considering has experts within driving distance that can take care of you and your family should the need arise.

The same goes for fire protection and law enforcement. Many small communities have volunteer fire departments with very limited crews and equipment. If you want to eventually purchase a plot of land, it is important to know if there are teams close by that fight forest or brush fires. In Maine, a lot of rural areas don't have a local police force and rely on a single sheriff or state highway patrol officers for emergency situations. That means that response time can be extremely delayed depending on where the officers are located when they are called. That being said, fewer people mean fewer emergencies and often times a more engaged police force. In my town, nearly everyone knows all of the police officers by name. They are aware of every change in the community and each new arrival. When we first moved they drove by our house constantly until we finally came out to introduce ourselves.

If you are bringing pets with you or want to raise animals after you move, you should know if there are veterinary clinics close by, if they do house calls and if they are available for after-hours emergencies. I've stopped counting how many times our dog has encountered a porcupine and we've had to drive her 45 minutes to the closest 24-hour vet to be treated. Not all vets care for larger livestock so if you are planning on getting animals to raise for meat, milk, fiber and/or companionship make sure there are vets close by that specialize in the type of livestock breeds you are considering.

Construction workers, carpenters, electricians, appliance repairmen and plumbers will all prove useful at some point, whether you buy your own property or rent. The more laborers there are, the higher the likelihood that these services won't cost you more than they did in the city and they will be available when you need them. If there is only one plumber or electrician in an area, they can set their prices at whatever they want and their response time is much slower because demand is higher. We waited six months to get our dryer fixed because the one appliance repairman within a 200-mile radius was completely booked when we called.

Personal care services like getting your hair cut or a massage might seem frivolous, but moving to a location where you can't get a decent haircut or occasional day of pampering matters to many of us. If you routinely get haircuts, facials, massages, etc. in the city, ensuring the location you are moving to has these services is important. Sometimes personal care services are cheaper in the country than they are in the city, but often times they are more expensive. You'll never find a $15 pedicure in a rural location. If you want to continue with the same beauty regime as you had in your city life, inquire about pricing when doing your research.

COST OF LIVING VS. MEDIAN HOUSEHOLD INCOME

Will you be able to afford living in the community you're considering? Compare the cost of living with the median household income in the town you want to move to. Even if you are taking your city job with you, it is still important to see what others are making just in case you should lose your job or decide you would prefer working at a local company. Some further reaching bedroom communities, tourist destinations and resort towns have very high costs of living compared to the local median household income. These are communities that cater to wealthy second-homeowners and can be cost prohibitive, even if you're still making city wages. Another way to determine whether or not you will be able to afford to live in the town you are researching is to go shopping. Go to the super market, the building store and a local restaurant—how much does everything cost? Is it more or less expensive than the city prices you're accustomed to? You don't want to choose a location only to find out that there is

no way you can afford living there for the long term. If you really like a place but find that the cost of living is too high, research surrounding areas to see if there is a community within driving distance that is more affordable and appealing.

TRANSPORTATION OPTIONS

It should come as no surprise that most rural towns don't have public transportation systems in place. You can't order an Uber or hail a cab, and most small communities don't have car rentals readily available. If you currently don't have a car and rely entirely on walking, riding your bike or using public transportation, get ready for a major life change. If the idea of spending lots of time driving each day doesn't appeal to you, walkable communities or small college towns are good places to start when narrowing down locations. Walkscore.com is an amazing resource that has walkability/public transit/bicycle ratings by zip code, neighborhood or city. My current seaside town has the worst rating possible (1 out of 100), while the small college town that I grew up in received a 59 out of 100.

Living in town can help limit the amount of time you spend in your car, but you will still need access to a car from time to time. In places with harsh winters, you will need a reliable car because biking, motorcycling or walking long distances in the snow isn't safe. One of the top things ex-city dwellers I've interviewed had a hard time adjusting to was the inability to walk places. I can say firsthand that this was very difficult to get used to when I moved from Seattle. I had a car in Seattle but only drove it when getting out of the city on the weekends. During the week I pretty much entirely relied on my feet or my bicycle to get me places. I didn't have to go to the gym because walking and cycling to and from work, the grocery store, the bank, out to dinner, etc. provided me with exercise and stress relief. Now I live a nine-minute drive outside of our town center, which is over an hour and a half walk and a harrowing (no shoulder) thirty-minute bike ride. Not all small towns are the same, but as a cycling enthusiast, I have found riding in the country to be much scarier than riding in the city. Most rural areas don't have shoulders or bicycle lanes and motorists aren't as aware or considerate to sharing the road.

Planes & Trains

Being close to a decent-sized airport and train station was a luxury I didn't appreciate before I left it behind. If you occasionally travel for work, or love to travel for leisure, you should choose a location that is reasonably close to an airport and/or train station. Beyond the convenience factor, ticket prices are generally much more expensive in rural areas than in urban metropolises. I remember fondly the days where I could buy a non-stop round-trip ticket from Seattle to pretty much any other major city in the U.S. for under $300 with enough planning and research. Now I live a two-hour drive from the Portland, Maine airport. There is a bus that we can take to the airport, but it stops at every town along the way so it can take upwards of three hours to get there. I am also cut off from the robust and convenient East Coast train routes. Every time I need to fly somewhere I have to drive two hours, pay for airport parking, fly a small connector to a major airport and then connect to my final destination. I've never paid less than $450 for tickets out of Portland. With most of my family still in rural Northern California, it takes over twenty-four hours to make it back to my hometown. I still travel quite a bit for work and love to travel for fun but I've had a sharp decline in leisure airplane travel since moving here. Being located so far away from the airport is my one lasting complaint about my life outside of the city. If travel is important to you, don't move to a place where you can't easily get to an airport or train station.

CULTURE & FOOD

First, ask yourself honestly how many times in the last year you've actually been to an art museum, play or a live show. If your answer is "a lot" or "too many to count," leaving the city will be a bit more challenging for you. For some food fanatics, losing the endless options that metropolitan areas provide is reason enough to never leave the city. Don't worry, I am here to tell you that you leaving the city doesn't mean you have to sacrifice culture and food. Certainly there will be fewer options, but rural revivals in many small towns across America have made it much easier to find small communities with things to do, see and eat. When you go to visit, ask people at the local coffee shop or watering hole about their favorite annual events. Look at town bulletin boards for art classes, theatrical productions and music shows. Although the year-round community is only 3,500 where I live, we have excellent restaurants (although many close for the winter), a photography/film school, two art museums, a documentary film festival, a monthly open-gallery night, some excellent theatre and lots of live music. Some small towns have gained national attention for their cultural or food offerings. A group of former New York City based musicians have made Woodstock, New York their home. Artists from around the world continue to move to the small community of Marfa, Texas. The towns that make up the Berkshires in Massachusetts have been attracting former city dwellers for years. Living close to, or in, a small college town is one way to ensure you will have lots of culture and food options. Try to visit and dine at local restaurants, attend plays, gallery openings, fairs and live music shows during your scouting missions. Even though I landed in a place that has fun things to do and great places to eat, that doesn't mean that I have everything I want (sometimes I would die for a bowl of pho, decent Mexican food or a Cuban sandwich), but honestly, that is okay. Not having access to everything I want all of the time has made me more resourceful and appreciative. I have started cooking ambitious dishes that I miss from my former city life and when I do return to the city I make the most of my time there by hitting up my favorite museums, restaurants and watching as many live music shows as I can. That said, if culture and food are important to you, don't move to a tiny rural area with no restaurants, coffee shops, artists or musicians. Small towns with growing culture and food scenes also tend to have faster home appreciation values and stronger job markets, so it doesn't hurt to find a place where these things are priorities.

Diversity

Many rural towns are relatively homogenous when it comes to cultural diversity. Leaving the city usually means that you will leave behind the wonderful melting pot of cultures living side by side. That said, just because you're leaving the city doesn't mean you have to move a place where everyone has the same cultural background. If moving to a place with diversity is important to you, it will require some time researching. The website city-data.com lists the median household income, home value, age, unemployment rate and the race percentages by town or zip code. This site can not only help you determine if the location you're considering is affordable and if there are jobs available, but it will give you a better idea of how diverse it is. Even in states with a high percentage of Caucasians, you can still find small communities with cultural variety, you just need to spend some time exploring and researching ahead of time.

MOVING SINGLE?

If you are moving to a place single and you would eventually like to meet a potential mate or even just have an active dating life, don't move to a place without first determining if there are enough suitable options within a fifty-mile radius. In Meeting Your Mates (page 117) I give some tips for dating in rural areas, but those tips won't help you if you move to a tiny town where everyone is married or over the age of seventy. If you haven't already, sign up for some online dating services and apps. It's easy to do a remote sweep and determine if there will be dating options in the area. You can also do some recon work in person when visiting by hitting up the local watering holes, going to a Contra or Salsa dance night or attending a farm dinner. Even if you are moving with someone you're dating, or a spouse, it might behoove you to check out the scene before deciding on a place. The number of incredible female divorcees in our town is mind-boggling. They all moved here with their husbands, had kids, got divorced and now are left with a handful of available single men. They can't move because this town is their home now and their children's home, but it certainly isn't easy not having local options for companionship.

RELIGION & POLITICS

Ah…church and state, the two things you should never bring up in polite conversation, and the two things that are supposed to stay separate, but often feel incredibly intertwined. Moving away from the city, you will no longer be able to keep yourself in an echo chamber of friends and acquaintances that have the same or similar core beliefs. When looking at locations to live, ask yourself if you are okay being an outsider when it comes to political or religious ideologies. For some, whether you're a conservative or liberal, religious or an atheist has very little weight. But for others, living in a place surrounded by people who don't believe in the same things they do is a deal breaker. No matter where you live, it is important to not judge people based on what they believe, but it can be hard to be an atheist and move to a small town where every yard has a political poster for a party you don't support and your new friends are constantly inviting you to attend their church. It is easy to feel like an outsider and not gain acceptance in your community if you're a religious conservative that moves to a non-religious hippie town or a liberal atheist moving to a town in the Bible Belt.

It is relatively easy to determine if the location you are considering is liberal or conservative by looking at county voting records. There have been some religious affiliation studies done in recent years, but the best way to figure out if the area you are considering is more or less secular is to visit on the weekends and attend some local church services. Are the services heavily focused on that particular religion or do they feel more inclusive? Although we have a number of churches in our small town, the majority of people who live here wouldn't consider themselves to be particularly religious. Most of the churches here aren't insular and welcome all faiths; they serve more as a town meeting place rather than strictly a place of worship. My father-in-law's parents, who live nearby, are Jewish but they regularly attend meetings, suppers and services at an Anglican church because it serves as their local social outlet. So if you aren't religious but the area you are interested in has a lot of churches, don't be scared away without doing some further investigational work. The best way to see if you jive with the people in the area is to socialize. You won't learn anything about a place if you don't spend time getting to know the people that live there.

CLIMATE

It is important to consider the weather when scouting locations. You might think you are a winter person in the city, but that doesn't mean you can handle long winters in a rural location. In the country, you have to deal with snow, plowing your driveway and shoveling your own walk. Rural country roads outside of town centers are the last ones on the snowplow route, which means you might be snowed in for several days. Some rural communities lose power for weeks at a time during extreme weather, which leaves those without a generator without heat or running water. The same rings true for summer heat—can you handle humidity, bugs and wood rot? How much will it cost to heat your home in the winter and keep it cool in the summer? If you plan on growing your own food, be sure to read Oh How Your Garden Grows (page 69), as you won't be able to grow all fruits or vegetables everywhere. Visiting the area in every season gives you a much better idea of what you're up against before deciding to make the move. Beyond the seasons, are there any natural disasters that commonly occur in the location you are considering? Asking locals and doing Internet research will help you find out about the prevalence of different potential disasters in the area. Was there a 100-year flood of epic proportions? Are ice storms common? Has the town been hit by hurricanes, tornadoes or wildfires? Are there any active fault lines running through the area? This information will prove helpful in choosing the right location.

RECREATIONAL ACTIVITIES

Reconnecting with nature and the natural world is one of the main reasons people relocate to the country. If staying active is a priority, make sure that the place you are moving to has recreational options. Test out hiking trails when you visit. While there is plenty of physical work to keep you active, the joys of recreational fitness are not to be overlooked. Go to the town office and inquire about organized sports leagues, fun runs, triathlons and pick-up games. Not all small towns have gyms or public swimming pools, so if these are an important part of your routine, do your research. People that work at local outdoor and sporting goods stores are incredibly helpful at giving you a lay of the recreational activity landscape. Many rural areas have mountain biking trails, ski mountains, river and lake spots, or at least a swimming hole. Learning about these places early on will make your transition much more fun.

SCHOOLS & TRAINING PROGRAMS

Whether or not you have kids, researching the local school ratings and training programs available can give you a good sense of the opportunities available in an area. Also, you don't want to get settled, have a kid and then realize that the school options are less than satisfactory. If there aren't great schools in the area you are looking, research homeschooling laws to make sure that you will have the option to homeschool should you decide that's necessary. The advances in homeschooling in the digital age are incredible. There are many online courses, distance learning programs, and online group socializing options with teachers and other homeschool students. Many people I've photographed for Urban Exodus homeschool their kids because the prospective schools in their area are either too far away or they just felt like the curriculum and standards were lacking. I photographed a family of six in the rural foothills of North Carolina and their mother has homeschooled all four of them since moving from Santa Barbara, California. Their 12-year-old daughter enrolled in an online college robotics course because she was interested in mechanics. She is constantly taking apart and rebuilding electronics in their house and wants to study nano-robotics in college. Partially supplementing homeschooling lessons online or having kids learn entirely from online courses is not a hindrance to college or a bright future—in many ways it will prepare them for the evolving job market. Homeschooled students can be taught at their own natural pace and don't have to fall behind or get bored if the curriculum isn't moving fast enough for them.

Beyond the primary school rating, what other youth programs are offered? Are there organized sports, summer camps, after school programs, advanced placement courses and art and music classes available? If you are moving with school-age children, their transition to small-town life can be particularly difficult. Leaving behind friends and moving to a place with fewer structured activities can cause previously well-behaved kids to act out and find trouble. Finding out about these activities and enrolling your kids early on can help ease their transition.

As an adult, secondary training programs can expand your rural career options. It's possible that moving to the country might even necessitate a career change. There are many online options available now, but nothing beats having a university, technical college or an extended education facility within driving distance. Quite a few ex-city dwellers I've met decided to get their nursing degree after moving to the country, as jobs in health care in their community are well paid and readily available. If you think you might have a desire or need to learn some new skills, don't choose a town several hours from the closest learning annex or college.

CRIME & DRUG ABUSE RATES

Just because a small community can appear idyllic and friendly from the outside, doesn't mean there isn't crime or pandemic drug abuse hiding behind closed doors. The town next to us has a thriving art scene and you would never know by visiting that it also has one of the highest per-capita rates of prescription drug abuse in the state. It's easy to find crime and drug use statistics online and search registered sex offenders in the area by zip code on nsopw.org. (A warning, search outcomes can be terrifying in densely populated areas and even some small towns.) You can also learn about drug abuse and violent and non-violent crime prevalence by reading the local newspaper, inquiring at the police station and asking people you meet. If you have young or high-school age kids, moving to a place with few after school extra-curricular options and high drug abuse rates doesn't mean your kids will get addicted to drugs, but it could be a recipe for boredom and excessive pressure from their peers.

LOCAL & STATE LAWS

If you are planning on leaving the city and moving to a new state, it is important that you know the state and local laws in the location you are considering. There are literally hundreds of laws that might pertain to your goals particularly, so this will just give you a cursory overview of some of the most common laws that people I've interviewed have been surprised/most affected by.

Gun laws: Moving to a state that is open carry when you are anti-gun doesn't mean you won't be able to grocery shop without seeing someone carrying a gun, but it does mean it's a possibility. The website nraila.org has gun laws broken down by state, but it is also easy to find this information just by Googling "(insert state) gun laws." In Maine, you can openly carry a firearm as long as you have a permit. Our town doesn't have a lot of people that carry guns around, but I have run into folks carrying firearms in smaller, more rural communities and have seen signs at the local businesses and schools asking people to not bring guns inside. Although I don't personally support open carry laws, the low violence and murder rates in our area make it less of a hot button issue. Also, after moving here, we realized that having a shotgun for our property was a good investment. We only use it to scare deer away from our garden and shoot rabid wild animals, but it's nice to know it's available should the need arise.

Environmental laws and policies: Many states have enacted laws that differ from federal guidelines. Although federal laws apply to all states, some states are more stringent than others when it comes to regulation and adherence. If recycling is important to you, make sure the place you are moving to has recycling options. I was surprised at how many small towns don't have recycling programs, as they don't have the funds available. Where we live, all of our garbage is either incinerated at the town dump or buried in old quarries. There is no telling the impact this has on the air and water quality over time. If you consider yourself an environmentalist and couldn't live in a place where you have to throw away all your recyclables and all of your garbage is burned, you should definitely do extra research to find a state with tough environmental laws and enforcement, and a town that has recycling and ecological waste management systems in place.

Homeschool laws: Homeschooling can be highly regulated, depending on what state you move to. If the schools in the area you are considering are sub-par, you will want to check on the homeschooling laws, even if you don't currently have children, because you never know what the future might hold. Responsiblehomeschooling.org has homeschool laws broken down by state.

Agricultural regulations: If you plan to farm, raise livestock or make your own food products to sell, you should first become well versed with USDA and FDA regulations, which apply to all states. Once you are familiar with those laws, research specific state laws as they could end up making or breaking your future business plans. Each state has different regulations when it comes to slaughtering, selling and shipping animal products. Some states require that any meat sold must be butchered at a certified slaughterhouse, while others allow on-farm slaughtering with certain stipulations. Some states have more relaxed regulations for smaller producers and CSAs. If you plan on starting a farm, check to see what the regulations will be on the products you plan on selling. Farmtoconsumer.org is a great resource for accurate information, legal advice and even legal defense if you get in trouble down the road.

Building codes and zoning laws: The tiny house craze is sweeping the nation and lots of city dwellers are toying with the idea of leaving the concrete jungle and erecting a tiny house in a rural locale. Although most tiny houses are portable, allowing you to pick up and move if the location you've chosen isn't a good fit, many states have laws that mandate lot and dwelling size, which make parking a tiny house on your own land very difficult. Zoning and building code laws can also prove problematic if you want to build your own home or business, restore an older home or run a business out of your home. Tinyhousecommunity.com provides lots of helpful information on building, financing and finding places to live legally. For all other building codes and zoning laws, you can consult the town or county offices in the area you are considering. Beyond just learning about the building codes and zoning, it would also be smart to inquire about the permitting process for rehabs, new builds, etc.

Hunting and fishing laws and licensing: Even if you aren't interested in supplementing your food production with hunting or fishing, you still might want to verse yourself on the laws as they will outline when hunting and fishing seasons begin and end. In Maine, the entire month of November is deer hunting season. With the exception of Sundays, when hunting isn't allowed, everyone wears neon orange when venturing outside to walk the dogs or go on a hike so they don't accidentally get shot. Even our dog wears an orange coat to stand out. Some communities don't allow hunting, while others have much longer open seasons. One thing to keep in mind is that if you are looking at an area with a high risk of Lyme disease, deer hunting is an essential element of managing and reducing tick populations. If you are moving to homestead and becoming more self-sufficient, an important component of your survival will be knowing ahead of time if you can hunt on your own land year-round, what types of fish you can catch and how many animals you can tag per year.

Tax laws: Don't decide on a location before knowing about the sales, income, property and business tax laws and rates. Taxes are broken down by federal, state and local and they can differ quite a bit, even between neighboring towns. The town we live in has higher property taxes than all of the towns that surround us, but it also has the highest rated school system in the area. If there are visible advantages—good schools, prompt snow removal and public parks—know that your tax money is going towards things that benefit the community. Know that most areas charge a higher property rate for waterfront properties—oceanfront and other bodies of water. If you are looking at a property on the water, make sure you can afford the annual property taxes, in addition to your mortgage and other expenses, before making an offer.

There you have it, those are some of the top things to do and consider before deciding on a rural location. One visit is not enough to fully understand the intricacies and complexities of any small community. Even if you've been visiting the same place every summer for years, that doesn't necessarily mean you can make it work there the rest of the year. Make a list of all of the things that you want from your new community and number them by level of importance. Compare the locations you are considering with your list of priorities. If accessibility, being close to an airport and having cultural offerings are at the top of the list, research small towns that fit that bill. If you are moving with your family, have everyone do this exercise and compare your results. Let everyone weigh in and have their voices heard as this will help prepare and excite everyone for the move. Doing your due diligence ahead of time and selecting a location that's a good fit for you will ease your period of transition, and you can then quickly begin enjoying this next chapter of your life.

HOUSE HUNTING

What to look and look out for in a home base

"Find a way to stay in the area you're thinking about living for a bit before moving there! We were in a total rush, and while we've grown to love our location, we probably would have chosen to be a little further north and have a different town as our nearest base. It takes a while to fully realize what you're looking for (and not looking for) in a home."

— Casey Dzierlenga, Furniture Builder

House hunting in rural areas and small communities can be particularly enticing to city people wanting to plant roots. The prices seem so affordable in comparison. In rural areas, many homes have barns, sheds or outbuildings that come along with the house. It's easy to dream up an incredible barn space where you can host farm-to-table meals or imagine the shed transforming into a perfect guesthouse or home office. As someone who has watched a few too many hours of HGTV, I am familiar with the vernacular of "charming" and "character" widely used to describe country homes.

Sure, a house with history, quirks and charm is hard to pass up. A lot of new rural transplants hear the siren song of an old farmhouse or colonial. It's easy not to look closely enough at the myriad of issues that may be lurking behind the walls and underneath the perfectly worn floorboards. A steal of a property can quickly turn into a money pit that will never recoup the investment required to keep it livable. Outbuildings, although enticing, initially require maintenance, repair and care to ensure they don't become a liability. Beyond just the home itself, there are many things to factor in when it comes to home and living expenses living rurally. Water, sewer and garbage—things maybe you never thought about in the city—are suddenly entirely your responsibility. Heating, cooling, snow removal and road repairs should also be factored into the equation. Having space, acreage and a beautiful farmhouse are all totally worth the time and investment, but preparing yourself for the search and doing as much homework beforehand as possible will ensure you find the right property the first time and don't get stuck in a money pit.

Choosing a place to call home can be time-consuming, frustrating and confusing and it is easy to make a bunch of expensive rookie mistakes. Even if you've bought a condo or a house with property before, buying a house in the country isn't a cakewalk. You might know all about mortgages, title insurance, home inspections and the like, but buying a rural property has many additional layers and it is important to not rush into anything. Do your research ahead of time and know that it can take well over a year to find a rural property that is right for you. A year might seem like an eternity, but jumping in and buying the first house you like and then discovering that there are many issues lurking that you never considered is not worth it. In the country, good things are worth the wait. Make that your mantra, not just in home buying, but also in this new chapter of your life. When you are settled in a home that is right for you, all of the hard work will be worth it.

BEFORE YOU START YOUR SEARCH, RENT FIRST

As discussed in the previous chapter, even if you have money available to buy a home in the country, it is wise to rent a place in or close to your desired location, at least for the first year. You may have chosen a general region to move to, but there are nuances to the villages and towns that make up that area. Take the time to suss out where exactly you want to be. Plus, renting for a year enables you to familiarize yourself with the maintenance required in owning a home. That will help you decide if you want to go with a smaller house on a smaller lot or if you are ready and willing to take on more house and a larger plot of land.

FIND A REALTOR YOU TRUST; LOOK AT ALL THE HOMES AVAILABLE

Alex, a local realtor, tells all of his customers who are relocating from the city to rent first, or at least visit for extended periods of time during every season, explore the wider area and get a feel for all of the surrounding towns within their targeted area. Once they've gotten to know the people and communities associated with each town, he has the prospective buyer decide on a few towns that they are interested in. He will then cast a ten-mile net around those towns and tour his clients through all of the available properties in that area that roughly fit their parameters. He often discourages buyers who don't have experience managing larger properties in taking on more than five acres. Alex recommends that home buyers don't hold back and look at all of the properties available in their targeted areas. Since the inventory is limited, it is important to see all that is out there, as you never know what home or property will resonate with someone. He's had several clients who were initially set on buying oceanfront, but after touring some well-appointed lake properties, they changed their minds and bought on fresh water. Alex has seen first-hand ex-urbanites who were enticed by the bucolic ideal of country life and dead-set on remote acreage, barns and outbuildings. He's discouraged clients from buying properties with outbuildings that require costly renovations, only to have them put in an offer, spend loads renovating the place, and then decide that country life is not for them and sell those properties at a loss. Alex's advice is solid when it comes to rural property hunting, "The best you can do is find a real estate agent that you can trust, think hard about what your needs are now and in the future and decide whether or not you have the energy and money needed to manage a more rural property or if you would be happier living in-town."

NEEDS NOW & INTO THE FUTURE

It's easy to imagine that you will grow old in whatever country haven your search finds you, so it is important to consider your needs not only now but also into the future. Remember that selling rural properties often takes much longer than selling homes in more populated areas. You don't want to get trapped in a situation where your home no longer serves your needs, but you can't find a buyer so you have to stay put. Making a list of your wants and needs now and into the future is the first step that anyone looking for rural property should take. If you are making the move solo, have some friends or family help you put together a list of your needs now, five years from now and ten years from now. Sure, life will throw you curve balls, but without thinking about the future you could end up in a place that only ends up working for a couple of years before you have to go through the stressful and costly process of selling your place, finding a new place and moving. If you are moving with a partner, this is a good exercise for more reasons than just finding a house, it will help align your goals and aspirations for this new life. It can begin the conversation for many things that will inevitably pop up. For example, do you plan on having children, and if so, how many? Do you want to have land for animals or crops? Are you ready to take on yard work and winter maintenance? Is it important to live in town or are you fine driving to get basic amenities? And so on.

GROWING INTO YOUR PLACE

My husband had already bought our farmhouse before we met, and when I first toured it I remember being overwhelmed by the size. I was twenty-nine and living in a 9 x 10 room in a small apartment in Seattle. The idea of upgrading to a 2,000 square foot house might have excited some, but I saw it initially as a place that would be time-consuming to clean and expensive to heat. While I was certainly correct on both fronts, I wasn't thinking further into the future, I was only considering my needs at the time. I would drive ten minutes to our town's center and imagine living in a small cottage that was walkable to all our basic conveniences, with a tiny yard that was easy to manage. Yet, after spending time immersing ourselves into our new community, I realized that with the non-stop social overload in the summer months, it felt essential to live outside of the town center so I could retreat and recharge my batteries. The empty rooms that felt daunting initially are now going to be put to good use: a space for our first child—we are expecting this winter—and for the family that will come to meet the newest arrival. The outbuilding that came with the house originally didn't make sense and we considered turning it into a rental unit, but once we started our own creative business, we realized that having an office outside of the house was an incredible bonus, as we didn't need to rent a place in town. Perhaps my husband was thinking about all of these potential possibilities when he made the offer on the place, but mostly I just think he fell in love with it. If you fall head over heels for a place, there might be something subconscious that is pulling you towards it—a future yet to be determined. It worked for us, but I would still recommend

really thinking about what you want now and into the future. If you buy a place that feels too big for "current you," you can always rent out the spare rooms to help with your mortgage or close them up until their purpose is revealed.

A GOOD DEAL ISN'T ALWAYS SO

So you've toured a myriad of local properties and stumbled upon a home that seems, on the surface, to be an incredible deal. It costs less than all the others you've seen, has a larger lot and more space. Proceed with caution. Properties are usually priced based on comparable homes in the area. If it is much less expensive, there is likely something wrong with it. The best way to investigate is to ask around. Go to the town office, the local library, bring a cake to a neighbor and inquire about the home. If the owner has recently passed, inquire about their family—do they live locally or away? If the previous owner has already moved to another house or out of town or their family is selling their estate, that might be why it is priced to sell. Inquire at the town office to see what building permits the property has had, if any. This information will let you know if additions have been added and if licensed contractors have made renovations or improvements. Research properties and homes within a five-mile radius. Is there a commercial farm that sprays their fields, a feedlot, a dump, a correctional facility, a gun range, etc.? All of these could be reasons why the home is priced lower than others. Also, check to see if there are any other homes available within five miles and see if they are also priced lower than comparable homes. If they are, it could mean that the area the home is located in is less desirable for one reason or another. Before you buy it is important to figure out why, as it could make your home harder to sell in the future should you need to. It is not to discourage you from taking advantage of a good deal, but you want to make an informed decision before making an offer.

ALWAYS GET AN INSPECTION & A SURVEY FOR ACREAGE

Is there anything worse than finding out you didn't get what you thought you'd paid for? When considering a home, the number one ABSOLUTELY essential thing to do is to get a detailed home inspection. If the property in question has outbuildings and barns, have the inspector look at those as well so you don't have any surprises. Make your offer contingent on this home inspection, as you don't want to learn after you've bought it that there are tons of problems with your new place. If your home inspector comes back with a laundry list of issues, you can then decide whether you are ready and able to take those projects on. You can also use the home inspector's findings to negotiate a lower asking price, or even negotiate with the seller that they make and pay for the necessary repairs.

If you are buying a home with acreage you should invest in a property survey, unless one has been completed in the last few years. Without a survey, you can't guarantee the number of acres you are buying. Also, if you go to the county surveyor's office you can see how many acres are currently being taxed. Sometimes their acreage figure is inaccurate and if it is you could be paying taxes on acreage that you don't own. You might also find that the listed acreage isn't the same as the recorded acreage. If there is a big discrepancy, you will want to do some additional investigative work. A surveyor can also determine if there are any easements or rights of way on your property that will grant other entities access to your land. Rights of way and easements are widely contested and lead to many property disputes. Know ahead of time if others will be able to use or access your land before you buy it, as it is very difficult to nullify deeded rights of way or easements.

PESTS THAT CAN DESTROY HOMES

For older homes, have your home inspector pay careful attention to the age of the plumbing and wiring, the type of foundation and for infestations. I hate to admit it, as I have spent the last three years trying to fight it, but all old country homes have mice. Sorry. It's just a fact of life. Mice are more than just gross, though. They can also nibble through cable and electrical lines. And other unwelcome guests can do even worse. Here is a list of these little menaces that can destroy your rural home:

1. *Termites:* Damage is not usually covered by your homeowner's insurance. These insects are responsible for over $5 billion worth of damage to U.S. homes every year.
2. *Powderpost beetles:* Infest structural hardwoods only, including cabinets, furniture, molding and flooring. Homes with this beetle must disclose that to prospective buyers, which can greatly reduce resale value.
3. *Carpenter ants:* They hollow out wood to make their homes in structural beams, inside doors and behind insulation. The best way to treat is to spray them, but you may need to replace wood if the structural integrity is compromised.
4. *Rats and mice:* As mentioned, rats and mice can nibble through wiring, cables and insulation. They can spread disease and leave behind feces and urine on cooking and eating surfaces. Rat poison is effective, but will often lead to vermin dying in your walls and leaving a terrible odor behind for weeks while they decompose. The best way to deal with infestations is to use snap traps. For a clever DIY mousetrap, see below.
5. *Squirrels:* These adorable creatures can be incredibly destructive to your home. They chew holes in siding and drywall, have babies in your attic and create giant messes. Having a one-way door installed is an effective way to keep them out of your house.

HOMEMADE BUCKET MOUSETRAP

No one likes mice or rats living in their home. This is an inexpensive, effective and long-term trap to catch mice and rats that can be used over and over again.

MATERIALS
Drill
5-gallon bucket
Metal or wood dowel
Paper plate
Peanut butter
Wooden ramp or stick

Drill two holes on either side of your bucket at slightly larger width than the dowel. Puncture the paper plate ¾ of the way with the dowel and secure in the drilled holes. Add peanut butter to the ¼ side of the paper plate, touching the ¾ side to the edge of the bucket. Run the wooden ramp or stick up to the ¾ side of the bucket. Mice will run up to get the peanut butter and will fall into the bucket when their weight tips the plate. You can add water or antifreeze to the bottom of the bucket to ensure they will die, but I prefer to turn them loose in the woods far far away from our house. It is entirely up to you.

TAXES, ZONING CLASSIFICATIONS & DEED RESTRICTIONS

No one should ever put an offer on a house until they first look up the yearly property taxes and zoning classifications and review the deed. This can usually be done online, but if the town or county you are considering doesn't have records online, you can go to the town office and ask for them. Can you afford the yearly taxes? Have they changed significantly in the last ten years? This might give you some insight on the property's history, as a jump in property tax could be linked with home additions or improvements. Another thing to look for is the assessed value. If the assessed value is lower than the asking price, you might have some negotiating room with the seller; you also might get a hefty property tax bump in a year or two if you buy the property at the asking price as the assessor often looks at this when updating taxes. If the assessed value is higher than the asking price, you might be able to contest the assessed value with the assessor and get your property taxes lowered after you buy your home.

Not only do you want to see what the yearly taxes and the assessed value are, you also want to determine what the land zoning classification is, which will sometimes be broken down by percentage. It is important to know what these classifications are, any restrictions associated with them and if they are taxed differently. For instance, if a percentage of your land is tree growth, you will receive a tax break on that land. If you want to clear the land (which could first require permits and/or EPA approval) you will lose that tax break and may even need to pay back taxes for the break you've already received. If you have wetland classification, you might not be able to build additional structures or make any changes to the land. Zoning classifications also might make it difficult to get financing and could limit your ability to raise livestock or certain animals. While you are in the town office, inquire about local zoning around the home you are interested in and ask to see any nearby development plans. A review of local zoning ordinances can give you an idea of what's planned around you. Finding out that there is a subdivision scheduled to be built close to your prospective home after you buy it could crush your dreams of a quieter life in the country.

Last but not least, review a copy of the property's deed. Some properties have deed restrictions or covenants that will limit what you can do with the property. Deeds will also outline any rights of way or easements on the land. Most deeds are (at most) two pages. Ours is seven pages long. We can't build any additional structures unless they are agricultural and limited to a certain footprint. We can't have a rental unit larger than 600 square feet. We can't run a business with more than five employees. Our home has to be our primary residence. It's all very restrictive and incredibly detailed. We also have a right of way on our land that grants a neighbor both personal and agricultural use of a gravel access road (which is also our driveway) to their field located behind us. My husband knew these restrictions going in and decided they weren't enough to dissuade him from buying the place. That said, wouldn't it be frustrating if you didn't take this step and found out after you bought your place that you can't build a mother-in-law unit or run a home business? Do yourself a favor and read the deed. It's painless and could save you a lot of heartache later.

LOCAL ORDINANCES & LAWS

We went over this in the previous chapter, but when looking for homes, it is important to know the local ordinances and laws where your prospective property is located. Some townships are very relaxed and don't have many restrictions, while others dictate specific days for rummage sales, if you can feed birds, keep animals, etc. Knowing the process of acquiring burn permits and what you can burn on your property will come in handy if you have land that you have to manage and keep cleared. Our town requires you to get a burn permit the day of the burn and you have to stand in line at the fire department to see if they are issuing that day. We've been turned away more than a dozen times because conditions aren't quite right for the fire marshal. Some towns have websites with local ordinances and laws listed. If you can't find them online, go to the town office and inquire. This is an easy step that could prevent you from learning later that you can't hunt on your own property without a license, or that you can't own a dog without licensing them every year.

FOR SALE BY OWNER

Most people in urban areas use licensed real estate agents to list, market and sell their properties. In rural areas you will see many more properties listed as "For Sale by Owner," or FSBO for short. Since 2007, the number of FSBO sales has increased by nearly 30 percent. Buying property without going through a real estate agent can be fine as long as you do your due diligence and make sure you are protected and that the paperwork is done correctly. A bonus of buying a house directly from the seller is that you avoid paying commission, which is on average 5-6 percent of the selling price.

My husband bought our house without a real estate agent. He knew the owners and they didn't even have to go through the trouble of listing the property on the market. Not having to pay the additional commission is one of the reasons he was able to afford our place, although when our property appraised at much lower than what he had paid for it two years later (after we had made some major renovations to the outbuildings), I realized that even though we love it here and wouldn't take back buying the place, he had likely paid too much for it. Things to be aware of when looking at a house for sale by owner is that the owner sets their own price without using a real estate agent to help come up with a number that is based on comparable homes in the area. Sometimes that means they will price their home lower than it is worth, but often times it will be priced higher, as they know how much money, time and effort they've put into it over the years and are trying to recoup that investment. Be sure to hire an attorney that specializes in FSBO sales to properly prepare and notarize all of your paperwork. Sometimes you can share an attorney with the seller to conserve costs, but it's always wise to have your own attorney, as they will be looking out for your best interest. The only difference between a FSBO transaction and a home bought through an agent is that you have to manage the negotiation and paperwork process yourself. You still need title insurance and an inspection and you should still look up the property taxes, zoning and deed. Don't trust that the seller will divulge any and all issues with the property or that they even know everything about the property they are selling. To summarize, do all your homework ahead of time like you would for any other property, hire a real estate attorney and title insurance agent you trust, and don't even think about not having an inspection done, even if you are buying the home from friends or relatives. You want to be sure you know what you are getting into before signing your name on a stack of legally binding papers.

FIXER UPPERS—DON'T BITE OFF MORE THAN YOU CAN CHEW

Watching endless hours of home improvement shows and YouTube videos does not make one a home improvement expert. When looking at homes, don't overestimate your abilities for DIY repairs. It is important to think about the real time and money that remodels and repairs require. Painting walls and refinishing floors is one thing, but updating electrical and remodeling a dated bathroom is quite another. Older homes in rural areas can hide a myriad of issues and botched DIY projects. A local carpenter in our area is constantly amazed at the horrors he finds just behind the drywall: cut structural beams, knob and tube wiring, mold from improperly installed bathrooms and kitchens, asbestos, colonies of mice and carpenter ants, you name it. Many of these problems aren't visible to a home inspector. If a home is obviously in need of a lot of work, but you are dead set on buying it, have a reputable and recommended construction worker or handyman join you on a tour of the property. Not only will this give you a more accurate idea of what you're in store for, but they may also point out problems that you didn't initially see or consider. Factoring the cost of renovations and repairs into the asking price will give you a much better idea as to whether or not you can afford the home in the long term. It can also be an effective bargaining chip when negotiating a price for the property. Comparing the asking price plus the estimate of cost of repairs with the price of other similar homes in the area will give you an idea of whether or not you will be able to get back what you put into the property should you need to sell it in the future. A big pickle many people get into with rural property renovations is that they end up investing more money into the property than it is worth. Going upside down on repairs and renovations spent on your new home right after you purchase it could lead to trouble should you lose your job or other unexpected expenses come up, as you won't be able to borrow on the property or sell it for what you put into it.

THE SIREN CALL OF THE MONEY PIT

Casey and Sam decided to check out a few real estate listings while visiting their family in upstate New York. Their now home, a stately but crumbling colonial revival in the small community of Salt Point, New York, was one of the first places they toured. These two furniture builders were siren called by the beautiful bones of the place. It was love at first sight. The house was a bargain, but also a total wreck. They bought it in the summer of 2011 and have been working tirelessly on it ever since. The first few years were extremely difficult: they lived without heat, running water or proper insulation through several harsh winters. They've done all the repairs themselves: peeling layers of wallpaper, replacing rotten exterior walls and floorboards and preserving the history of the place while making it more energy-efficient and livable. Even with the knowhow and skillset to take on a historic renovation, coming home from a long day's work of building furniture to start a full evening's work of renovations hasn't allowed them much time to really appreciate their new country life. In hindsight, they wish they had spent more time house hunting and purchased a home that required less upfront repair investment.

NEW BUILDS VS. RENOVATING

Perhaps you have always dreamed of building your perfect dream house in the country. Or maybe after an exhaustive home search you've decided that the style and condition of homes in the area you are considering aren't to your standards. Before you start scribbling home designs on napkins, contacting builders or touring pre-fab home websites, know that more often than not, building in rural areas is more expensive than renovating. Rural areas have less competition when it comes to contractors, electricians, plumbers, etc. so hourly rates are usually more expensive than city prices. Also, unless you're located in close proximity to a big box home improvement store, building materials will definitely be more expensive. If you think going the pre-fab route will ease things along and make the project finish faster, consider that most rural areas don't have experts who know how to set up pre-fabricated homes and you may need to hire and provide housing for an outside contractor to manage the job. Installing septic systems, running electrical and drilling wells can also cost a pretty penny depending on the slope of the land, the soil and whether or not there are ledges or bedrock that need to be drilled through or blasted. Also, finding financing for new builds in rural areas can be much more challenging than getting financing on a fixer-upper property. This isn't to squash your new build dreams but rather to rein them in.

Before embarking on a new build, it is important to have built relationships and a positive reputation in the area you are planning on building. You want to put together a team of craftspeople that you trust and that are honest, available and easy to work with. You need to have financing in order and a place to live lined up for at least double the time that they estimate your project will take. Lastly, you should crunch numbers and determine whether or not it is okay with you if your new build appraises at lower than what it cost you to build. You may never get back what you put into your new build but the payoff of living in a home that you dreamed up might be worth more to you than its resale value.

PROXIMITY

We talked about this in the previous chapter, but finding a home within reasonable driving distance to basic amenities, schools, hospitals and your place of employment is important. The main gripe ex-city dwellers have with moving rurally is the inability to get anywhere by foot and the constant necessity of a car. If you have a thirty-minute drive to work every day, that is one hour out of your day that you can't mow the lawn, hang out with your family or get caught up on household projects. A thirty-minute drive on a scenic rural byway with no traffic is a vast improvement from a daily rush-hour commute in the city, but are you willing to make that drive for the next five, ten, fifteen years? If there are no medical facilities or schools within a thirty-minute drive, do they have ambulatory services or school buses that will be available to drive you to the hospital or bring your kids to school? Proximity is also important for property value and appreciation. If you are located far away from basic amenities, your property value will have a much slower appreciation rate than properties with closer access to town, healthcare facilities and schools.

CONNECTIVITY

If you are like most ex-urbanites, the idea of living without breezy Internet access and cell phone reception is unimaginable. Finding a home with decent Internet options and mobile reception in rural areas can be like finding a needle in a haystack. Sure, satellite Internet has improved in recent years, but to people used to fiber-optic speed, satellite can feel glacially slow. Ask your realtor what Internet provider serves that particular area and call them to see what their options are. Forget your cheap city Internet bundle. Internet in the country can be expensive because often there is only one provider and they are able to set their prices at whatever they want. If satellite Internet is the only option, ask what their standard megabits per second rate is. Nearly every ex-urbanite I've interviewed considers Netflix part of their winter coping ritual. To stream movies seamlessly at SD quality, you need 3.0 megabits per second, which jumps to 5.0 for HD and 25 megabits for Ultra HD. Anything less than 3.0 will have most former city dwellers tearing their hair out.

Can you survive living in a place where you get no cell phone reception and have to rely on—gasp—a landline? Again, this is not something to learn the hard way. When you are doing your home tours, check your cellphone in every home you enter. Can you make a clear call without it cutting out? Can you upload a photo to Facebook? Send a text? A month after I moved from Seattle to our small town in Maine I received a text from my cell phone company, AT&T, saying they were suspending my data plan because they didn't have any towers in the area. It had worked fine for the first month, but that was because AT&T was paying Verizon to use their towers. Most cell providers will only do this for a short period of time before suspending your data plan. I had to go through the irritating process of changing my carrier and porting my number. The only benefit was that since AT&T could no longer provide me with the service I was paying for they waived the hefty contract termination fee that they usually charge when you switch carriers. Even living in-town doesn't guarantee you will have reliable Internet and phone service, so add this to your list of things to research. This is especially important for anyone who will be telecommuting or running a home business.

NEIGHBORS & NEIGHBORHOOD

It is never too early to start reaching out to your (potential) neighbors and staking out your (potential) neighborhood. Living rurally, you likely won't have to suffer through a loud club-footed upstairs neighbor or music blasting through your walls, but that doesn't mean you will mesh with your new neighbors or neighborhood. Living outside of the city, you have a lot more flexibility with what you can do on your land and very little control of what others do on theirs. Are you okay living next to a person who hoards broken automobiles in their yard? What about a neighbor doing nightly target practice with live rifle rounds? Or a neighbor whose livestock consistently get out and trample through your yard? How about a neighbor who constantly operates heavy machinery or sprays chemical pesticides on their nearby fields? In the country, it's pretty critical to stay on decent terms with your neighbors, so do your homework ahead of time.

Knock on doors, bring some baked goods (see Neighbors and Community [page 57] for my mom's famous shortbread recipe) and introduce yourself. "Hi, I'm _____, I'm looking at purchasing the (insert last name of current owner) house. I just wanted to introduce myself and ask you a few questions about the neighborhood." You can learn a lot of valuable information about your prospective home from neighbors: the reason the owners are selling, how long they lived there, if they took good care of the property, etc. Ask about driving on the roads during foul weather, whether there is school bus service, whether they ever lose power and, if so, how long those outages tend to last. Nobody can tell you more about your potential home and neighborhood than the people who have been living there.

If you are introverted and averse to stopping by unannounced, you can look up the names of the nearby property owners in the town registry. You can even do Internet searches to determine what they do for a living, if they have a criminal history, etc. Sure, this is borderline stalker-ish, but no one wants to find out their next door neighbor has a violent criminal past after they've closed on their house. Even if your neighbors are beyond shouting distance, fertilizer/animal smells, pesticides, gunshots and machinery noises carry. Spend a few evenings and early mornings staking out your potential neighborhood. Sit in your car, windows down, and just listen, look and smell. Finding out your neighbor starts hammering away in their woodshop every morning at five is something you want to know ahead of time. You also don't want find out that the livestock farm a few miles down the road has a horrible stench that carries all the way to your house on windy days.

IN TOWN OR IN THE COUNTRY

A big thing to consider and think about is if you would like to live in town or outside of the central village in the "country." In-town properties are much easier to sell and often stay on the market for shorter periods of time than country homes, simply because there is a smaller market for rural properties. Homes located in the town center or within a five-minute drive to town are more desirable and usually more expensive per square foot than country properties. If you want acreage, you will get the best deals looking outside of the town center. Another thing to consider with in-town or "country" properties is if you'll be on town water and which electricity grid you'll be on. If you are considering an area with harsh winters or frequent natural disasters, being located closer to town will ensure your power will be restored and you'll receive help faster than those living in the further reaches. Some in-town properties have additional conveniences like garbage pick-up, sewer and pre-treated town water. If you live outside of town you may have to take your garbage to the dump yourself, maintain a septic system and have a well for your water, along with any filters and treatment devices necessary.

If you have kids or plan on having them at some point, there are pluses and minuses to living in town. In the country, your kids will have more space to explore, but when they are old enough for school and sports, you might feel like you've turned into a full-time chauffeur. If you would like to live closer to town but want to grow your own food or raise animals, look into the laws in the area you are considering to make sure you can keep animals. Sometimes there will be a lot size required for certain animals, which will help guide your search. If you are on the fence about in town or in the country, see if you can find a rental in both and compare. Do you prefer the quiet and privacy of the country, knowing it comes with the additional work of keeping the grass mowed, trees trimmed and roads clear? Or do you prefer to be able to walk around town and spend time outdoors in public spaces rather than on your own land? This is a personal choice everyone must make and it should be made after careful consideration. If you are leaning towards the country, remember that it takes longer (in most instances) to sell a country house so you really want to be sure the house you find is right for you.

HEATING & COOLING

Chances are that no matter where you decide you want to move, you will need to have some form of heating or cooling or both. Moving from a city, this is often the biggest sticker shock, as many apartment dwellers have their heat included in their rent or HOA fees. The price of heating oil in the winter can be jaw dropping, just like the price of continuous AC in the sweltering summer months. You don't want to find this out the hard way. Not only should you have your inspector carefully look at your heating and cooling systems, but you also want to see if your oil and propane tanks are owned or leased. If they are leased it means that you don't have a choice of which oil or propane providers serve your home so you won't be able to do any price comparisons. Also check to see if the warranty and/or coverage for the water heater, air purifier, water filter and so forth are voided when the property transfers hands. Another crucial step is to call the oil company and electric company and ask for their most recent bills for the extreme weather months for the home you're looking at. Not only will this give you a very good idea of what you are in store for, but it will also help determine if the house is well insulated. Many folks I've met through Urban Exodus bought their house and discovered the first winter that many of the walls and ceilings in their home had little to no insulation. This is an easy but expensive fix, and it is better to know ahead of time if you'll need to update your home's insulation or heating and cooling systems. If the home has a system you aren't familiar with, you should research it before making an offer. Heat pumps, solar, geothermal, radiant floor heating, etc. are all recent technological advances that can help offset the costly electric and oil alternatives, but you shouldn't just buy a place without understanding the repairs, costs and upkeep these systems require.

NATURAL DISASTERS & AIR QUALITY

We talked about this briefly in the previous chapter, but once you've decided on a location, you should research the natural disasters that have occurred in the area where the home that you are considering is located. What flood zone is the property in? What is the 100-year flood expectancy? Your property could be fine in floods, but roads surrounding it could become inaccessible, meaning you will be cut off from the rest of the world until the waters retreat. Was the home damaged in past earthquakes, floods, hurricanes or tornadoes? If it was, be sure your home inspector knows so that they can keep a close eye out for any residual damages. Knowing the natural disaster history of the home will also help determine how high your home insurance premiums will be. In higher-risk areas premiums can be quite expensive.

Where I live in rural New England, a natural gas called radon has a high presence in the air, and it has been linked to lung cancer. When looking at homes in an area with radon present, it is important to have a radon level test done. If the radon levels are measured at an unsafe level, you should factor the cost of a radon mitigation system into your offer—these systems can cost thousands of dollars and, if there aren't many local service providers, sometimes have a long waiting list for installation.

I'VE GOT THE POWER...OR NOT

Rural areas are often amongst the last to be served if a power line goes down. Homes located in town or on the same grid as the area hospital are usually the first to be restored in a power outage. In the further reaches, people may be forced to go days, or even weeks, without power. Before deciding on a home, go to the town office or call the electricity company to see what power line grid the home is located on. You might also want to inquire if they have a record of the longest time that the home has been cut off from power during an outage. If you decide to move to a home where losing power for long periods of time is a possibility, a back-up power generator is a must. Even if you have a generator, if you have an electric pump for your well, you won't be able to use tap water, so make sure you've got plenty of water and other essentials stored in case of an emergency. A wood stove in a place where long power outages are possible can be a lifesaver if you don't have a generator—it can help keep your pipes from freezing and melt snow for water.

Unfortunately, I know this from first-hand experience. Our second winter in Maine we were hit with several ice storms. We lost power for a week and a half, while our friends in town had their power restored in less than twenty-four hours. We had no running water, which meant no flushing toilets, no showers, no laundry, nothing. We also had to do our best to keep the house warm so our pipes wouldn't freeze and burst in the negative temperatures. Our small woodstove became the hero in this story. Cooking around the clock, it kept our house temperature just above freezing and fortunately we didn't have the expensive mess and heartache associated with busted pipes. This cautionary tale isn't to dissuade, simply to inspire you to take the time to inquire about the power grid and factor the cost of a generator into the price of the property if you don't have a woodstove or other heat source to protect your home during harsh weather.

WATER QUALITY & QUANTITY

Are there any water features on the property you are considering, such as natural springs, rivers or a lake? Unless you are lucky enough to find a property on municipal town water, most rural properties draw their water from private wells, which may be contaminated with minerals, sewage, radon, lead or even dangerous chemicals. Insist on a water test before making an offer on the house. If you discover problems with the water, factor the cost of a treatment plan into your offer. Water treatment and softeners can be really expensive. If you don't treat the water before you buy your home, you will be saddled with handling the entire cost. Your home inspector should evaluate your well equipment and will occasionally do a basic on-site water quality test, but that should not serve as the only water test done before making your offer. A certified lab should test a sample of the well water for bacteria, high concentrations of minerals, pesticides, etc. In some areas, the local health department offers free or low-cost water testing. If the home you are looking at is in an agricultural area, it is important to have a full spectrum of lab tests done to ensure your water is potable. If the home you are looking at already has a functioning water treatment or water softening system in place be sure to check to see if the current owners own or lease the system. Sometimes businesses will lease these systems to homeowners, which requires monthly payments.

Another thing that's important to check is the well water quantity, well water flow rate and the well recovery rate. Droughts are common, even in places with steady rainfall, and you don't want to be caught in a situation where your well runs dry and you have no water for days, months or even years. Some key questions to ask: 1) What kind of well is it (driven point, drilled, hand dug, spring, stream, etc.)? 2) Where is it located (that includes the pump, pressure control switch, reservoir tanks, pressure tank and water treatment equipment)? The well water quantity will tell you how much water is available to the pump after the water has risen to its maximum height in the well, before the pump has turned on. The well flow rate is measured over a 24-hour period and is often called the well yield. This will tell you the maximum rate that water can be taken out of the well once the reserve and storage tanks have been fully consumed. The well recovery rate describes the rate at which water runs into the well and the rate at which water can be pumped out of the well without running the well dry. Typical well recovery rates run from less than a gallon per minute (bad) to more than 10 gpm (great for residential use). If you plan on farming and irrigating your crops you will want to ensure you have both high flow and recovery rates, along with a high well water quantity. It is also important to know that these rates can change over time. Someone drilling a nearby well can tap into the same water table and cause your levels to drop, dryer seasons and droughts can significantly affect water levels and recovery rates, local blasting for construction or fracking can reduce your levels and also contaminate your well water with silt and lastly, global warming has caused permanent water level shifts that drop water tables permanently. Why scare you with this information? Because you want to make sure your water and well are kick-ass just in case a drought hits or a subdivision is put in nearby and they start drawing off the same water table.

LEARNING THE HARD (WATER) WAY

When we bought our property it already had a purification treatment system in place. Our water was cold, clean and delicious. It wasn't until year two when we had three pin-hole leaks in our pipes that we realized the high mineral content in our water was eating away at the inside of our copper pipes. The only solution was to buy an expensive water softening system that required us to measure and add natural softeners to our system every month. When we go out of town and the water sits in our pipes we need to let the water run for a few minutes or it tastes like old fish (the taste of the natural softener). Knowing how hard our water was and that it could eventually disintegrate our copper pipes would have been something we would've loved to know before we made our offer. You live and you learn. Don't make the same mistake we did.

SEWER AND SEPTIC SYSTEMS

Well, we've officially gotten to the dirty nitty gritty of home buying: what happens to your waste. First things first, you need to figure out if the house you are considering is connected to a public sewer or if it has its own septic system. If you live in town you might have the luxury of being connected to the public utility sewer system. That means everything that flushes and flows down the drain leaves your home and you never have to think about it again. Being hooked up to the town sewer does come with a monthly fee, but you won't be responsible for maintenance or repairs aside from any issues your pipes might have connecting to the public sewer system.

A septic system is a whole other ball of wax. It doesn't have a monthly fee (bonus!) but all of the repairs and updates are your responsibility (ouch!). Ask anyone living rurally and they will tell you that septic systems can be a terrible and costly headache from time to time. Modern septic systems are composed of a holding septic tank and a leach field. The septic tank contains microbes that digest organic matter and allow solids to settle on the bottom while the liquid flows out to the leach field via perforated piping. When installed, the health department will inspect the size, design and location of the septic system, so you should be able to find this information in their records. One important thing to consider is the size. If there were only two people living in the house before and your family is larger, or you plan on having big dinners or parties at your new home, you should pay careful attention to the size of the tank. Smaller septic tanks need to be pumped every one to three years, while larger tanks can have longer intervals between pumps. The more people you have using the facilities, the faster your tank will fill.

Some homes in rural areas still have the older "cesspit" septic system. These systems are no longer legal to install, as they have been known to contaminate well water because they consist of either a perforated tank or just a hole in the ground that leaches untreated sewage into your soil. If you can't find information on your septic system, hire a septic system inspector to determine which system the property has and what condition it is in. If you have a cesspit, it is an easy point of negotiation for getting the price down. A new septic system can cost anywhere from $1,500 to $25,000 depending on the site location, size and design. The bedrock in New England can be a costly hindrance to septic overhauls and well digging, as some locations require dynamite blasting in order to get below the rock. Don't get in a shitty situation: do your sewer and septic homework before making an offer.

ACCESSIBILITY & PRIVATE ROADS

If you're looking for a house in an area with heavy snowfall, make sure that the property is on a road that will be safe to drive on and plowed regularly by the county or town. If not, prepare yourself for dangerous driving conditions by investing in studded snow tires and a four-wheel or all-wheel drive vehicle. Add this cost to the home price so you can begin to figure out what the actual cost of the home you're considering will be. If the home is located on a private road you could be facing thousands of dollars in extra expenses each year, as you will need to split the bill of road maintenance, paving and plowing with your neighbors on the road. That lovely winding road leading up to the home you're touring might belong entirely to that property, which means all of the maintenance costs will be your responsibility. It is amazing what heavy rains and snow can do to both unpaved and paved roads. If the home is in an area that has snowfall in the winter months, call around to local plow truck drivers and determine what the cost will be to plow your drive during the winter season. Even a short driveway can be a big added expense, especially since it coincides with winter's higher heating bills.

HOMEOWNERS INSURANCE

Things that may increase your rate:

-Being further away from a fire department
-The age of your house
-Outbuildings (barns, sheds, silos; Even if you aren't using them they can cost extra.)
-Keeping pets and livestock
-Woodstoves or fireplaces
-Treehouses
-Swimming ponds and/or pools
-Living in a flood plain or in a high-risk natural disaster area
-Running a business out of your home

BUYING A RURAL "COUNTRY" HOME

Searching for country properties located ten minutes or more from rural town centers requires a bit more consideration. You should be ready to set goals, establish what your purpose is and, above all, try your best to avoid instant gratification. If you are in a big hurry, you will most likely not be able to find what you are looking for. Rural properties have fewer interested buyers, but there are usually lots of interested dreamers who are not considering the realities of rural property upkeep and maintenance. It may seem romantic to own a property with many acres of land and outbuildings but, in reality, it is TOUGH work. Unless your land is mostly forest, you will have to cut back brush, clear fallen trees and maintain access roads. You'll be responsible for maintaining the structures, mowing the lawn, clearing debris, and plowing snow in the winter, among other strenuous tasks. Make sure that you are physically able to do these projects yourself, or that you're able to afford to hire helpers. Properties with acreage may have lease agreements in place so it is important to ask if the timber, mineral, hunting and water rights convey with the sale of the property.

If you are interested in buying a rural home with outbuildings, make sure you have your inspector look at these as well. Sometimes inspecting additional structures will cost extra, but it is worth it to know if there are hidden issues with your outbuildings before you buy. If you are buying a property with acreage and there are sheds, chicken coops and farm equipment, don't assume that these will come with the property. It is important in your offer to include a detailed list of the inclusions (e.g., John Deer 2210 tractor, 10 x 12 foot hen house, portable 8 x 7 foot utility shed, all existing gates, all existing fences, etc.). If you don't include a detailed list of included items, you might arrive on closing day to find that the sheds and equipment have all been removed.

BUYING FARMLAND

If you are buying acreage specifically to farm or raise livestock and you don't have much experience with growing crops or raising animals, you will want to have a skilled farmer or rancher help you in your search. I can't even scratch the surface of what someone needs to consider before deciding on a piece of farmland. Unless you have loads of extra money at your disposal, I might consider buying a small piece of land to begin your farm, with potential adjoining land that you could purchase in the future when you expand your operation. You don't want to bite off more than you can handle or manage. Farmland can be much more difficult to find financing for and it can take a very long time to sell, so it is best to pace yourself and use an expert to find a parcel that is right for your purposes. One thing that is absolutely essential to do when considering a piece of farmland is to have the soil tested, and to determine the water table and flood zones. If there are any wells on the property, figure out their draw and recovery rates. If you want to move rurally to farm, this is definitely not the only book you should be reading. Go to the library and check out every book you can on farming, do an apprenticeship position on a farm or take some agriculture classes at a local college.

IN CONCLUSION, DON'T BE SCARED, BE VIGILANT

Okay, wow, that was intense wasn't it? I bet you never thought that you would need to consider or research so many things when looking for a home outside of the city. This chapter is not meant to scare you away, but to prepare and protect you from making expensive rookie mistakes. By following the advice in this chapter you will not go blindly into the home buying process; you will be informed and know what you are getting yourself into so that you don't have any surprises down the road. After a property meets your initial requirements (size, location, acreage, number of rooms, etc.), start ticking off these other important things before making your offer. You can always make an offer contingent on a home inspection, soil/water tests and other discovery-period line items. If you are afraid that putting the time in to do this additional research might mean that you lose out to another buyer, that is a great way to secure the property before making a final decision. Inventory in rural areas is slim, and patience is not only a virtue but also a necessity when searching for a rural property. You don't want to close on a house that is just okay only to have the perfect house come on the market a few months later. Take your time, breathe, do research, and most importantly, have fun. This home signifies your next chapter and it is important that with all of the other growing pains and difficulties you will undoubtedly face while making this transition, you are able to come home at the end of a trying day, look around and give yourself a pat on the back for taking your time and choosing wisely.

GETTING SETTLED

How to make a smooth transition

"What's proving toughest to get used to is the utter lack of anything resembling anonymity. There is no getting around the fact that there just aren't all that many people, and sometimes that can feel totally suffocating. When someone stays overnight at your house you get asked about it at dinner parties because people wondered whose car was in your driveway."

— Jesse Ellison, Writer

Many city folks want to know what the transition will be like and what they should expect to go through their first year adjusting to country life. While this is different for everyone, there are some common threads woven through the experiences of the hundreds of ex-urbanites I've interviewed. Getting settled and making your new place feel like home, learning to sleep without the hum of the city, adjusting to the odd combination of the lack of anonymity and isolation, missing the conveniences and endless options of your previous city life, contending with the elements of the natural world and having trouble fitting in are normal components of the transition that nearly every ex-urbanite goes through. In this chapter, we will go over these common, sometimes difficult, changes you'll experience and give you creative ways to adapt, cope and feel satiated in your new environment. While what I cover in this chapter might not end up being part of your story, it can still be comforting to know that if you struggle, stumble or feel regret from time to time, you are certainly not alone. Hang in there, once you get settled, you're going to love this new life.

MOVING IN & GETTING SETTLED

For most, moving rurally means moving to a place that has more space than they had in the city, sometimes significantly more. Moving the contents of a crammed city apartment into a larger rural house or apartment feels liberating, but also can invoke a powerful human desire to nest and immediately fill the vacant spaces with new stuff. It takes time to quiet that fast-paced, instantly-gratified city brain and many new arrivals find themselves attempting to quickly fill the empty rooms of their new home via late night

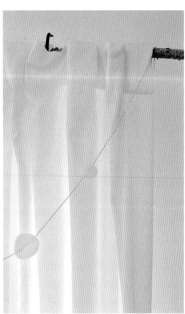

online splurges. I encourage you to relax and not give in to the urge to get settled immediately. Let this be the chance to practice your first country mantra of "good things take time." In this case, the good thing is making your new place feel like home. Why move in slowly? First, it's expensive to buy everything all at once and I guarantee that you'll be happy you saved that money for other pressing expenses later on. Second, you no longer have a myriad of stores and delivery options, so this is an opportunity to get creative, take your time, and put your own stamp on your place as opposed to just filling it with Ikea furniture.

For the first six months that we lived in our house, we slept on a mattress on the floor, had one small dining room set from my Seattle apartment, a vintage 50s hairdryer chair and a ratty hand-me-down loveseat as our only seating. I look back on those days with incredible fondness—it was almost as if the pace of us moving in paralleled the pace of us adapting to this new chapter, one where slow and steady wins the race. Having both physical and mental space readily available, partnered with being surrounded by sticks, stumps, and natural building materials, we decided to try and build as much of our furniture as we could—what we couldn't build ourselves, we would try to source locally. Not only did this help us make friends and become familiar with the area, but now nearly everything in our home has a story—a friend's painting, an old stump we found in the woods and refinished and a dresser we bought at a neighbor's estate sale.

Our first summer, we traded workshop space to some carpenters in exchange for them building our bed out of old boards from our barn's hayloft. I scoured thrift stores, junk shops and flea markets to find diamonds in the rough and put in a little elbow grease to make them shine. We took any hand-me-downs offered to us, and the things that didn't immediately work for us we kept in our basement for future use or gave to friends that had use for them. By taking time, getting creative and curbing our desire for instant gratification, we saved loads of money and have created a place that we love to come home to. Here are a few easy and inexpensive projects for your home. You don't need to be an expert carpenter to build your own furniture. These projects require less skill and patience than putting together anything from Ikea.

BRANCH WINDOW COVERINGS

Something I didn't realize in the city is that window coverings are freaking EXPENSIVE! In the city, I never had more than two or three windows that I covered with the crappy pre-existing rental mini-blinds and softened with a curtain or two. Being faced with lots of windows to cover, I nearly passed out when I totaled up what the cost would be for curtain rods alone. Then I got crafty. These branch window coverings I made out of necessity, but they have become the most complimented thing in our house. Lots of friends have followed suit.

MATERIALS

Long, thin branches cut 6–12" (15–20 cm) longer than the length of your window(s)

Cast-iron j-hooks that fit the branches (can be bought online or in a garden store—often labeled as a plant hanging hook)

Stud-sensor

Screws

Electric screwdriver

Curtains—you can make these out of inexpensive drop cloths and sew them to work with the tree width, buy curtains with wide cloth loops or buy curtains with hook holes and use ball chain loops to ease them over the branch.

First, use your stud sensor to determine where the studs are for your cast-iron j-hooks (or you can screw into the window trim if you prefer). Once you determine where they are, mark a location for your hole using a pencil (I like about 3 inches [8 cm] outside the window pane and 3 inches [8 cm] above it). For a snug and secure fit, use your electric drill to drill a hole slightly smaller in size than your j-hook. Screw your j-hooks into the wall in the pre-drilled holes. Measure the length between the two j-hooks and add 6 to 12 inches (15 to 30 cm) to the overall length. Once you have that number, head out into the woods. Your ideal sapling is about 1 to 1.5 inches (2.5 to 4 cm) in diameter, without many branches. These are best found on the edges of clearings or in thick woods where saplings don't receive a lot of light. Measure before you cut and remove any branches. Add your curtains to either side of your branch curtain rod before lifting up to secure in the j-hook. Enjoy your new window coverings!

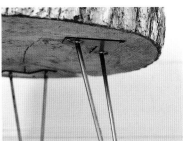

THREE-LEGGED STUMP TABLE

Guess what, you can build one of those sexy hairpin leg "handmade" tables that cost a pretty penny in the city yourself—for cheap! There are many places you can buy hairpin legs online—hairpinlegs.com is my favorite. Once we started building tables with hairpin legs we were hooked. Three legs are easier than four because you don't need to balance them to keep them from wobbling, but honestly it isn't too difficult to balance them.

MATERIALS

1 thin stump or flat surface (you can find old table tops at junk shops)

3 hairpin legs at your desired height

Screws about ¾ the width of the stump or top you are using

Electric drill

Electric screwdriver

First, find a stump, round tabletop or chunk of wood you would like to use. Try to make sure the table top is flat and not warped or lopsided, as that will create a lopsided final table. Prep the table top by sanding or painting it to your specifications. Once your table top is fully dry, cleaned and prepped, flip it over on a flat moving blanket or piece of cardboard. Place the legs in an equilateral triangle shape, about 3 to 4 inches (8 to 10 cm) from the edges of the tabletop.

(continued)

Make a mark in pencil where each of the screws will need to be drilled for the legs. Remove the legs and grab your electric drill. For a snug and secure fit, use your electric drill to drill a hole slightly smaller than your screws. Put the legs back in place and use your screwdriver to screw the legs on. Flip your new table over and enjoy.

SLEEPING—WHY IS THE QUIET SO LOUD?

It's your first night in your new place. You're exhausted and excited. Maybe you had to break your lease, or maybe you had a harrowing journey navigating your U-Haul through city streets and freeways. But you've done it. You're finally ready for your first night of restful sleep in the peaceful, quiet, dreamy country. No sirens. No drunk people yelling on their way home from the bars. No honking invading your dreams. You lay your head to rest and wait for sleep to set in. You wait. And wait. And wait.

Argh, why is the quiet so loud? Your first few nights of sleep in the country can be excruciating. Every creak, every peep, prickles the ears and paints shadows where they do not linger. If you have moved into an older house, of which there are plenty in the country, your mind might be imagining ghosts or some nightmarish Hollywood take on hillbillies lurking outside your window. Never fear, this paranoia eases to a lull after a couple of weeks of tossing and turning.

If "delicate sleeper" is a term you've used to describe your sleep patterns in the city, you might be tempted to seek instant relief for this temporary problem. Adding a white noise machine, a fan, earplugs or even sleeping pills can do the trick. But relying on these aids will only diminish your chances of ever experiencing that blissful goddamn peace and quiet you promised yourself. The best advice is to give it time. For now, just wallow in the silence. Your body and your mind will get used to it. Stretching your legs and venturing out for a night walk before you go to sleep can help you become familiar with your new evening soundscapes.

It can also help to identify the noises, both to dispel your fears and pass the time, as you lay in bed: the banging, popping, high-pitched squeals of an old furnace; the blood curdling cries of a red fox or barn owl (both sound almost exactly like a woman screaming); the skittering of mice (sorry, unless you live in a brand new house, mice will most likely be in the walls); the guttural "glumb" of the bullfrog, the chorus of spring peeper frogs or the summertime chirping of crickets.

In the daylight hours, be sure you have made friends with your neighbors (read Neighbors and Community [page 57]). Knowing dependable folks are just down the lane and ready to come to your rescue can put even the most paranoid mind at ease. Your neighbors also might be able to identify any unusual or unnerving sounds you've heard: a deer warning call, a squeaky floor board, morning duck hunters or the creepy whispering sounds of roosting guinea fowl. And remember, sounds can carry much further in a place without noise pollution, so even if something sounds like it's right outside your window, it could be coming from more than a mile away.

SCARY ANIMAL NOISES

Animals that can sound like a woman screaming or baby crying: Cougars, peacocks, red foxes, an injured or scared rabbit, goats, sheep, owls, fisher cats and even some frogs and lizards.

HOW TO SILENCE A SQUEAKY FLOOR

Squeaky floorboards are common in old homes, where the house has settled or the floorboards have dried out and shrunk. There is good news though: this is one of the few sounds in the country that you can easily quiet. Start by walking over the floor, listening closely to pinpoint the exact location of the squeak. Then use a stud finder to find the closest floor joist (the floor support beam that typically runs perpendicular to the floor boards). If you haven't picked up a stud finder at the hardware store yet, you can use a hammer or another heavy object to knock on the floor, listening for a flatter, thinner sound. Use a heavy-duty wood screw and a drill to attach the squeaky board to the joist, and voila! No more squeak. If all else fails, remember, many people think the squeak of a floorboard underfoot is charming.

GOODBYE ANONYMITY

By far, losing anonymity is the most commonly cited thing that ex-urbanites had trouble adapting to. Even if you didn't like being anonymous in the city and passing a sea of nameless faces every day in your daily existence made you feel lonely, no one fully appreciates anonymity until they've lost it. Once you've relocated to a small community, it is impossible to stay mysterious for long. People gossip and new arrivals are a hot and interesting topic of conversation. You might find that people already know of you even if they've never met you. You might also find that if you aren't proactive about meeting neighbors and making friends, people will start to fabricate their own rumors about you. It will no longer be possible to do errands without running into someone who wants to chat or introduce themselves. It is important to be kind to everyone you meet because any missteps or curt interactions could come back to haunt you.

If you find yourself struggling to adapt, it can prove helpful to occasionally take weekend drives to new communities so you can enjoy a precious moment of anonymity in a restaurant or coffee shop. Not only will it help give you a taste of privacy again, but it also can help you get a wider lay of your new landscape. Visiting a city every couple of months can also really help put things in perspective and make you better appreciate this new life you're building. When we first moved, I had a really hard time adjusting. Staying with friends in New York for a weekend every three or four months really helped get me out of my head and remind me of all the positives of living rurally—including the lack of anonymity. Watching cabbies yell at each other, getting pushed on the subway, and receiving cold glares from people passing me on the street made me yearn for the friendly, familiar faces in my new small community. Each visit to New York got harder and less enjoyable; after only a day or two I was ready to get back to the place where everyone knew my name. The frequency of our visits slowed and now I haven't been back in a year and a half. When we have to go for work, I get excited about eating food, going to museums and seeing friends, but during my entire visit I'm anxious to get home.

Eventually most people warm to their new lack of anonymity. Although initially it totally freaked me out that people already knew who I was before I had ever had a conversation with them, I now appreciate the many positives of living in an area where you can't be anonymous. Living in a community where everyone knows everyone requires that people be on their best behavior. You can't get away with being a jerk or a busy body without building a bad reputation that will stick with you. You can't get away with ripping people off, acting superior or being cruel; lack of anonymity keeps people on the up and up. You also can't avoid people, so if you have a problem with someone you have to be proactive and work it out. When I lived in the city and someone burned me, I would just write them off indefinitely; I can't do that here. There is tremendous merit in having to swallow your pride from time to time and face your problems head on instead of avoiding them.

LONELY ISOLATION

Another common theme in making the transition is feeling lonely or isolated. Even if you move to the country with a significant other or with your family, it's still easy to feel lonely or isolated, as you are now cut off from your other social outlets. It's easy to hide out at home, distract yourself with crossing things off your endless 'to do' list and wallow in your loneliness. If you move in the wintertime, it can be even more difficult to fight feelings of loneliness and isolation. The only way to curb these feelings is to be proactive and face them head on. Throw yourself into a project, try your hand at a new hobby, enroll in a cooking class or put effort into making new friends and acquaintances. In Meeting Your Mates (page 117) we discuss how to make friends and date in the country. If you're feeling sad and alone, use that advice to help pull yourself out of your slump and build and nurture your local social circle.

GOODBYE CONVENIENCE & ENDLESS OPTIONS

In most small towns you're lucky to find anything open past 9:00 p.m. Even grocery stores, pharmacies and gas stations close up for the night—in some places, in some seasons, at 6:00 p.m. Coming from a city that never sleeps, it can be difficult to adapt to earlier close times and fewer options. I remember driving home from the airport late at night and panicking because I couldn't find a gas station open to fill up my tank. Somehow, I made it all the way home on fumes. You can't get your groceries delivered. There are few, if any, food takeout places. It can be tough to find a decent cup of coffee. And the variety and endless options you were accustomed to in the city are gone. These are just the facts. They can't be changed. But you can play an active role in adapting and coping with the lack of instant gratification and endless options to choose from. Sure, you will probably always yearn for those soup dumplings or French pastries from that place you used to frequent in the city, but guess what, when you go back to visit, you can still get them, and I guarantee you will savor and appreciate them so much more than you ever did when you had the luxury of getting whatever you wanted, whenever you wanted it.

THE JOY OF COOKING

First thing's first, if you don't already know how, you're going to have to learn how to cook. Before I moved rurally I was good at making salads, pasta sauce and eggs—that's it. Being single in Seattle, it didn't make sense to cook for myself every night. It was expensive and messy and I didn't like having to eat tons of leftovers. Plus, I had amazing, inexpensive food within walking distance of my house. Why figure out how to make a pulled-pork sandwich when you can just go buy one from one of the best Cuban sandwich shops around? Spend three days making stock for pho when you can get the real thing from the Vietnamese restaurant down the street?

Everyone I've featured on Urban Exodus said they now make most of their meals at home and eat out way less than they did in the city. When you get home from work in the country, there usually aren't bars or happy hours to go to; you have the rest of your evening at your disposal for developing your culinary prowess. I'd start by checking a few cookbooks out of your library. Make it easy on yourself and don't start with complex ethnic cuisine that requires spices and ingredients that could prove difficult to source locally. The best cookbooks are ones specific to your region so you can learn how to best prepare ingredients that are readily available in your area. Working with fresh and local ingredients makes it easy to make great food. If you are like me and are intimidated by the time commitment and mess associated with cooking, start with one-pot slow cooker recipes. You can prep and put everything in the pot before you start work, and by dinnertime you'll have dinner ready to go.

Cooking, like any skill, takes time to develop. Living rurally without knowing how to cook will definitely make your life less rich. You can't live off of greasy spoon diner food and boxed cereal for the rest of your life. You have moved closer to where food is grown and raised, so make the most of it. With enough practice it is easy to go off-recipe and start experimenting on your own. Don't be scared to mess up—that is part of the process of learning. I've cooked some total flops, but I've also made some impressive meals. If there is something from your previous life that you are desperate for, see if you can figure out how to make it yourself. I was amazed at how many recipes I found online developed by home cooks and chefs replicating famous city eats. I successfully copied a chicken sandwich I had been dreaming about for months by experimenting and combining some recipes developed by others for the same sandwich (apparently many people dream of this sandwich).

SCHEDULING CONVENIENCE

If losing the conveniences of city life has got you down, streamline your new country life and build a rough schedule to make your life feel more convenient. It is easy to just go to the grocery store whenever you need stuff, but living rurally that might mean a long drive—and many social run-ins— between you and your groceries. Write a list, plan out the meals you're going to cook for the week and buy everything in one trip. If you want to avoid getting stuck in lots of conversations, go in the early morning when the store opens.

Schedule your time: for housework and yard work, and also for relaxation and exercise. Figure out what it costs you hourly vs. what others would charge to do certain tasks, and then decide whether it makes sense to continue managing those things or if it's better to hire someone else to do it. Trying to do everything yourself will not only exhaust you, but will take time away from making money, doing things you are efficient at and actually getting a chance to enjoy your new life in the country. If going to the dump twice a month cuts into your work schedule, hire someone to haul your stuff away. When we moved we felt like we needed to do everything ourselves, both to learn how and to save money. Once we learned how to do everything that was required for our daily existence, I realized that certain things weren't cost efficient to manage ourselves. A website or illustration project pays me more hourly than what someone would charge me to prune my trees or haul brush. While I still do these things when I have bandwidth, I have been able to grow my business by outsourcing some of my 'to do' list when my plate is full with paying work.

The digital age has, without question, made the transition to country living easier. Not only are we able to stay connected with friends and family on video chats and social media, but we also can participate in the global marketplace where convenience is the name of the game. Sadly, I don't know of a place that ships Chinese takeout to your door, but there are lots of online stores where convenience is one click away. Many folks I've interviewed don't know how they would survive without their Amazon Prime account. I know…I know…many feel like Amazon is the online equivalent of Wal-Mart, but the convenience of free two-day shipping and access to Prime entertainment can be very enticing. At the click of a button you can get toiletries, pantry items, clothes, electric fencing, tools, gardening supplies, etc. Several new moms I know rurally have diaper subscriptions and diapers are dropped on their doorstep every two weeks. When we first moved, I relied heavily on online shopping. Now, four years in, I try my best to source things locally before going online—both because it helps our local economy and it helps me meet new craftspeople and small business owners. Here are some of my favorite resources for online shopping convenience:

Sierratradingpost.com—Discounted practical clothing and outdoor gear. I shop here for winter boots, jackets, long underwear, etc.

Overstock.com—Great deals on housewares, furniture, tools and home improvement stuff (faucets, hardware, etc.). Free shipping on everything.

Wayfair.com—They sell everything from throw pillows to water tanks. Free shipping on nearly everything they sell.

Asianfoodgrocer.com—Just like your favorite Asian market in the city, you can buy ingredients that are hard to find rurally, get recipes, buy housewares, etc.

BATTLING THE ELEMENTS

A common reality that comes with transitioning from city to country life is being much more intimately connected with the natural world. There are obviously many positives associated with reconnecting with nature, but it can also be tremendously difficult to adapt to living in a more natural environment. In the city, for the most part, the environment is man-made. The streets are smooth and paved, the landscape has been planted and manufactured, and the natural world has been tamed and curated for our ease and enjoyment. The temperature in city apartments and office buildings is usually managed for you, so extremely hot or cold weather can pass by without much notice. Living in the city I can't recall ever getting a bug bite, a sunburn or having to clean up after a storm. The city's infrastructure protected me from experiencing such things. I had little use for practical clothing and could make it through even extreme weather days wearing heels and a light jacket.

FASHIONISTA TO PRATICALISTA

Living rurally means having to prioritize function over fashion. There is no such thing as bad weather, just bad clothing, and an easy way to adapt to the elements is to embrace practical clothes. Even the most stylish ex-urbanite can't last long living in the elements without caving and getting some practical outerwear. Fortunately, the new lumbersexual trend popping up in cities all over emulates practical country attire, so it's easier than ever to bridge the gap between being stylish and being sensible. It took me the better part of a year before I embraced technical clothing. I spent my first winter in a soggy, miserable wool pea coat and wet leather ankle boots before I gave in. Sourcing relatively stylish, practical clothes became a fun and challenging game. Turns out Canadian footwear and clothing brands (Canadian Goose, Sorel, Santana, Muttonhead) are amazing at blending winter practicality with urban style, and L.L. Bean actually has some pretty cool looking sensible clothes with a lifetime guarantee.

My advice for new arrivals is to invest in a few crucial practical pieces (if you don't have them already): an insulated coat for the cold, a waterproof shell, waterproof boots, thin long underwear, a wide-brim sunhat and some breathable long sleeve shirts for the summer. Your style and clothing will inevitably change as you settle in and find out what works best for your habits and environment, but it's important to know that being a slave to fashion doesn't work in the country. No one cares what you look like, and honestly dressing too "city" will not make it easy to fit in and make friends. Eventually it will feel incredibly liberating to throw on any old thing and not care as much about your appearance. Just yesterday I was clearing out a closet where I had been putting things I hadn't worn in a while. It was filled with heels, corporate work pantsuits, and skin-tight dresses. Guess what, I don't miss any of those clothes now. I'm much more concerned about staying dry and warm through my hike or, in my garden, protecting myself from the sun and biting insects, than I am about looking cool.

Speaking of biting insects, we can't talk about making the transition without talking about bugs and creepy crawlies. In the city maybe you had a couple of run-ins with a scary spider or two on your ceiling, but in the country there is no hiding from the biting insects of the natural world. When I first moved to Maine I couldn't believe how many different varieties there were: black flies, mosquitos, no-see-ums, horseflies, ticks...my skin crawls just thinking about them. My first summer I was literally covered in welts from black fly bites. I pulled fifteen embedded ticks off me, followed by mosquito bites, no-see-um bites and then the painful bites of the horsefly. By the end of the summer I was nearly ready to throw in the towel and go back to my bug-free life in the city. I tried nearly every repellent on the market, wore a DEET fan hiking, bought permethrin soaked clothes, and still I couldn't shake them. My advice for adapting to bugs might not be welcomed advice because honestly there is nothing you can do to completely remove yourself, aside from locking yourself inside, but that's not why you moved to the country, is it? Here are some things I learned about bugs that have made my springs and summers so much more enjoyable:

Don't wear dark colors: New Yorkers aren't the only ones who love dark colors—so do bugs. In the spring and summer months transition your wardrobe to lighter colors. Not only will you get fewer bites, but ticks will be easier to find if you're not wearing black.

Invest in a beekeeping hat and veil: Biting insects love the warming months of spring, perfectly timed with planting your garden and doing yard work. Keep bugs from biting your face and around your eyes by wearing a beekeeping hat. Who knows, maybe you'll decide to keep bees and it will serve dual purposes.

No exposed skin when working outside: Even if it's a hot day, don't garden or do yard work in shorts and a tank top. Not only will you be susceptible to sunburn and cuts but you will also be a bug magnet. If you are still wearing skinny jeans, rub some bug repellent on them or mosquitos will bite you right through them. If you are hiking in the woods, pull your socks over your pants to keep ticks from crawling up your pant legs and cover your shoes and socks in repellent. When you get inside, take off all your clothes, pop them in the dryer for twenty minutes to kill any ticks and do a tick check while you wait.

Invest in some natural bug oil: I've tried nearly everything on the market. Seriously. I felt like spraying myself with DEET every day was putting me on the fast track to some sort of cancer. I found this all natural bug oil called White Mountain that is made in New Hampshire, and it has protected me from nearly every biting insect I've come across in both Maine and out on the West Coast. The only thing you should know is that you need to reapply every hour or two. I honestly should be their spokesperson as I have gotten loads of friends hooked on the stuff. Will it work for you? I hope so! If not, ask your friends and community as there might be something that locals swear by.

Wind and dry weather are your bug fighting friends: Flying insects can't navigate through windy conditions. If it's a windy day, prioritize outdoor work and save indoor work for still days. Dry weather keeps most biting insects at bay—even ticks. Insects need water to survive and reproduce so if it's been dry for a few weeks, there will likely be fewer insects to contend with.

Don't water your garden or do yard work after the sun has gone down: Bugs love the evening hours, which is when they most like to come out and feed. If you can wake up earlier and get your outdoor chores done before you have to go to work (as opposed to after) you will save yourself from being a bug buffet.

Build a screened-in space for evening outdoor enjoyment: If you haven't bought a house yet, add screens to your list of must-haves. Some homes don't have screens on the windows and if you have a lot of windows adding screens to all of them can get expensive. If you are moving, or have moved, to an area that is known for its bugs, a screened-in porch or pop-up screen tent is an incredible way to enjoy the outdoors at night without being attacked.

Lastly, time helps. I can't prove this scientifically, but I honestly think that biting insects are more attracted to "fresh" meat. When I first moved to Maine I was a novelty—cuisine from a far off place— and I'm convinced it made bugs more interested in biting me than others. I would go to a BBQ and be covered in bites and no one else would. Also, I was much more reactive than locals who had built up an immune tolerance. Now, after four years, my black fly and mosquito bites no longer swell up to the

size of baseballs and I receive far fewer bug bites than I did when I first moved. By getting wise and making adjustments to wardrobe, schedule and lifestyle, I have made summer a time to be celebrated and enjoyed, not a time to be scratching and swatting at endless bugs.

SETTLING IN

Your first year living rurally can be tough—filled with highs and lows. Many ex-urbanites feel like they don't fit in with their new community initially. Some of the nicest small communities to live in can feel closed off to outsiders, and it's important to not get discouraged if you feel like things aren't going your way your first year. Even if you feel like you are adapting and your city ways are melting away, you still need to put effort into finding friends, getting involved in your community, and trying new things. If your community gets particularly excited about an activity, seasonal sport or event, make sure you participate and, better yet, see if you can volunteer to help run things. Becoming a recognizable and helpful face in the community will make fitting in easier. Remember, good things take time to establish in the country. Making the transition can be easy for some, but for others it can take years before they feel like they've fully hit their stride.

NEIGHBORS AND COMMUNITY

*Meeting the neighbors and becoming a member
of your new community*

*"One funny thing that I had to get used to is nearly everyone in our small town waves,
whether they know each other or not. Now I wave too."*

—Sean Fields, Painter

You made it! You've packed up your city life and made your way to the next chapter. You've either found a home to rent or you have planted permanent roots and bought a place. Congratulations, you've arrived! It might feel like your journey is finally done, but this is when the real work begins. Just because you've found your little piece of heaven doesn't mean you can just sit back and wait for neighbors and your new community to come to you.

If you thought you moved out of the city to get away from people, you will be disappointed to know that living rurally requires people to nurture their relationships with those around them and become an active member of their community. Your survival in the country is integrally connected to the relationships you build with your neighbors and your surrounding community. There will most certainly come a time when you need help or advice. By establishing friendships with those around you, you will ensure you'll have people willing to lend a hand or offer invaluable guidance in difficult times. Meeting the neighbors is an easy and painless way to begin building the foundation of your new life in the country. Although it might seem easy to some, a lot of former city folks have a hard time putting themselves out there initially. People can be quick to make assumptions about new arrivals. But postponing meeting your neighbors will mean extra effort to establish your social footing later on.

SMALL WINDOW FOR MAKING INTRODUCTIONS

It only takes a month or two before neighbors lose interest or make their own postulations about the new city folks who have come to town. Usually these assumptions don't paint you in the best light, so it is important to be proactive. Even if you're introverted or painfully awkward, I promise that it will be more uncomfortable to wait and find out the whole town is talking about the rude, anti-social new people who moved to town. Meeting your neighbors is easy, relatively painless and can even be fun. All it takes is some baked goods, a positive attitude and an afternoon. For extra credit, you can even use Whitepages.com to reverse address search your neighbors so you can greet them by name when you arrive on their doorstep to introduce yourself.

WHEN IN DOUBT, BRING DESSERT

My parents moved us from Los Angeles to a remote lumber town in northern California in the early 1980s. My mother knew that as a stay-at-home mom to four young girls, she would need the friendship and support of our new neighborhood. With our closest neighbors almost a quarter of mile down the road, she immediately got to work whipping up batch after batch of her signature giant shortbread cookies. My mother emigrated from England in her teens and although she didn't inherit any prowess in other culinary pursuits, her baking game has always been on point. Shortbreads are a perfect way to break the ice with neighbors. They are relatively easy to make, require just a few key ingredients, have a long shelf life and nearly everyone enjoys their flakey, buttery goodness. After her feverish baking, she packed up each shortbread cookie in a festive tin and set out to knock on doors. In the course of an afternoon, she met nearly every one of our neighbors within a two-mile radius. Delivering the shortbreads in a tin encouraged neighbors to pop by our house to return them and visit a little more. Creating a tight and aligned neighborhood became very important a year after my parents moved when all the neighbors came together to fight a proposed housing development on our quiet country road. My mother already had the friendship and support of her neighbors, which made it easy to quickly come together and stand united against the proposal. Never underestimate the power of dessert.

LENDING A HAND

Offering your services to your neighbors is the very best way to make friends and allies in your community. Do you have an elderly neighbor whose lawn is overgrown? Offer to mow it for them. Do you have a neighbor heading out of town? Offer to feed their animals or watch their house while they are away. Do you know how to change oil, fix computers, take photos, etc.? Offer your help with things you know how to do and let them know you are a phone call away. Sure, you might end up with a neighbor that takes a little more than they give, but there are many things you can learn from someone who grew up in the area, has experience working the land or has machinery and tools you might need to borrow from time to time. Being a good neighbor is a two-way street and it is important that you always pull your weight.

GRANDMA ANN'S "MEET THE NEIGHBORS" SHORTBREAD RECIPE

Yields 1 (8–9" [20–23 cm]) shortbread, serves 4–8 pieces

This recipe was passed down to my mother from my British grandmother. It makes one thin shortbread. You can bake this recipe in an 8-inch (20-cm) cake pan and make your own pattern or design using utensils, but I would recommend investing in a shortbread mold as they add a pretty special little touch to the final dessert. You can easily find shortbread molds at antique stores, cooking stores or online. Before my mom got her first shortbread mold at a department basement sale, she would use a heart-shaped cake pan that she had and prink patterns into it with a fork. I'll often make four times the following recipe to use up a full pound of butter and make four or five shortbreads all at once. It's super simple.

INGREDIENTS

1 stick of butter (½ cup [115 g]) at room temperature—salted is fine

⅓ to ½ cup (64–96 g) white sugar—castor (fine grain) is nice if you have it, but hardly necessary

1 cup (100 g) unbleached white flour

DIRECTIONS

Preheat oven to 350°F (176°C). Blend the butter and the sugar, mixing by hand. Slowly add the flour, also by hand. Knead if necessary to combine the ingredients. Pat firmly and evenly into a well-greased 8-inch (20-cm) cake pan or shortbread mold. Prick through the entire surface with a fork (mixing ingredients with a machine mixer usually adds enough air that the shortbread bubbles and ruins the mold shape). If in a cake pan, sprinkle the surface with sugar (optional). Bake in the oven for about 30 minutes, turning the pan around after about 15 minutes. Cook until slightly brown around the edges and no longer moist looking in the middle. Let cool in the pan for 5 to 10 minutes before moving to a cooling rack.

Note: The shortbread will continue to cook in a hot stoneware mold, so don't let it brown too much in the oven. If in a cake pan, score with a knife into bar sizes (you can also just break pieces off the shortbread to eat). Flip the shortbread out onto a cooling rack when firm and let cool to room temperature. If not eating right away, wrap when cooled to prevent the shortbread from losing crispness.

Note: For all you chocolate lovers out there, add extra oomph by drizzling melted semi-sweet chocolate across the top. Let the chocolate harden before eating it or wrapping it up.

BE KIND, BE HUMBLE

Things in the country move at their own pace and people do things their own way. In urban areas, we are used to speed and efficiency; in the country, living a life well lived takes precedence—thank goodness. It is easy to arrive in your new town and immediately notice that the processes are slower and the technical aptitude is delayed. Your neighbors might still be stuck in what you consider "the old ways" of doing things, but restrain yourself and don't give them your smart city advice on how to streamline their operations. Only offer your advice when asked, and be humble. No one appreciates a know-it-all in the country, especially one that recently moved from the city. It might seem like a no-brainer, but being a kind observer willing to help when asked is much more treasured than being a city slicker who is constantly critiquing the ways things have been done forever. I myself was guilty of being a bit of a braggart when I initially moved rurally as I still felt like living in the city and working for a big company was something worthy of praise. Guess what—it is not. I quickly realized that all of the skills that I had acquired living in the city wouldn't help me survive a year living in my new community. I didn't understand the way of life yet, so how could I possibly critique it?

SLOW TO JUDGE, QUICK TO LEND A HAND

When Thomas McCurdy and Bailey Hale moved to the depressed reaches of Vermont's Northeast Kingdom, they weren't sure how their neighbors would react to two young, gay, first-time farmers from Philadelphia. They were committed to one another and to making this new chapter of their life work. They knew that in an area with long, harsh winters, they would need the help and expertise of their neighbors and the support of their community to stay alive. With the mantra, "slow to judge, quick to lend a hand" they introduced themselves to their neighbors and fellow farmers in their community. They were pleasantly surprised that their kindness and wiliness to lend a hand was reciprocated and in very little time, they became woven into the fabric of their community. Certainly some of their new friends and neighbors had different beliefs and political inclinations, but by proving themselves as friendly, hardworking and trustworthy neighbors, they overcame any previously held prejudices and were welcomed with open arms.

Judgment and prejudice goes both ways. Country folks are stereotyped just as much as urban dwellers. When you arrive in your new community, it is important to not rush to judge the man whose yard looks like a junkyard or the family with political rants on foam core in their front yard. Every person is entitled to their own beliefs. Our life experiences are what guide our beliefs, and those beliefs do not separate the "good folks" from the bad. The homogenization we might have been used to in the city doesn't exist in the country. Living rurally, you can't just surround yourself with only people who are exactly like you (same education, same socio-economic level, same profession, etc.) and have the ability to ignore everyone else. In the country, everyone has to live together, support one another and be a good neighbor.

HOW HARD IS IT TO WAVE?

Remember that thing on the end of your wrist that holds your coffee cup and types your emails? Well guess what, it is also your most valuable tool for making friends and building community in the country. In the country, waving is just something nice that people do to acknowledge one another. A wave goes a very long way and, in some small communities, it is what separates the locals from the outsiders. There are very few excuses for not waving. This goes both for waving when driving in your car and also when people pass by your yard. Do you hate waving? I would suggest moving to a home on a long private drive, as that is really the only way to reduce the frequency of waves. You might move to a community where waving is less of a common practice, so observe local behavior when visiting your perspective new community. If the wave is only used amongst friends, don't feel obligated, but if you live on a road or street with traffic, it is always a good idea to wave to people passing by.

COUNTRY GREETING ETIQUETTE

If you think you can continue going about your day the same way you did in the city, think again. Living in the country requires that you invest a bit more time and energy into building relationships and community. Sure, you can be the weird anti-social person who doesn't talk to anyone, but don't expect any help if your power goes out, you get snowed in or a bunch of trees fall down on your property. In the country, people need each other for survival. In the city, we compete for resources and survival. There is a real mental shift that you need to make when moving rurally. You need to be familiar with country greeting etiquette or be labeled the new rude city slicker—a label that can be very difficult to remove. To help you master the art of country greetings, I have included a number of everyday social situations and the expected level of interaction for each:

Working in the yard: Wave at passersby unless you are in the process of carrying something large and unwieldy or in the middle of some sort of vigorous task. If your arms aren't free, a head nod and a smile will suffice.

Grocery store (bank, post office, etc.): A wave usually isn't enough interaction to make it through a grocery store run in. If you need to make a quick trip to the grocery store, best to plan your excuse if anyone stops you for conversation. Need to pick up your kids, rush off to an appointment or get home before the ice cream melts are all decent excuses for cutting short a grocery store conversation. Another way to cut down your grocery store time is to go in the early morning.

Walking in town: If you are across the street, a wave and a smile to people you know will suffice. If you pass someone you know on the same side of the street, a brief conversation is in order. Try to be the first one to inquire about how their (insert season) is going. If they pass in a car, a wave is sufficient unless they pull over to chat.

Dropping your kids at school: Wave at crossing guards, parents that you have interacted with and teachers. If you are dropping them off in person you should plan to spend more time and have a few conversations with parents and teachers.

Going out to eat: When you run into people at a restaurant, a wave, smile and a quick hello to people you know (if they haven't started eating yet) is an appropriate greeting. If they are mid-meal you can just smile and wave politely.

Sporting or community events: Wave to friends and acquaintances if they are already seated and there is no space around them to sit. If they have space near them and they wave you over, you should join them without protest. If you are at your child's sporting event, don't get overly verbal and yell—be respectful and refrain from getting upset if the game isn't going well or the ref makes a bad call.

TRADING, SHARING & GIFTS

Trading with, sharing with and gifting your neighbors with extra things you have is a great way to build lasting friendships. Our friends trade their raw goat milk with their neighbors who raise pigs for meat. Now they can both benefit from the merits of their collective labor. You could arrange a trade with a neighbor who has a snow plow to plow your drive in the winter in exchange for you mowing their lawn in the summer or help build a business website for a neighbor who runs a mechanic shop in exchange for fixing your car. There is no telling how much easier you can make your life by working with your neighbors. We have other friends who share poultry hatchling orders with their neighbors, as many poultry suppliers have minimum order numbers and smaller farms and hobbyists don't have space or need for a full order. Gifting your neighbors with extra plant seedlings you have, excess tomatoes at harvest time or scrap wood from a construction project are also great ways to show that you care. Before hauling old car parts, furniture, tools, etc. to the dump or salvage ask your neighbors and see if anyone has use for them. Remember that one person's trash is another person's treasure.

NEVER UNDERESTIMATE THE POWER OF A PARTY

Depending on what time of year you are moving, throwing a seasonal party is an excellent way to break the ice and meet all of your neighbors at once. A BBQ or block party in the summer, a bonfire in the spring, a holiday party in the winter or a harvest or costume party in the fall are all good excuses to invite your neighbors over and get to know them. You can have alcohol at your party—just make sure you don't overly indulge, as you want to make a good first impression. Be sure to have plenty of non-alcoholic options as you could have some recovering alcoholics and abstainers in attendance. If you don't have extra money to invest in buying food and drinks for your party, you can always bring your neighborhood together by throwing a potluck. Your party doesn't have to be fancy. Don't stress yourself out by trying to make everything perfect. Just keep things simple and relaxed. Keep reading, as there are more ideas for throwing get-togethers and dinner parties in Meeting Your Mates (page 117) and Embracing the Seasons (page 135).

THE COUNTRY STOP BY

In the city, most of us would never consider stopping by a neighbor or even a friend's house unannounced. In the country any time is fair game. The "country stop by" or "dooryard call" was initially bizarre. I would be out working in the garden or hauling brush and someone would turn down the drive to come say hello, ask if I needed help, offer advice or ask if they could climb an oak tree to forage mushrooms. Although originally I found it unnerving, I came to really enjoy the occasional impromptu visitor. It became a way to take a breather, share a laugh or get an extra set of arms or knowhow for a pressing task. Although I must say, I still haven't been brave enough to stop by neighbors' and friends' places without letting them know ahead of time. I'm certain that in a few years my qualms about this practice will lessen and I'll be the one popping in when I'm in the neighborhood. So when a strange car appears in the driveway or you receive a few too many slow drive-bys from the same car, know that it is likely a neighbor either wanting to introduce themselves or ask a question. Diffuse your city tendencies to think they might have malicious intent and give them a wave, a smile or go up and introduce yourself.

GOOD FENCES DO NOT MAKE GOOD NEIGHBORS

I can't tell you how many times I've seen new city arrivals move to town and immediately erect a giant fence around their property. I understand the reasoning behind this action; they finally have access to the privacy they so desired in the city and now they are going to wall off their kingdom so they can hide from prying eyes and go about their business in peace. Of course it depends on the area you are moving, but tall fences aren't commonplace in most of the rural towns I've visited. Building a tall fence before making friends with your neighbors is an instant way to ostracize yourself. Before you begin fence construction, go meet all of the people living around your house and determine if you even feel like you need a fence. Pricing out fencing materials and ongoing maintenance is also a way to determine if you really want/need a fence. If you are still hell bent on building a fence, let your neighbors know ahead of time and tell them the reasons why (so they don't think they are the reason). Having a dog or small children is a good reason—just wanting to hide is not.

Also, before you invest in purchasing the materials to build one, go to your town office to see if there are any ordinances dictating fence height, materials, etc. A friend of ours learned the hard way that she could only build a five foot fence around her property after completing construction on one that was six feet tall. One thing to consider when thinking about constructing a fence in an area with harsh winters is that snow removal can completely destroy fences located closer than 15 feet to the road. A better solution for privacy, that doesn't feel separatist, is a hedge of bushes or trees. These fare better in the winter, aren't an eyesore for neighbors, and don't immediately single you out as the anti-social person on the block. A short fence to keep your kids and animals contained isn't going to upset anyone, but before building a substantial fence, make sure you have fully thought it through, made friends with your neighbors and told them about your plans and have received approval from the town.

PROBLEM NEIGHBORS

Sometimes no matter how hard you try to be a good neighbor, you end up having a neighbor that just doesn't play nice and isn't willing to be neighborly in return. The best thing to do in this situation is practice killing them with kindness—keep waving, keep smiling and don't let them know that their attitude or aggression is getting to you. Don't air your grievances to your other neighbors and friends, as you never know how intimately connected they may be with your problem neighbor. If word gets back to your difficult neighbor that you have been talking behind their back it will only make things worse for you. If they make a lot of noise, get into yelling matches in their yard or are polluting the ground water or land by dumping, do the neighborly thing first and address your concerns with them directly. Calling law enforcement without speaking with your neighbor beforehand can label you the town crier and will not win you any popularity contests. If you have a problem neighbor, don't worry, just continue to be kind and make friends with your other neighbors and they will either come around eventually or avoid interacting with you. If your neighbor is aggressive and you continually have trouble with them, go to your town office and ask, without mentioning the neighbor by name, what your options are to help deescalate the situation. Some communities have free mitigation or conflict resolution offerings, while others will just refer you to the police station to file a formal complaint or restraining order.

BE A JOINER

Is there a rummage or bake sale your community is running to benefit the volunteer fire department? Volunteer your time to help, contribute items or bake cookies. Being a joiner is a great way to both connect with your neighbors and weave yourself into the fabric of your community. Ask if you can lend a hand and try saying yes to experiences and things that are offered to you. Helping your neighbor fix their greenhouse when it blows down means that they will be more likely to help you should you get into a pickle down the road. Attend your neighbor's gallery show, reading or presentation; show that you care and are interested in what they are doing and they in turn will support you in your endeavors. In the city it is easier to only do the things that are of particular interest to you. But you never know where a new experience may lead you. Watching a lecture presented at our library by a friend and neighbor inspired me to do a better job rotating my garden crops and managing pests using organic methods. By being a joiner you are both opening yourself up to new experiences and solidifying your bond with your neighbors and community.

This chapter might be pretty self-explanatory to some, but a lot of former urbanites find it difficult to leave their former closed-off comfort zone. You can stay anonymous in the city and go about your day ignoring people without suffering any consequences. In the country, it is impossible to be anonymous—whether you put yourself out there or not—people will quickly talk and know all about the new arrivals. First impressions are important—be proactive and reach out to them immediately, and don't let your neighbors make up their minds about you without meeting you first. Living rurally, your neighbors are much more intimately connected to you and whether you like it or not, you will need people power and friendship to get you through the inevitable hardships that will pop up from time to time.

Making friends with your neighbors is easy—do it early with a dessert, throw a party, keep waving, be courteous, be humble, share and be willing to offer a helping hand. Avoiding someone isn't an option in the country, so you can't just write people off that you don't immediately get on with. Be accepting beyond just being tolerant. You might not see eye-to-eye with a neighbor's political or religious beliefs, but that doesn't mean you can't still learn things from them and build a lasting friendship. The better quality of life you are trying to achieve will quickly be squelched if you get labeled the know-it-all jerk from the city. Listen, learn, be kind, be helpful and, in return, helping hands will come to your aid in times of need. It's full circle in the country and you get back what you put in in every facet of your existence. Welcome, neighbor.

OH HOW YOUR
GARDEN GROWS

The basics of growing your own food

"The place where I find inspiration is in silence on the land and in nature. There is a calm and magic in those spaces that can both be seen and felt. It is meditative, reflective and spiritual, and I am fed in ways that we as human beings scarcely admit we have need, but we no less feel a real hunger that cannot be satisfied by what we consume."

— Robin Emmons, Non-profit director of Sow Much Good

It really wasn't that long ago, in the grand scheme of things, that nearly everyone on Earth played an active role in their own food production. People in WWI and WWII grew victory gardens in backyards, city windows and on public lands to help prevent food shortages. Growing up, my parents raised a couple of cows for our own personal meat consumption and I'm only three generations removed from sharecropping ancestors in Kansas and peasant farmers in England. No matter how citified and growing disinclined you may feel, every human being on Earth has subsistent farmers in their bloodline. Before moving rurally, I couldn't even keep a houseplant alive. I assumed I was not blessed with a green thumb and gave up the chance to plant a container garden in the city, even though I was given permission to use a small plot of land behind my apartment. I occasionally would shop at weekend farmer's markets, but mainly bought my produce at Trader Joe's because it was cheap and convenient. I didn't have any concept of buying "in season" because I had easy access to whatever bizarre ingredient I wanted at any time of year. I, like so many Americans, paid very little attention to where my food came from. Looking back, my disconnect from what nourished my body every day was not healthy or wise. Not only do fruits and vegetables have more nutrients when eaten immediately after they are harvested, but when you grow your own food you know exactly what you are eating, as you yourself planted those seeds, and tended and harvested those crops. I consider my habits now to be much healthier, and I have gained a better appreciation of food and flavors. I am happier knowing I'll leave behind a smaller footprint on the earth.

After surviving my first winter in Maine, I decided to try my hand at gardening. I wanted to play an active role in my food production, and I was ready to put in the work to become more self-sufficient. There were some stone-lined beds on our property in a sunny spot with good drainage that the previous owner had long since abandoned. It took nearly three weeks to shovel out the weeds and old root systems. I Googled and read my way through a myriad of farming and gardening guides before adding lime, compost and topsoil to rebuild the integrity of the soil. That first year I made a ton of mistakes, but guess what, I also grew a ton of food—so much food that we only went to the grocery store a handful of times between June and September. I can still remember biting into that first tomato; I realized I had never eaten a "real" tomato before that moment. It was still warm from the sun, sweet and bursting with flavor. I would come home from a hard day at work and decompress by pulling weeds and watering. Gardening became my therapy. The cultivation of food feels primordial, cathartic and incredibly rewarding. I feel connected to my ancestors as I shovel compost and manure, prune tomato plants, dig potatoes and save seeds for the next year. The other day I made a frittata for friends visiting from the city. The eggs were from my friend's chickens and every other ingredient I grew in my garden—a true locavore meal—and it was hard not to beam with pride.

Not everyone who moves away from the city grows their own food and that is okay! Just because you move rurally doesn't mean you have to become a kitchen gardener or homesteader. I have friends who tried to grow their own food. After several failed attempts, and lack of passion for the drudgery of caring for crops, they gave up. Guess what? They still love living rurally and eat well. A girlfriend who moved to our area from Boston had a container garden for her first few years but decided that she much preferred going to the local farmer's market and supporting an off-season CSA than growing her own produce. Instead of growing her own food, she now has a thriving flower garden that provides her with much more joy and requires much less upkeep.

Gardening in a tight-knit community is also a great way to meet your neighbors and make friends. My friends can't wait for summer harvest season when I drop baskets full of extra heirloom tomatoes on their doorsteps. A common practical joke in my area during zucchini harvest time is to leave a giant forgotten-until-it's-too-late zucchini on the hood of a friend's car or in their mailbox. Seed sharing, giving away extra seedlings to other gardeners and sharing harvest excess with those who don't garden is always appreciated in the country. Specializing in certain crops and trading with others who grow different things can streamline and ease your growing operation and is a great way to build community. If you happen to be particularly good at growing tomatoes and root vegetables, but never fair well with other crops, set up a trade with others in your neighborhood who grow the crops you are lacking. Or you could trade produce for eggs, milk or meat shares with folks that raise livestock. Gardening is a great way to not only nurture your soul and body, but also your friendships.

There are ample resources—books and websites—that go into detail of how to best utilize your growing spaces, how to effectively grow pesticide-free crops, how to compost, how to prune, how to preserve—how to do pretty much anything and everything. This chapter will outline the basics. My gardening journey has been exactly that, a journey, with highs and lows. I learn something new every year and just when I think I've mastered a particular crop, a new pest or blight arrives to humble my gardening ego. I don't think I will ever consider myself a master gardener and that is okay. I can still produce a bounty of food. I garden because I love the process, from start to finish, even the hard and arduous parts I find tremendously invigorating and rewarding. Each year I get closer to perfecting preserving and saving the fruits (and veggies) of our labor for the cold, dark winter months. Pulling a jar of homemade salsa or pear ginger sauce out of the freezer in February is so gratifying and reminds me that it won't be winter forever. Even if you decide that growing your own food isn't a good fit for you in your new rural lifestyle, I encourage you to try it out. If you have little ones, let them grow their own little garden patch. Every child I've worked with in the garden has fully appreciated the magic of growing food; like a wizard, you plant the seeds, water, weed and wait for the food to appear.

START DEVELOPING YOUR GREEN THUMB NOW

If you are still living in the city and planning your escape to the country, don't let that be your excuse for not trying your hand at gardening. Practicing in the city is a great way to familiarize yourself with the process, seasons, varieties, harvests, etc. and gain valuable know-how that will be invaluable when you finally uproot your city life and plant roots in the country. Many cities have community gardens with plots available for rent. If you can't find or afford to rent a plot, build a small container garden on your fire escape or ask your landlord if you can build a small rooftop garden on the top of your building. If you are lucky enough to have yard space, put in a couple of raised beds. A sub-project of Urban Exodus is Urban Haven where I tour the urban gardener's spaces. I've been amazed by the inventiveness and year-round yields some urban gardeners have achieved. In the city, you don't have to spar with as many pests but be prepared for lots of soil, plant waste and water hauling if you plant a container or rooftop garden.

TIME & INVESTMENT

Many people want to grow their own food but they are daunted and unsure of the time and financial investment needed, so they postpone their foray into gardening indefinitely. Gardens give back what is put into them. You can grow a small kitchen or container garden with minimal time and resources and still yield enough to cover a majority of your food consumption during the growing season. If you want to grow enough food to sustain you and your family for most of the year, you will need more space, more supplies, and more time to harvest, store and preserve your food for the off-seasons. In my experience, the most time-consuming stages are the initial planting, fruit tree pruning and picking/processing/preserving your harvests. In mid-August through early October, I spend insane amounts of time food processing our fruits and vegetables, making and freezing soups, sauces and salsa, and canning jar after jar of pickles, dilly beans and jams. New gardeners will need to invest more time and more money to get their gardens built, soils ready and crops established. Some plants will only need to be planted once and will come back year after year without much coaxing, while others need to be planted every year. My suggestion is to start small with just a handful of your favorite crops in a location where you have room for growth. If you find that you love it, you can always add more plant varieties and expand your garden footprint.

My garden is less than a quarter of an acre and our orchard has roughly fourteen trees that produce fruit yearly. I start growing seeds in late February/early March to plant in late May/early June when they have matured into seedlings. Tending those seed starters takes a couple of hours a week of my time. I spend roughly fifteen to twenty hours in the late spring prepping our beds for early summer crops and planting spring crops. Every other spring, I spend forty to sixty hours pruning back all of the water sprout growth on our fruit-producing trees. In early and mid-summer, I spend at least five to eight hours a week planting, watering, pruning and weeding our beds. In the late summer, I spend six to twenty hours a week succession planting, watering, weeding, harvesting, processing and preserving what I've grown. We run our own design business, so during slow workdays I have the flexibility to pop out of the office for an hour or two and tie tomato plants or weed. When I planted our first garden I was working for a non-profit and the only time I had available for the garden was in the early mornings, early evenings (oh, the bug bites!) and on the weekends. It was hard to juggle, but still totally doable. If you don't want to jam up your summer weekend schedule with yard and garden work, you might consider a small self-watering container garden or a few raised beds with weed suppressors in place and a basic irrigation system on a timer. By investing in your infrastructure and putting a little extra time in on the front end, you can lessen your time commitments without reducing your yield.

HARD COSTS OF GROWING YOUR OWN FRUITS & VEGETABLES

There are many hard costs associated with setting up your garden. Fortunately, the most expensive items on the list are for the initial set up. After you build and put together your garden infrastructure, the reccurring costs are minimal—seeds, compost (which you can make yourself—keep reading), natural fertilizers, natural pest deterrents and plant starters. I probably only spend about $75 a year on our garden now, while my initial investments were at least five times that amount and I started with already established stone beds. Container gardens can cost more to set up than building raised beds, as you need lots of pots to grow the same amount of food as a four by six (12 x 18 m) foot box. If you are worried about start-up costs, start with just one or two raised beds and expand your growing space each year to spread your investment out over several years.

MAIN SUPPLIES & TOOLS TO ESTABLISH YOUR GARDEN

1. Soil testing and soil amendments: compost, manure, lime, sulfur, peat moss, etc.
2. Infrastructure set-up: raised beds, tiling, fencing, row covers, cold frames, etc.
3. Garden tools: shovels, spade, pitchfork, rakes, hoes, post driver, wheelbarrow, etc.
4. Seed starting supplies, starter plants and trees (grow lights, heat mat, potting soil, seeds, plastic nursery flats)
5. Watering supplies: spray bottle, watering can, hoses, hose attachments, irrigation system
6. Processing and preserving tools: pots, canning materials, food processor, blender

TOP TEN COMMON ROOKIE GARDENING MISTAKES

1. Not supplementing the soil with the nutrients it needs. Get a soil test every couple of years and keep amending your soil for healthy plants.
2. Choosing the wrong plants and/or varieties for your growing zone. Consult a growing zone chart online to determine your zone and only choose varieties and plants that will grow in your area.
3. Planting too early or too late. Follow the guides on your seed packets and consult your growing zone for frost dates before planting.
4. Planting crops too close together. Follow the seed packet guide to allow enough space and plot your garden accordingly.
5. Overwatering, under watering or watering during the wrong time of day. Consult the Internet or reference books for watering guidelines for specific crops. Some crops require very little water, while others like a lot.
6. Letting weeds take over. Weeds steal nutrients and water from your crops. Keep reading for weed barrier and suppression ideas.
7. Over-pruning, under-pruning or pruning during the wrong time of year. It's best to prune when trees are dormant (no leaves), after the coldest months of winter and before the spring bloom begins. Keep reading for a basic introduction to proper pruning.
8. Not supporting and/or trellising heavy or climbing plants. Tomatoes are heavy and won't produce high yields without pruning and proper support. Use stakes, trellises or cages to keep them supported. Peas, pole beans and other climbers need a trellis to climb. Leaving them on the ground will greatly reduce yields and not provide proper sun exposure.
9. Not dealing with pest or predator problems before they wreak havoc. Use fences, prep beds with barriers and deal with insects early on to avoid crop destruction.
10. Planting your crops in the same location year after year. Use crop rotations to avoid depleting certain areas of particular nutrients and prevent reoccuring blights and pest problems.

CHOOSING A SITE

Choosing a site for your garden is the first step to growing your own food. If you have a lot of land available, choosing a site that is close to a water source is crucial. You don't want to have to move a super long hose every time you need to mow. You also don't want to haul water buckets or go through the costly process of installing a water line. Even if you only have a small space with a few hours of sun each day, you can still grow a garden, but you will want to make sure you plant varieties that will work in the site you have. The three most important things to consider when choosing a site are sun exposure, drainage and soil quality.

Sun exposure: An ideal spot for a fruit/vegetable garden is in full sun. "Full sun" means that the location receives eight or more hours of direct sunlight during peak summer season. In a location with full sun, you will be able to grow nearly all crop varieties suited for your area. "Partial shade" refers to more than two hours of sun per day—usually between two to four hours of sun a day. In partial shade

locations you will not be able to productively grow any fruiting crops, but you can still grow some leafy greens, root vegetables and herbs. A location with "full shade" gets less than two hours of sun a day and isn't going to be a productive growing area. If you only have a plot for raised beds in "full shade" you can creatively spread your crops into pots, building a container garden in the full sun patches around your property.

Drainage: Finding a location with proper drainage is an essential step to ensure a productive garden. In poorly draining soils, plants have a hard time establishing healthy roots and they risk having their roots freeze in colder temperatures. You don't want water to collect around your plant without proper draining. Well-drained soil is important not only for crops but also for fruit trees. Draining between one to three inches (2.5 to 8 cm) per hour is good for garden plants as ideal soil drainage is two inches (5 cm) per hour. If your drainage rate is more than four inches (10 cm) per hour it is too fast, and less than one inch (2.5 cm) per hour is too slow. You can make amendments to the soil to improve drainage but you might decide that it is easier to find another location with better drainage to save you the headache and cost of improving the soil.

How To Test Your Soil Drainage
Step 1: Dig a hole 12" x 12" x 12" (.305 m) with straight sides.

Step 2: Fill hole with water and leave overnight to saturate the soil.

Step 3: The following day, fill the hole with water again and measure the initial water level.

Step 4: Measure the water level every hour until the hole is completely drained.

Soil quality: In order for your garden to get the nutrients needed to be productive and grow healthy plants, the soil needs to be well balanced and healthy. It is easy to get your soil tested to determine what supplements it needs to grow healthy crops. Most state universities have agricultural departments that offer soil testing. I use the University of Maine, and UMass Amherst has a well-respected soil testing facility that tests for home gardens, landscaping/ornamentals, commercial vegetable/fruit growers and forage or grain crops. Because soils differ by region, you should find a university or testing facility in your general area, as the test will likely be more geared towards that region's general soil properties. There are also home soil tests that you can buy at most home improvement stores, but those tests are not all reliable, so be sure to check the online ratings for each. No matter how good your soil is when you first plant your garden, you will need to continue monitoring it and amending it, as growing crops deplete nutrients from the soil.

THINGS I WISH I WOULD'VE DONE EARLIER

With almost five years of country living under my belt, it's easy to look back and wish I would've prioritized a few items on the to do list instead of delaying them for later years. Even with the best-laid plans, you will have lots of early expenses when you move and will have no choice but to delay a few things (likely why we didn't get to these until year four). In an ideal world, these are some things to move to the top of the list if you can manage it:

Plant fruit trees and bushes: Fruit trees take several years to get established and depending on the type, they can take anywhere from three to seven years to bear fruit. Fruit trees and berry bushes aren't as hardy when they are small, and in areas with extreme cold or heat spells they can easily die. We planted ten fruit trees and ten berry bushes this spring and seven have already died. If you want to start eating fruit off of your land early on, it is important to prioritize planting fruit trees and bushes. Once you plant them, make sure you fence them off to keep them protected from deer and other creatures. Fruit trees and bushes are particularly fragile while they are getting established and require a little extra attention and TLC.

Plant perennial crops: We had some perennial plants already established when we moved, and to salvage them we weeded around them. I do wish I would've planted more perennials—a large patch of asparagus and an allocated spot for an herb garden. I kept moving these plants for the first few years and continue to have an ongoing battle with horseradish popping up all over.

Fencing our garden: Every October, when other food options become scarce, we have a full-on deer invasion. It's like they know the perfect time to eat our Brussels sprouts—just after the first frost has sweetened them for harvest. To fend off deer, you need at least a 6-foot (1.8-m) fence, although I've heard stories of deer clearing fences that high without a problem. To make the most of a garden fence, use chicken wire or tightly woven sticks to keep out other garden munchers like rabbits and woodchucks. There are lots of different garden fence designs out there. Do some research and price out your options to choose one that is right for you. The free version—using sharpened sticks—works just as well as a fence made with lumber and wire, although it tends to not hold up as well over time.

TYPES OF GARDENS

There are many types of gardens out there. You don't have to follow the rules when it comes to what you plant or how you set your garden up, but knowing the pluses and minuses of various configurations will help with problem solving later if you have certain crops that aren't thriving.

Containers: You can grow a myriad of plants in containers; tomatoes, herbs and other high-yield crops do particularly well. For small spaces and places that don't have a spot sunny enough to put a raised bed, a container garden can still provide you with a lot of produce during the growing season.

Raised Beds: There are many different ways you can construct and lay out a raised-bed garden. Raised beds can be short to the ground or several feet high. The beds can be constructed using milled wood frames, logs, sticks, stones, bricks or even cinder blocks. If you take time to design and construct sturdy raised beds you will greatly reduce maintenance required down the line. In areas where rabbits and gophers are a problem, adding tight wire fencing to the bottom of your raised beds before filling with soil will keep those creatures from destroying your crops. To avoid constantly battling weeds, you can line the bottom with landscape cloth to prevent them from shooting up into the new soil. The taller your raised bed, the easier it will be to prune, weed and harvest, as you won't have to constantly crouch down to a lower bed. With a taller raised bed, you will also have more soil depth to establish healthy roots and allow ample space for soil amendments. The one downside is the expense, as you will need more topsoil and compost to fill the taller beds.

Tilled field beds: If you want a larger growing space or don't have money to invest in building raised beds, you can also plow or till a field on your land. If the place you are planning on putting your garden is thick with vegetation it could save a lot of weed suppressing time by renting a sod cutter to remove the first two to three inches (5 to 8 cm) of grass before plowing, double digging or tilling the soil beneath. For a productive garden you will still need to add necessary soil amendments once the space is clear and the soil is dug. Weeds tend to be particularly voracious in garden beds dug in fields, so you might want to invest in weed barriers.

WEED BARRIERS & SUPRESSION

There are many things on the market to help suppress weeds. You can use straw, landscaping fabric, plastic sheeting or burlap. My favorite biodegradable and cheap alternatives are wetted cardboard and newspaper. Cardboard and newspaper break down over time, help maintain soil moisture and attract earthworms, which improve your soil aeration. I put cardboard down in between my larger rows for tidy paths and less time spent weeding. I avoid using newspaper with color inks and prepare my cardboard by breaking it down and removing glue, tape, staples, etc. before laying it down. Once you lay it down, wet it with a hose to weigh it down and begin the decomposition process. You might need to stake it if your garden is in a windy location.

PREPPING BEDS

To prep your garden for planting, you will want to make sure your soil is loose and not compact. If you are planting larger beds, make defined pathways in-between crops where you will walk, as compacted soil will lead to poor germination and root development. Some gardeners swear by rototilling to cut up weeds, mix in soil amendments and aerate the soil, while others say that double digging is the way to go. I've done both and honestly I can say that certain crops seem to fair better after double digging (tomatoes and peas), while others did better when I tilled (kale, greens and cucumbers). There may have been other variables that swayed my results, but if you have access to a rototiller, it will save you the extra time and energy that double digging requires.

How To Double Dig

1. *Start at one end of the bed and dig a 12 inch (.305 m) wide by 12 inch (.305 m) deep trench, placing dirt in a wheelbarrow or garden cart.*

2. *Use a pitchfork to loosen the soil on the floor of the trench by rocking it back and forth.*

3. *Dig a second trench next to the first, adding the soil from the second trench to the first trench hole, along with any soil amendments.*

4. *Repeat the cycle for the remaining trenches, adding the first trench's soil to the final trench.*

COMPOSTING & SOIL AMENDMENTS

The key to a healthy garden is healthy soil. There are many natural things you can add to your garden to amend your soil, including planting a cover crop. Soil is different all over the country, so research regional specifics. If your soil isn't working well for you (your plants look sickly, yields are low and/or pests are a huge problem), consult a soil expert on the best ways to rebuild the integrity of your soil. Pests, like carnivorous hunters, tend to attack sickly plants first. Common soil amendments are peat, lime, bone and blood meal, compost, manure, phosphate, worm castings, sulfur, potassium and magnesium. Once you have a soil test, you will know what elements are missing from your soil. It's worth spending time researching products and natural elements you can use to restore your soil's balance.

Cover crops: Also known as green manure, cover crops can help reduce soil erosion, increase soil fertility and quality, suppress weeds and help control pests and diseases. Before the cover crop flowers or goes to seed you must kill them and dig them into your soil (if you plant them in the late fall the frost will do this for you). For spring cover crops, kill them by cutting off the heads and digging and flipping over the soil. Some common cover crops are clover, rye, oats, buckwheat and sorghum. There is quite a bit to read up on when it comes to selecting the right cover crop for you, so do your homework before using this method to improve your soil.

Manure: It is important to use animal manure correctly, or you could burn/dehydrate your plants or spread weeds in your garden. Gardens love poop and a bonus of having animals is that you get free garden food out of the deal. The best way to use animal poop is to age it for six to twelve months. The longer it ages, the more it will break down, reducing the odor and preventing it from burning your plants, spreading weeds into your garden or contaminating your harvest with E.coli. Pile up your manure and use straw or black print newspaper between layers. Let it sit and decompose for at least six months before applying it to your garden in the spring. A quicker way to use manure in areas with colder winters is to spread fresh manure on your beds in the fall and let it overwinter before digging or tilling it in the spring (note: this is a smelly solution in warmer climates). Horse, cow, goat, rabbit, turkey, alpacas, llamas, etc. all produce manure that can be used in the garden. Hot manure from chickens and sheep is rich in nitrogen and can easily burn plants even after being aged; this manure should be used sparingly or only on certain crops. Some zoos sell exotic animal manure from elephants, zebras, etc. for garden use. Never use pig, dog or cat manure because parasites can survive the composting process and remain infectious to people.

Compost: It is ridiculously wasteful to throw away food scraps in the country. Even if you don't garden, you can still have a designated compost pile for kitchen waste. Word to the wise, don't throw meat, dairy products, fish, bones or diseased plants into your compost pile. These will make your compost smell, attract animals and could harm your plants if you eventually use the compost in your garden. You can use a compost bin, build a compost pile contained by pallets or just pile it in a heap. Your compost decomposes from the inside out, so in order to speed up the process, you will need to turn your compost after it gets taller than three feet (1 m). You can turn your compost by digging out the center and moving it to the sides so that the sides then become the center. Don't use your compost until it resembles dark soil; this is what compost looks like when it is fully decomposed. There are two types of compost material categories: brown (carbon rich) and green (nitrogen rich). You can pile both brown and green together, but you will need a bit more brown than green to evenly cook your compost.

Brown: Eggshells, woodstove ash (don't use too much as it's very alkaline), black and white newsprint and brown paper bags (shred these first), straw, leaves, sawdust, wool and hay.

Green: Grass clippings, fruit and vegetable scraps, garden waste (cucumber vines to pulled weeds), coffee grounds and animal manure.

GROWING ZONE & FROST DATES

Before choosing what you want to grow, you need to first determine what your growing zone is and the frost dates. Your growing zone and frost dates will narrow down the crops and varieties you can successfully grow in your area. If you are planting in a zone with a shorter growing season, you should choose varieties with faster maturity rates so crops can be harvested before the first frost arrives. When it comes to fruit trees, a good rule of thumb is to plant varieties that are suited for a colder zone above your zone to ensure they survive a harsh winter. I planted three cherry trees—two suited for my zone 4 area and one for zone 3. Only the zone 3 tree made it through a particularly brutal winter. Just because you live in an area that has cooler summers doesn't mean you can't enjoy growing warmer weather crops. You can help along crops in cooler areas that like warmer temperatures (peppers, melons, squash, tomatoes, basil, okra and cucumbers) by growing them in a greenhouse or laying down black plastic to increase temperatures. If you live an area with hot summers, you can still grow crops that prefer cooler temperatures (tender lettuces, kale, peas, spinach and chard) by covering with shade netting or planting mid-season successions in partial shade. You can also extend your growing season by using a cold frame, greenhouse or row covers. If you are planning on planting heirloom varieties, check to see where they originated and try to buy varieties that are particular to your region as they will already be adapted to your growing conditions.

PERENNIALS VS. ANNUALS

Many city people know the difference between perennials and annuals, but since I was pretty clueless when I first started growing my own food, I thought I would explain the differences here. The majority of vegetable crops are annuals. Annuals need to be planted every year and perennials are plants that come back on their own year after year. The ease of perennials makes them a gardener's best friend, at least theoretically, but there are some drawbacks to be aware of. Some perennials spread rapidly and can totally take over a garden. If you live in a colder zone, some plants that act as perennials in milder climates won't overwinter and will need to be planted annually. Before planting a perennial garden, check your zone to ensure the perennials you want to include are hardy enough for your area.

Perennial fruits, veggies and herbs: Raspberries, strawberries, berry bushes (blueberries, blackberries, etc.), asparagus, rhubarb, lovage, watercress, artichokes, chives, lavender, rosemary, sage, thyme, tarragon, lemongrass, lemon balm, marjoram and tarragon.

Annoying spreading perennials: Oregano and mint (spreads like crazy and can even cross pollinate to make a weird minty pizza smelling hybrid). Keep these two herbs contained in their own separate beds to avoid them creeping all over your garden. Horseradish pops up year after year in new places and is nearly impossible to remove. If you want to plant horseradish, plant it away from the rest of your garden so it doesn't pop up and destroy other plants.

OPEN-POLLINATION VS. HEIRLOOM VS. HYBRID SEEDS

Open-pollination: These seeds require natural pollination methods (bees, birds, wind, etc.). They adapt to the environment they are grown in and will pass down their adapted traits (hardiness, flavor, heat tolerance, etc.) to their seeds.

Heirloom: These seeds are all open-pollination, but not all open-pollination seeds are heirlooms. Heirloom seeds are passed down through families and communities. Heirlooms have been saved for generations and offer unique varieties you won't find anywhere else. Heirlooms can be somewhat finicky, as they are adapted to the environment in which they were raised. Using heirloom seeds gives gardeners unique crop varieties that others won't have, which can be an advantage at farmer's markets. With crop varieties diminishing every year, it is imperative in a larger environmental sense to continue growing and nurturing diverse crops.

Hybrid: These seeds are created by human intervention using a controlled method of pollination where two species or varieties are crossed. This is done to breed a desired trait such as yield, size or hardiness. Hybrid F1 seeds can't be collected and used the following year because they tend to be sterile or grow significantly less vigorous plants.

DIRECT SEED OR PLANTING SEEDLINGS

Some plants prefer to be direct seeded (sown from seed) into your garden, while others thrive if they are transplanted as pre-established seedlings. Planting seedlings can also allow you to harvest crops early, plant more successions and have higher yields. Here's a list of plants that prefer to be sown from seed and those that prefer to be grown from started plants:

Direct seed: Beans, beets, carrots, corn, cilantro, radishes, turnips and parsnips

Seedlings: Basil, broccoli, cauliflower, Brussels sprouts, chives, melons, parsley, peppers, strawberries and tomatoes

Your choice: Arugula, lettuces, spinach, cucumber and squash (direct seed cucumbers and squash only when the soil has warmed)

GROWING SEEDLINGS

Growing your own seedlings is fun and can be a nice late winter/early spring project to get you excited for warmer days to come. I start my tomato and pepper plants in late February/early March when we still have many long days of cold before planting season. Growing your own seedlings can also allow you to grow unusual and heirloom varieties that aren't readily available in garden stores (most stores only carry popular hybrid varieties). To grow your own seedlings, you will need seedling flats, seed starting soil, a heat pad and grow lights if you live in an area with a dark and cold early spring. If you live in a warmer area, you can grow seedlings without grow lights in a greenhouse or cold frame. Seed packets and catalogs will give you

seed start times. Back date those start times a couple of weeks after your last projected frost date and put together your planting schedule. I suggest labeling all your crop varieties the first year so you can keep track of how they do in your garden. This will help you narrow your selection for next year to the most successful varieties. Keep your planted seeds moist and warm with a heat pad to encourage germination. Once the seeds have sprouted you can move the heat pad to the next batch of newly planted seeds. Seedlings like fifteen hours of sunlight per day. Putting your lights on a timer will help ensure they receive the same amount of light each day. If you are growing in a greenhouse but there are fewer than fifteen hours of natural daylight, you might want to add a couple of hours of grow light time for maximum results. Water regularly and don't allow your seedlings to dry out. A week or so before you transplant the seedlings, it is important to "harden them off," meaning slowly prepare them for the elements of the great outdoors. If they have been grown inside, start by putting them in a greenhouse or cold frame to get used to cooler temperatures. After a few days, bring them outside to a wind-protected, partially-shaded area for a few hours, bringing them back in before nightfall. Up the number of hours every few days, gradually move them into full sun and expose them to wind.

PLOTTING YOUR GARDEN

There are many online tools and apps available to help you plot your garden. Each year I draw out my garden on graph paper, list the crops I want to grow, consult seed packets for spacing and start plotting.

There are four main things to consider when plotting out your garden:

Spacing: Your seed packets will tell you the ideal spacing for your crops. Planting too close together will lead to lower yields and stunted crops. Even if your tomato seedlings look way too far apart when you put them in the ground, they will get much bigger. If you plant them too close together, their yield will be lower and it will be difficult to tie them up, prune them, find and remove hornworms and harvest them.

Companion planting: Some crops prefer to be planted close to others as they assist each other by repelling pests, attracting beneficial insects and providing structural support, nutrients or shade. There are lots of companion plant pairs but here are a few of my favorites to pair together: *

-Tomatoes <u>next to</u> basil (basil improves flavor and growth of tomatoes)
-Broccoli or Brussels sprouts <u>next to</u> nasturtiums and marigolds (nasturtiums repel aphids; marigolds repel cabbage moths)
-Radishes <u>next to</u> cucumbers (radishes repel cucumber beetles)
-Carrots <u>next to</u> leeks (leeks repel carrot flies)

*Just as there are companion plants, there are some plants that inhibit each other's growth (like kohlrabi and tomatoes). Do your research ahead of time to make sure you are plotting a garden that will thrive.

Yields: Growing enough food without having too much excess is difficult to master. There are resources online for crop yields that will give you the estimated number of plants to grow per person that can help you decide how many plants to grow for your family. There are also guides online for how much a crop will yield based on the number of feet in your garden. I have used both methods, but nothing is more reliable than trial and error. Our first year I planted 30 tomato plants and I spent two months trying to figure out what the heck to do with my excess harvest. The following year I planted 18 and

that gave me a high enough yield for both fresh eating and winter storing without being chained to my food processor full time. This year I grew far too many leeks, so next year I will scale back. Keeping a garden notebook where you can log your yields will help tremendously.

Crop rotations: Rotating your crops each growing season will help increase your soil fertility and yield, and prevent soil erosion. Growing the same crops in the same locations year after year depletes the soil of certain nutrients and can make crop yields much lower and plants more susceptible to diseases and pests. Research crops that do best planted after other crops, and crop family categories that shouldn't be rotated together to maximize results. I'm a bit lazy and just don't plant the same crop in the same place it was the year before—that's it. Save your plotted garden chart for the following year so you can make sure that you don't accidentally plant something in the same place as last year.

SUCCESSION PLANTING

In order to keep a steady supply of fresh greens and veggies during the growing season, one must succession plant. Succession planting is a way to extend your harvest season by staggering your plantings so you have staggered harvest dates. There are a few different ways you can succession plant to help increase your yields and extend your harvest seasons.

Same crop, staggered plantings: Space out your crop planting every two to four weeks. A lot of vegetables pitter out after the initial harvest period and produce smaller and smaller yields before dying or bolting (prematurely flowering). For example, instead of planting all your arugula seeds early in the season, plant one to two rows every two weeks and keep yourself rich in arugula salads all season long. When your arugula crop bolts, let it bolt, go to seed and then save the seeds for the following year or succession. (See page 86 to learn how to save seeds.)

Best seeds for succession planting: Arugula, beets, broccoli raab, bush beans, carrots, chard, cilantro, dill, kale, lettuce, mixed greens, mustard, pak choi, radish, spinach, tatsoi and turnips.

Early season crop/late season crop succession: Peas and radishes are early, quick harvest crops. While you can continue to replant radishes, peas usually prefer the colder, wetter conditions of late spring and early summer. It is difficult to replant peas and get another harvest. Instead of leaving dead pea plants in your beds to take space after you've harvested them, plant a warmer season crop in their place like hot peppers or eggplants.

Same crop, different varieties: Different varieties of the same vegetable will have different maturity rates. Choosing an early, mid and late season variety of the same type of vegetable will give you a larger yield and longer harvest period. And you will have the bonus of tasting different varieties and seeing which fair better in your garden.

GENERAL GARDEN MAINTENCE

Once you've done your initial planting, your garden will require weekly attention. You can do a little or a lot; the more you care for your garden, the more it will care for you. In addition to succession planting, you will also need to fertilize, water, weed and prune certain plants to ensure they have a bountiful harvest.

Water: In sixty-degree weather your gardens need about one to two inches (2.5 to 5 cm) of water every week. For every extra ten degrees of temperature, add half an inch (1 cm) of water to that number. Over-watering or under-watering your plants can harm them. Water before or after the sun, so you don't burn your leaves with residual water droplets. You can go the hands-off route (after some up front labor) and irrigate your crops with a timer, or you can monitor rainfall each week with an inexpensive rain gauge to see how much rain your garden has received naturally and water accordingly. Seedlings and newly planted seeds need to stay moist and should never dry out, so water these a bit more until they get established.

Fertilizer: Some gardeners fertilize every week using all-purpose fertilizers. You can go crazy researching fertilizers specific to each of your crops. I personally don't use fertilizers. Occasionally I will add an organic tomato booster to my tomato crops and I usually top dress (spread compost in a circle around the base of a plant) all of my plants one to two times during the growing season. Sure, my beets and carrots are smaller than the ones at the farmer's market, but I still have bountiful harvests without fertilizing. Fertilizers are merely a tool to help grow bigger crops and produce higher yields.

Weeding: Even if you add weed barriers and suppressors, you will still need to remove weeds throughout the growing season. Weeds rob your crops of water and essential nutrients, and they can prevent your plants from establishing healthy roots. Be vigilant and don't let weeds get too established. Established weeds are a pain to remove, while young weeds are easy to remove.

Pruning: Pruning is not just for fruit trees and bushes. Pruning tomato, squash and cucumber plants will help increase your yields. You can prune these plants by cutting off excess foliage. On tomato plants, remove any suckers that shoot up from the base of the plant, remove excess flowering (about one third of the flowers), and remove sickly or deformed fruit on crowded vines so that the plant can put its energy into the healthy fruit.

PRUNING FRUIT TREES

There is an art to fruit tree pruning. Pruning fruit trees will help increase yields and fruit size, make harvesting easier, and prevent your tree's limbs from breaking under the weight of too much foliage or fruit. There is a lot to pruning fruit trees, but I am going to give you the basics. The best time to prune is after the coldest days of winter, but before the spring bloom. You don't want any leaves on the trees, but it is okay if buds are just starting to form. You want to cut off all of the new upward growth (called water sprouts). These are usually smooth vertical growing shoots that pop up all over the tops of the established branches and even out of the base of the trunk. You want your trees to resemble an umbrella, encouraging the downward growth to ease your harvest. A great expression in pruning is the old timer "cat method," which means thinning the branches wide enough that you can throw a cat through (but don't actually throw a cat!). This will ensure that when leaves form, the branches

will not be competing for sunlight or space. After you prune the tree and before the buds break, add a fruit tree fertilizer to encourage a healthy and bountiful season. You can also help fruit trees along by adding mulch in a four to six foot (1.2–1.8 m) circle around the base. This will keep trees moist, regulate soil temperature and suppress weeds. You can use store-bought mulch or woodchips, grass clippings, pine needles or shredded leaves.

FIGHTING PESTS!

There are tons of insects and critters that can destroy the fruits (and vegetables) of your labor. It feels like every year I wage a new war against a newly introduced garden pest. Since each region has different pests, here's a list of some of the most widely prevalent pests and some advice on how to deal with them.

Aphids: Small soft-bodied insects that suck the juice from various garden plants and congregate together in clumps. They can be green, brown, white, black, grey, pink or almost colorless. They love my Brussels sprouts and cabbage, but they can infest nearly any garden crop.

Solution: Use a high-powered jet setting on your hose and spray the little jerks off all of the infected areas, being sure to also spray the plants around them. This works well if you catch them early. If the plant is too far gone, tear it out and dump it far away from your garden. Ladybugs eat aphids, but if the infestation is bad, they might not be able to handle it completely.

Cucumber Beetles: Small yellow and black beetles that can be either striped or spotted. They attack cucumber plants (hence their name), but they can also destroy squash and melons.

Solution: You can either smash them by hand, spray neem oil, row cover your crops until they are established and start flowering or buy yellow sticky traps. Sticky traps are essentially yellow fly paper that attracts cucumber beetles.

Cutworms: These little worms can destroy your newly planted seedlings by literally cutting them off at the base. If you notice that several of your seedlings are cut off, run your finger in a circle around the root and you will likely find this little brown worm. The only solace is that cutworms can't cut through more established stems and their larva period is short.

Solution: The best way to curb any devastation is by adding paper collars around your seedling stem. This collar should be at least three inches (8 cm) tall and at least one and a half inches (4 cm) of it should be beneath the soil. I make my collars out of strips from a brown paper bag and put them on preventively when planting my seedlings.

Colorado Potato Beetle: These squishy beetles are striped and yellowish/orange in color. They can greatly reduce your potato yields and completely destroy your potato foliage.

Solution: Shake them off your plants in the morning, or pick them off by hand and dump them in soap to kill them. It's gross, they are squishy, but those delicious potatoes are worth saving. Check for eggs on the undersides of leaves and remove them; eggs are small, orange and laid in clusters. Ladybugs, lacewings and spined solider bugs also eat the potato beetle's eggs and larva.

Flea Beetle: Tiny black and iridescent beetles that leave pinhole-sized bites on your greens and other plants. They love my arugula and kale.

Solution: Covering your affected crops with row covering (transparent fabric) is the best way to keep flea beetles from chewing holes into your crops.

Squash Bug: A brown bug that resembles a stink bug. These bugs move quickly on the underside of squash and pumpkin leaves. Their eggs are brown and laid in clusters on the underside of leaves. These bugs can completely destroy your squash plants and need to be caught and dealt with early on; once they reach maturity they are hard to fight.

Solution: Place a board in the garden overnight; both adults and nymphs will congregate underneath. In the morning, squash the underside of the board on a hard surface. You also need to check for and scrape off their eggs every week or so until they are gone. It only takes ten days for their eggs to hatch. Any remaining bugs you can hand pick and drop into soapy water.

Tomato Hornworms: Green squishy caterpillars that can destroy an entire tomato plant in just a few days by eating the leaves and the tomatoes. They start small and continue to grow as they feed. The largest one I've ever removed was about four inches (10 cm) long and very fat. They also eat peppers, eggplants and potatoes, but they seem to prefer tomatoes. I have such contempt for these caterpillars that my husband included a line in his wedding vows that he would continue to help me remove tomato hornworms until death do us part.

Solution: Hornworms are very well camouflaged and difficult to spot. You can try to find them by looking for their brown pellet poop, but the best way to hunt them is at night using a black light. Hornworms glow in black light, while tomato plants do not. Pluck them off the plant and squish them.

Slugs and Snails: These little buggers pretty much like to chew on everything in your garden and can destroy a multitude of crops. Slugs and snails dry out in the heat so you will see more of them during rainy spells.

Solution: Since slugs and snails like moist conditions, moving your watering to the morning so the soil is dry at night can reduce your slug and snail problem considerably. Another way to deal with slugs and snails is to set up a beer trap. Bury mason jars up to their neck in your garden and fill half way with cheap beer. Slugs and snails are attracted to beer and will have a blissful drunken drowning demise.

Deer: Bambi doesn't care how long you've been tending to your garden; he will cause massive destruction in just a few visits. Deer eat nearly everything grown in a garden and they can clear a bean or lettuce patch in less than an hour. They will also tear all of the low-lying fruit and branches off of your trees.

Solution: Lots of companies make deer deterrent out of predator urine, musk, etc. but the ones I've tried smell awful and have never worked for me. The best way to stop deer is by building a fence over six feet (2 m) tall. You can build a permanent fence around an established garden, or you can invest in an electric netted movable deer fence that can be packed up at the end of the season and moved if you change your garden location.

Rabbits, Ground Squirrels, Woodchucks/Groundhogs and Gophers: These furry rodents love nibbling on gardens. Remember Mr. McGregor from Peter Rabbit? There is a reason why he was always trying to seek out and destroy Peter Rabbit.

Solution: The two best ways to curb these voracious rodents is to build raised beds with wire-mesh bottoms to keep them from digging their way to your garden goodness. You can also build a perimeter fence that goes all the way to ground to prevent these critters from sneaking in. The best solution is to do both, but that can be expensive and time consuming. A dog or barn cat hanging around can also help deter rodents.

HOT TIP: FLOWER AND HERB FRIENDS

There are many flowers and herbs that help repel pests. The two most widely used are marigolds and nasturtiums. Aphids, bean beetles, potato and squash bugs don't like marigolds, and nasturtiums repel aphids, potato beetles, squash bugs, pumpkin beetles, bean beetles and white files. Plant these pretty edible flowers in with your plants to repel pests naturally.

SEED SAVING

Farmers have been saving seeds for generations. Not only will it save you the cost of purchasing seeds, but if you keep the seeds from your favorite, highest yield, heartiest and best tasting plants, you will become like your own plant breeder, selectively weeding out the least desirable traits and encouraging the more desirable traits for your future crop plantings. There are two types of seeds (open-pollinators and hybrids) for the most popular vegetable varieties. Open-pollinators produce seeds that have the same characteristics as their parents, while hybrid seeds can be sterile or produce plants that aren't like their parents. While you can still collect seeds of hybrids, I would recommend focusing your efforts on open-pollinators. Seed catalogs and packets will state whether they are open-pollinators, "OP," or hybrids, "F1 Hybrid." If you can't locate this information, call the seed company or ask someone at your local garden store. Once you've collected your seeds, be sure to properly label them and store them in a dark, cool, dry place for the next growing season. Seed germination rates decline rapidly after the first year, even if you are buying seeds from the store or catalog, so try to use all your seeds up every year, as you will inevitably have trouble with germination if you save them too long.

Cross pollination: If you are planting multiple varieties of the same crop and you want to save seeds from each variety, it is important you separate the varieties so they aren't cross-pollinated. If you are seed saving and want to grow the same type of acorn squash the following year, don't plant it next to a zucchini or miniature gourd without erecting a barrier like a row cover to prevent cross-pollination. You can also prevent cross-pollination by staggering their blooming and harvesting dates.

Easy seeds for saving: Beans, corn, peas and peppers are easy to collect and just require you to let seeds dry before storing. Melons, squash, tomatoes, eggplants and cucumbers have wet seeds and require a bit more effort. Rinse the seeds and dry them fully on a paper plate before storing. To store, pour the seeds into an envelope or plastic bag, label and keep in a dry, cool place for the following growing season.

Long game seeds: Greens like lettuce, arugula and spinach need to continue growing past their harvest time to produce seeds. You can leave just one or two of your favorite plants to go to seed and tear out the others to replant a new succession. Weather conditions can cause some plants to bolt—meaning to go to seed prematurely. When a lettuce or spinach plant bolts it begins upward growth and the leaves begin to taste bitter. Arugula will grow tall, flowers will bloom and it will produce small seedpods. When seeds or seedpods are visible, pull up the entire plant, put it head first into a paper bag, and let dry. Once fully dry, shake the bag vigorously, letting the seeds fall to the bottom. Pour the seeds into an envelope or plastic bag, label and store in a dry, cool place for the following growing season or plant succession.

Tricky seeds to save: Certain plants like kale, onions and carrots only go to seed in their second year so it's not always possible to save their seeds, especially in areas with long cold winters. Unless you are super ambitious or have a year-round growing season, plan to continue to buy carrot, kale, radish, beet, broccoli, cauliflower, Brussels sprout and onion seeds each year.

SAVING AND PRESERVING

If you decide to grow extra food for off-season use, be prepared to allocate some time to cure, prepare and store your bounty. My late August and September weekends are usually spent processing, cooking, curing and drying the massive amount of vegetable matter I've harvested. In order to get the most out of your garden harvest, it is important to have some basic kitchen tools. Here's my dream list (granted I don't have all of these, but someday I will): Food processor, blender with puree ability, set of good knives, big cutting boards, large cook pots (one for boil-water canning, one for sauce simmering), sterile mason jars and lids, heavy duty freezer bags, food dehydrator, pressure canner and chest freezer. With these supplies you can literally prepare and store any veggie or fruit you want. Here are a few ways to preserve your crops for later use:

Drying

Herbs, flowers, hot peppers and beans can all be dried for future use. For freshly dried herbs all winter, I harvest extra herbs and hang them in bunches to dry, or leave them pressed between two screen drying racks that I made using old picture frames and window screens. Once they are dry, I crumble them up and put them in labeled mason jars. For winter tea, I pull the leaves off my peppermint and the flowers off my chamomile and dry them using the same screen drying racks and store in mason jars. I string hot peppers (habaneros, fish, Thai chilies, cayenne, etc.) using a needle and thick thread, being careful to string them through the stem and not pierce the pepper itself (which can cause it to rot). For beans, I let them dry on a rack in their pods and then transfer them to a pillowcase and hit it against the floor until the pods have broken off. Then I throw away the pods and save the beans in dry mason jars.

Dehydrating

Dehydrating fruits and vegetables is a wonderful way to preserve your harvest. You can snack on them in the winter when you crave something sweet or use them in a multitude of recipes. Apricots, strawberries, tomatoes, peaches, apples, pears, raspberries, blueberries, cherries, grapes, dates and plums are all excellent fruits to dehydrate and use later. Beets, carrots, squash, mushrooms, onions and peas make great snacks or additions to soups. You can use your oven to dehydrate, but machines meant for dehydrating yield the best final results and store longer than oven-drying.

Curing

Potatoes, squash, onions and garlic can keep for a long time but fare best if they are cured for a few weeks before storing. Cure them by spacing them out (not touching) on newspaper in a cool dark place for several weeks. After they are cured, you can put them in bins in your root cellar, basement or another cool dark area of your house until you want to use them.

Freezing

I freeze a ton of produce every year—so much, that I needed to invest in an extra freezer for our basement to store everything. If I'm in a time crunch in late summer and can't devote enough time to making canned jams and sauces, I will just freeze the raw ingredients and make my canning recipes in the late fall and winter when I have more time. I also like freezing sauces, salsas and cut fruit instead of canning because I don't consider standing over a hot stove for hours in the summer a particularly fun time. Before you freeze tomatoes and most veggies you will want to blanch them first. Blanching means dropping the veggies in boiling water for a short time to preserve the flavor, color and texture. Blanching also helps clean your produce and reduces vitamin loss. Different veggies have different blanching times, but you generally submerge them in boiling water for one to three minutes and then immediately plunge them into an ice bath before bagging and putting in the freezer. I freeze beans, broccoli, pesto, peppers, berries, asparagus, kale, chard, leeks, spinach, tomatoes, etc. When freezing produce, you want to prep it for its future use as best you can (chopping, pureeing, juicing) because when you do pull it out to use, you will want to avoid thawing it first (it can get mushy) and just start cooking with it frozen. I store nearly everything in plastic freezer bags as it helps conserve space. I also make sure to label the bags with dates and contents using a sharpie pen so I don't keep stuff too long or have a hard time identifying it later. In the Staying Alive chapter (on page 161), I list out freezer expiration dates for all different types of food.

Canning

Drying and freezing food is a very forgiving process, while canning requires strict recipes and guidelines to ensure the food is safe to eat later on. You don't want botulism in your food (even though you might inject it into your face). To prevent the risk of foodborne illness from canned foods, the safest method is to use a pressure canner. Simply canning and submerging in boiling water (i.e., boil water canning) is not 100 percent safe with low-acidity foods. I water bath can a lot of tomato sauce, apple sauce, jams, dilly beans and pickles every year and always use canning specific recipes to ensure my canned goods are safe.

FRESH SALSA RECIPE FOR FREEZING
OR EATING STRAIGHT AWAY

One of my favorite ways to extend the enjoyment of summer's tomato harvest into the colder months is by making and freezing salsa for winter.

Makes 6–8 cups (1.5–2 ml)

INGREDIENTS

2 medium-size onions

4 cloves garlic

2 hot peppers (I use cayenne or diablo peppers— sub these for mild peppers if you hate spicy salsa.)

1 sweet/mild medium-size pepper (I use a banana or ancho pepper.)

1 bell pepper (no color preference)

1–1 ½ tbsp (15–22 ml) apple cider vinegar (to taste)

1–2 tsp (5–10 g) salt (to taste)

½–1 tsp (2.5 g–5 g) freshly ground pepper (to taste)

3–4 lbs (1.4–1.8 kg) tomatoes (enough to fill the food processor without overflowing it)

Squeeze of lime (about 1 tsp [5 ml])

DIRECTIONS

Cut the onions into four sections and throw into a food processor. Add the garlic cloves and pulse until the onions and garlic are chopped. Add the peppers, breaking/cutting them apart to make processing easier. Pulse the food processor until they are chopped and mixed in. Add 1 tablespoon (15 ml) apple cider vinegar, 1 teaspoon (5 g) of salt, ½ teaspoon of pepper and a squeeze from a lime wedge. Cut the tomatoes into slightly smaller chunks to make processing easier, and remove the full stem. Pulse in the food processor until everything is evenly chopped and blended together. Taste and add more salt, vinegar or pepper if needed. Let sit for a few minutes while labeling the quart-size freezer bags with the month/year and then ladle them into the bags. Save a bowl to enjoy immediately.

GROWING OUT OF SEASON

Extending your harvest season into in the fall and winter months is easier in the warmer zones, but there are still plenty of four-season gardeners in the northern reaches. Growing out of season can be more accurately described as harvesting out of season. When the weather gets cold and there are less than ten hours of daylight, plants do very little growing. The key to late fall and winter harvests is to plant a bunch of cold hardy crops in the late summer/early fall so that they are established and ready to harvest when you want to use them in the winter months. You can group off-season plants in a greenhouse or hoop house while you still have your summer garden growing outdoors. You can also use thick or layered row covers to tent over your garden before the first frost and keep them covered through the winter. Heavy-duty row covers will prevent frost from killing your plants, but your plants can still freeze in cold temperatures. Greenhouses and hoop houses tend to keep the soil a bit warmer than row covers so plants can still slowly grow even when the weather goes below freezing. Unless you heat your greenhouse though, you won't be able to plant and germinate new seeds or grow crops at the same rate they were growing in the warmer months once the weather cools. A cheap way to keep winter crops alive is to surround your crop with hay bales and put an old window on top. Some cold hardy crops that can survive winter harvesting are: garlic (plant cloves in October and spread hay to protect them in the winter, harvesting garlic the following summer), carrots, beets, parsnips (cover with hay and harvest when needed), cabbage, spinach, kale, lettuce, parsley, Brussels sprouts, collards, peas, broccoli, chard, mache, tatsoi, turnips, onions and leeks.

OVEN-DRIED CHERRY TOMATOES

I love fresh small tomatoes; they are sweet garden candy I enjoy while weeding and harvesting. I usually end up with too many to enjoy all at once so I started to oven-dry them to save for fall snacking, pastas, frittatas and other recipes that call for sun-dried tomatoes.

INGREDIENTS

A bunch of small tomatoes (sungold, cherry, black cherry, grape, etc.)

Salt

Thyme

DIRECTIONS

Cut the tomatoes lengthwise and lay them cut side up on an olive oil–greased pan (or better yet use a Silpat to prevent sticking). They can be very close together, as they will shrink while they dry. Fill the entire pan with tomatoes. Sprinkle course sea salt and crushed thyme over the tomatoes. Put tomatoes into a preheated 250°F (121°C) oven and set the time for 3 hours and 30 minutes. Check on the tomatoes when the timer goes off. If they need more time, add it in 15-minute increments to ensure they don't get burned or overly dried out. Store in olive oil in your fridge for quick use or freeze for future use.

ESSENTIAL GARDEN TOOLS
(WHAT'S WORTH SPENDING MONEY ON AND WHAT'S NOT)

Here are my favorites—my tried and true garden tools. I've made the mistake of buying cheap tools or "garden tool sets" that broke their first season of use. Most professional gardeners invest in quality tools that stand the test of time. You don't need much in the way of garden tools, so try to get quality tools and keep them in good condition by cleaning and storing them in a dry place after the season is done.

Scuffle hoe: The fastest, easiest tool for weeding. A metal stirrup that moves back and forth and pulls up weeds quickly and easily. I broke my back hand-weeding until my father-in-law introduced me to this amazing tool.

Garden Hod: A sturdy harvesting basket with a wooden handle and wire basket to clean vegetables with the hose before bringing inside. This is a true time saver and sturdy enough for pounds of harvested food.

Hori-Hori: A weeding or soil knife. This is an amazing tool for pulling up deep roots like dandelions and for transplanting, splitting perennials, harvesting, etc.

Weeding tarp/mat: There are heavy-duty mats and tarps with handles made specifically for weeding. You put weeds on the mat/tarp and haul them away when done. Any tarp will work but make sure the one you buy is durable; cheaper tarps have ripped on me when hauling thorny brush to the burn pile.

Pitchfork and point shovel: For potato harvests, replanting and turning the soil you won't find better tools. Choose a height that works for you. I bought both a pitchfork and shovel that were too short for me and it was back breaking to use them for long periods.

Wheelbarrow or garden cart: It is a contentious debate amongst gardeners whether a wheelbarrow or garden cart is more useful. I think it depends entirely on your garden, what you'll use it for and your terrain. We chose a garden cart over a wheelbarrow because our garden has wide rows and beyond just hauling soil, we also use the cart for hauling leaves, brush, etc. Only a small amount of our property is flat—most is at a steep grade, so using a wheelbarrow felt too unstable when moving stuff up or downhill. If you have narrow rows and flat land, a wheelbarrow might be the better option.

Sharp, quality hand pruners: Spending a little more money on good pruners is absolutely worth the investment. I've had cheap pruners quickly get dull and break. Fiskars and Felco make some great ones.

Trowel: I've had four trowels break on me. I'm no Hulk Hogan so I can only assume many trowels are made poorly. Invest in a good sturdy trowel with an ergonomic handle.

Garden gloves: I have two pairs—a fabric summer pair that are breathable with rubber palms to protect my hands from blisters and a heavy duty leather spring/fall pair for pruning trees, roses and raking leaves.

Garden apron: I began using an apron in the garden by accident. I went to take the compost out after washing dishes and ended up getting distracted in the garden. I couldn't believe how nice it was to have pockets to easily access my tools. A sturdy canvas apron will do the trick, or you can buy a waxed canvas apron for easy clean up. You can also buy a regular canvas apron and wax it yourself.

GROWING FOR A LIVING

If you want to try your hand at farming for a living, apprenticing or working on a farm will prove invaluable and save you from making expensive mistakes on your own land. Once you have the skills necessary to grow crops for market, reach out to farming organizations that can help you find and finance farmland and source grant money to offset the high start-up costs. Once you start farming full-time it will be harder to allocate time to write grants and find funding, so do as much of this research and work ahead of time to help you start off on the right foot. If you can't afford to buy land right away, leasing is always an option, but make sure you establish a good relationship with the landowner and have a lawyer prepare a thorough and protective lease so you don't end up getting booted off the land in the middle of the growing season or after you've invested time and money into setting up your farm. When you start looking at property, look for good soil and sun exposure, but also take into consideration if it will be easy to sell the food you grow in that area. Some areas have farmer's markets with waiting lists several years long, some have lots of CSAs that have to compete for the same customers and some have farmers that specialize in certain crops so growing those crops wouldn't make sense for your bottom line. Being within a two-hour drive to a city center will ensure that you can reach a wider customer base if you can get into some city farmer's markets, and sell direct to restaurants.

PRACTICE MAKES YOUR GARDEN BETTER, NEVER PERFECT

I know that was a lot of information to digest, but I guarantee you that I just scratched the surface. There are a million things to learn and experiment with in your garden each year. Some years, harvests will be plentiful and pests few, while other years, harvests are lean and pests are plentiful. Even people that have been farming for decades will tell you that there is always something new to learn each growing season. I think that is one of the reasons I love gardening—it is dynamic and doing the same thing every year doesn't mean you'll have the same results. This is also why gardening can be frustrating as there is no way to control all of the variables. Growing my own food has taught me some important country lessons that extend beyond the perimeters of my garden beds: good things take time, you get back what you put into something, being in nature is good for the soul, some things are beyond your control and if at first you don't succeed, try try again. Now get out there and start growing!

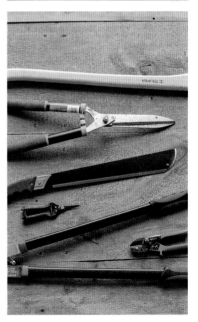

FURRY FRIENDS
AND FOOD

An abridged first-timers guide to raising animals

*"Having animals that depend on me gives me a feeling of purpose.
There are no days off. As a close friend once said, 'obligation is a hell of a motivator.'"*

— Tommy Enright, Black Rabbit Farm

A field of happy sheep munching away and mowing your lawn. A barnyard of playful goats hopping onto anything and everything they can reach. A backyard filled with gossiping chickens scratching about and a rooster that wakes you up every morning. Farm animals are one of the more overly romanticized elements of country living. Caring for livestock on a summer day can be idyllic, but shoveling manure in sub-zero temperatures on a winter morning can break the spirit of even the most dedicated animal owner. People don't often think about the time investment required to raise animals. They dream about the fresh eggs, fresh dairy, pasture-raised meats, mowed lawns, alarm clocks and companionship. Choosing whether or not to keep animals is a big decision and demands serious thought before impulse buying hatchlings or goat kids over the Internet. People with animals are literally tethered to their homestead. Unless they can find someone to house sit, they can't take vacations or even go for long day trips.

You shouldn't acquire furry or feathered friends without doing some research first. Find a veterinarian in your area and ask them about the most common problems with the type of animals you are planning to raise. If you can find a neighborhood farmer or home gardener who raises the same animal and breed, consult them as well. After much consideration, we decided not to get animals (aside from our dog) until our incomes are steady, our kids are in school and the travel bug is out of our systems. Although we love the idea of having fresh eggs, a hog to gobble up our garden waste and adorable goat friends, we don't want to be tethered to our home. Consider that you may have to pay someone upwards of $50 a day to watch your creatures when you're away if you don't have any friends or neighbors willing and able. We are blessed with lots of young farmer friends in our area and prefer to support their farms by buying our eggs, meat and dairy products from them instead.

One creature we did add to our family after moving was a dog. Dogs are easier to find sitters for and easier to care for than other feathered and furry friends. Dogs are excellent country companions—they provide protection, friendship and certain breeds can help reduce your rodent population. We have a terrier mix and she is amazing at warning us whenever people drive down the driveway. She's killed hundreds of mice and even two pesky woodchucks that kept eating our garden. I love taking her on walks in the woods because even though I know she wouldn't be able to take on a bear or other large predator, I know her presence helps keep them away. People that move rurally also frequently get cats. Whether kept indoors or outdoors, cats are much more independent than dogs and they are great mousers. If you have a rodent problem at your house or in your outbuildings, adopt a cat from your local shelter. While you can let your domesticated animals roam more freely in the country, be cautious of the road. If your pets don't respect the road boundaries you might need to invest in fencing or an invisible fence to keep them away from the road. There are many more predators in the country that would be happy to eat a cat or small dog, so bringing your pets inside at night is a good idea. We've had bald eagles circle our dog in the middle of the day, and hungry foxes and coyotes have eaten many of my friends' cats. If you've never raised an animal or pet before, starting out with a dog or cat is a good first step.

In this chapter we will give you a rundown of the most popular rural creatures people raise in the country: bees, chickens, goats, sheep, pigs and cows.

BEES

WHY BEES?

Beyond the luxury of having a supply of honey and beeswax from the foraging of fields and farms within several miles of your house, keeping bees can help replenish the world's rapidly diminishing bee colonies and ensure your crops will receive pollinator attention. Beekeepers might feel like a secret society—their skills passed down through generations—but once you show interest and enthusiasm, most beekeeper communities will be happy to take you under their wing. All beekeepers know how important it is to share their knowledge so that the bee colonies across the globe have a fighting chance for survival. Beekeeping isn't easy. You will definitely get stung, you will need to lift heavy bee boxes and you will suffer your fair share of heartaches. It is inevitable that you will have some colonies fail. Even experienced beekeepers battle with colony collapse caused by disease, pests and pesticide exposure. Before heading down the apiculture yellow brick road, visit with some experienced beekeepers, watch them go through their routine and only move forward after you've had up close and personal contact with a noisy and bustling colony. A great place to get started is by attending a local or regional beekeeper meeting (yes, such things exist). Or you can always "dooryard call" a neighbor with hives in their yard—who knows, you might just end up meeting your beekeeping mentor or a new friend.

TYPES OF BEES

Apis mellifera is the only species of honeybee specific to Northern American and European beekeepers. Within this species there are several races with varying temperament, color, disease resistance, productivity, heartiness and swarming habits. Before buying or collecting a new swarm, consult with local beekeepers on the best race to suit your area. Bee colonies are composed of the queen bee (boss lady, egg layer, biggest bee in the hive), the drones (bigger than workers but smaller than the queen, only job is to fertilize the queen and then they die) and finally the workers (do all the work, grow from indoor "house bees" to outdoor "collectors," far outnumber drones, smallest in size).

SPACE REQUIRED

Oddly enough, the first space requirement is determining if beekeeping is legally allowed in your area. Even some rural areas have ordinances banning people from keeping bees. If you live in town you might come across opposition, as some people are deathly allergic to bee stings and inexperienced beekeepers can run into issues with swarming and agitated bees that may sting nearby neighbors. If it is legal to keep bees where you live, it is the neighborly thing to do to reach out and tell those living nearby your intentions. If they have no objection, they might even give you helpful information or introduce you to area experts. Bees don't need a lot of space. Urban beekeepers keep their hives on apartment rooftops and balconies. A medium size backyard is all you need for a hive, but keep in mind that they will be actively working during the warmer months. If want space for your family to enjoy BBQs, yard games, etc. it makes sense to put them as far away from heavily trafficked areas surrounding your house as possible, but not so far that it is a nuisance to get to them for routine inspections. Positioning hives near places you want them to pollinate (orchard, garden, etc.) and in a location that is south-facing, near a water supply and out of the wind is ideal.

EXPENSE

The startup costs for beekeeping are significant, but continued maintenance costs are low. To start your colony, you will either need to purchase bees from an online company, sold as either a package (bunch of bees funneled together to make a colony, not yet established) or as a nucleus colony (established colony sold in boxes and frames). You can collect a swarm of feral bees but this is not an easy thing to do and you should get an experienced beekeeper to help you!

Housing: There are a number of different types of hives to choose from but all are essentially boxes and frames. Plan on spending around $200 per hive. You can go foundationless and let the bees build their own foundation, but most novice beekeepers start with a hive that has a foundation—these can be wax, wire or plastic. Don't buy used housing or equipment as they may harbor diseases that could quickly kill your colony. After choosing your hive, paint the boxes different colors or patterns using outdoor latex paint so that bees can identify their own hive.

Food: Bees forage their food. They need nectar (carbs, sweet mix of sugars and water that plants produce to lure pollinators), pollen (protein, essential for producing new bees), water and propolis (sticky sap-like substance from the buds of trees). In cases where hives aren't producing enough food to stay healthy, bees will need to be fed honey or sugar water.

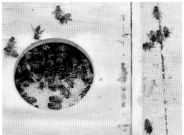

Gear: You'll need a bee veil and jacket (to protect against stings), a pair of thick bee gloves (also for protection), a hive tool (to unglue the strong propolis when you inspect the hive and frames), a smoker (to make the bees docile for inspection) and a brush (to clean out dead bees and gently brush bees off of places you don't want them while inspecting). Also, remember Winnie the Pooh and how much he loved honey? If you have bears in your area, put an electric fence around your hives to prevent bear attacks.

TIME INVESTMENT

Unless you move to an area that doesn't get colder than sixty degrees in the winter, beekeeping's workload is very seasonal, requiring more time and attention in the spring (swarming season of April–June) and in the fall when the weather starts dropping into the fifties (to get ready for the winter). Experienced beekeepers estimate about fifteen to thirty hours tending to each hive every year. Keep in mind that your first few years will require extra time to learn the lay of the land. Good keepers routinely inspect their hives to make sure there is enough room for the bees and nectar, to check for disease and abnormalities, to ensure there is enough food stored until the next inspection and to make sure the queen is laying. They also open the hives to clean and replace full frames so the colony can continue to grow. Opening the hives is jarring to the bees so it shouldn't be done more than once a week or so during peak swarming season. Keep an inspection record book for each of your hives to monitor production, health and behavior.

SEASONAL NEEDS

Bees are sensitive to temperature and rarely work when it's colder than fifty-five degrees. Temperatures below fifty degrees are too cold for bees to fly. In order for your bees to survive the colder months, you will need to prepare your hives for hibernation. First, it is important that your bees have enough to eat to sustain them through the winter, so don't harvest their honey in the fall. Second, mice like to nest in combs through the winter so adding mouse guards across the entrance will help prevent an infestation. Once you've prepped your hives for winter, don't open them again until the spring swarming season, no matter how much you want to.

CHICKENS

WHY CHICKENS?

Chickens are the animal equivalent of a gateway drug, ushering many former urbanites into raising livestock as both friends and food. A small backyard flock of chickens can be extremely simple to keep and, if desired, expanded into a more complex operation over time. Keeping chickens still requires daily care but they are less maintenance than other larger farm animals. If you are interested in raising animals, chickens are a good place to start. You can raise chickens both for meat and to keep your fresh egg supplies stocked. If you live in an area with a tick or mosquito problem, chickens are a great ally as they love eating ticks and mosquito larva. Hens have hilarious mannerisms—they like to gossip and scratch around their run. Roosters can be boisterous, pugnacious and courageous. A good rooster will be protective of his hens and non-aggressive towards his keeper—a bad rooster will be the opposite. If you're ready to dip your toes into raising animals, give chickens a try. If they end up not being a good fit, you can either find someone to take them in or harvest them for meat.

CHICKEN BREEDS

There are many different breeds of chicken and several hundred varieties. Breeders are continually creating new varieties of chickens to improve their traits for specific purposes. There are breeds raised primarily for meat, others for egg production and some serve dual purpose as both layers and meat birds. Different breeds and varieties produce different colors and sizes of eggs and are better suited for certain environments. It's best to ask friends and neighbors in your area about their experiences with different breeds and varieties. If nearly everyone in your area gravitates towards a few breeds, it is likely those birds are better suited for your location. You can have a mix of different chicken breeds in your flock, as chickens tend to get along well with one another if they grow up together. If you want a variety of different types of eggs (the rich dark brown eggs of the Maran, the blue of the Araucanas or the brown variety of the Rhode Island Red), get a bird or two of each breed for your flock. Because there are so many breeds and varieties available, it is best to do some research up front, inquire with locals and read some books to find the breeds and varieties that will best suit your needs.

SPACE REQUIRED

Before investing in chickens and the infrastructure needed, first make sure you can legally keep them. Some rural towns and areas have laws or ordinances that restrict the number of chickens, dictate whether or not you can keep roosters or ban keeping chickens entirely. If you find out you can keep chickens in your area, the size of your flock will dictate the amount of space you will need to allocate. Chickens need a coop for bunking up at the end of a long day, for laying eggs and for protection from predators. Your coop size depends on the number of birds in your flock. Each bird needs a bare minimum of one and a half square feet (929 cm^2) of floor space in the coop but three to four square feet (2787 to 3716 cm^2) is recommended. If you start with a small coop for a small flock don't expand your flock without upsizing their coop. If you plan on letting your chickens free-range throughout the day you don't need to worry about run space restrictions, but if you instead have a protected chicken run for daily exercise, each chicken will need at least four square feet (3716 cm^2) of space in the run. Remember, these are minimums—more space makes for happier and healthier chickens.

EXPENSE

Raising chickens requires both an up-front investment to set up their housing, fencing, feeding and watering equipment, and also a long-term investment in feed. A chicken can range in price from around $3 to $30, depending on their age, sex and breed. Chickens do eat kitchen scraps, but you will also be buying a substantial amount of feed. Meat birds cost anywhere from $3 to $5 to be butchered at a facility, although many people butcher their own chickens. After looking at the up-front and long-term costs, you may decide that it makes more sense to forgo raising your own birds and instead buy eggs and meat locally from your neighbors. That said, many people love having laying hens as pets and eggs are just a bonus. It's worth weighing the cost versus what you consider the pay offs to be.

Housing: Chickens need a coop for protection from the elements and from predators. Although they won't spend all their time in the coop, it is important that any coop you get provides adequate space, cleanliness, security, ventilation from heat and to prevent moisture (adjustable windows or vents are ideal) and is weatherproofed for rain and cold. Chicken coops come in a wide range of shapes and sizes. You can buy pre-builds, assemble one from a kit, build your own out of new or scrap wood or repurpose an old shed or outbuilding. For eggs layers, you will want some nest boxes in a dark corner of your coop so that your eggs will stay clean and unbroken. Ideally, these nest boxes should have an easy access flap on the outside so you can collect the eggs without having to climb inside the coop. Chickens love sleeping on a perch, so having a couple of staggered perches located at least a one and a half feet (46 cm) from the ground will give them a place to roost at night. Some coops have a removable dropping tray or poop boards that make cleaning the coop faster and easier. Straw or wood chip bedding will need to be refreshed weekly. Finally, your coop will need a sturdy door to keep out predators at night. If you are raising chickens just for meat and not for egg production, you can have a much less elaborate set up. Most commercial chicken producers harvest their birds at six weeks of age, while free range farmers tend to harvest at eight to fourteen weeks. A fenced in free-range area and enclosed structure to protect your birds overnight will suffice.

Food: Chickens love to eat. Use a good quality chicken feed pellet that is at least 15 percent protein. Tailor the amount of feed to the number of chickens you have. If your chickens are free-range or have a rotating run, up to 20 percent of their diet can be composed of foraged greens and insects. You can also feed them kitchen scraps and garden waste, but be wary of strong tasting fruits and veggies like garlic, lemons and onions, as they can affect the way a chicken's eggs taste.

Gear: Beyond the coop, there are several other tools you will need to care for your chickens.

1. *A suspended, automatic or trough feeder with a wire or protective covering to prevent birds from walking on their food.*
2. *A moveable elevated waterer. Chickens need access to water at all times so you should invest in one for the coop and one or two for their range.*
3. *Proper fencing for their chicken run or moveable range. If you have a predator problem, investing in secure fencing for your run or in a moveable and secure free-range pen for your chickens will help keep them safe throughout the day.*

Nice To Have But Not Necessary

Solar automatic coop door: Don't like waking up early or remembering to open and close the coop at night? A solar door will do that for you.

Coop interior lights: Lighting your coop in the winter can boost egg production, but it can also tire your chickens.

Exterior motion lights: Helps scare away predators.

Dust bath box: Dust baths are how chickens stay clean and healthy. If you don't have a box for them, they will inevitably tear up your yard to make their own.

Heated waterer: For areas with cold winters, investing in a heated waterer will ensure that your chickens' water will never freeze in icy temperatures.

TIME INVESTMENT

Chickens need daily attention to keep them healthy and happy. First, they need to be let out of their coop every morning and then they need to be fed and watered. In the summer you should check on your chickens throughout the day to make sure they have adequate water available. Their coop should be cleaned and their bedding replaced weekly. A deep cleaning is required twice a year; everything should be pressure washed, chicken-safe cleaning solution should be used and the coop should dry completely before letting your chickens back in. For layers, you will need to collect their eggs daily. At the end of the day, you will need to lock your chickens up for the night. If you go out of town, you will need chicken sitters. You can alleviate some of the time commitment by installing a solar coop door and automatic feeders and waterers, but it is still important to have someone keep an eye out to make sure their supplies don't dwindle and continue to clean their coop. Building, maintaining and/or moving your chicken's coop, run or free-range fencing will also demand some of your time. Chickens are also susceptible to mites, pest infestations, diseases and parasites. Most health problems can be avoided by keeping their coop clean and their diet balanced. Smaller flocks require far less time investment than larger ones, so starting small is best for beginners. Chickens can live as long as eight to ten years, but a lot of people harvest their laying hens at one to two years of age to prevent the meat from getting stringy. Laying hens continue to lay eggs throughout their life, but after the first initial few years their egg production will decrease.

SEASONAL NEEDS

Most chicken breeds are hearty and can handle colder temperatures. But if you live in an area with long, cold winters, make sure you select breeds and varieties that are known to withstand extreme weather conditions. Chickens still like to go outside, but they don't much care for snow. Even when the temperature drops you need to continue opening the coop in the morning and closing it up at night. Shovel your chickens an area to roam for a few hours to encourage them to get some exercise. If it's really cold, you can create a little cold frame chicken run that will act almost as a sunroom they can play in. Hen's egg production goes down when the days get shorter and temperatures drop. You can increase their egg production by introducing timed lights in their coop, but know that this can stress your birds and reduce their egg laying lifespan.

BREEDING

In order for your chickens' eggs to be fertilized and produce new hatchlings you will first need a rooster. Many keepers of small flocks decide against a rooster to lessen their chances of accidentally growing their flock. Some roosters are helpful and protect their hens, while others can be mean and aggressive. If you have a rooster that mates with your hens, chances are your hens are laying fertilized eggs. Fertilized eggs taste the same as non-fertilized, but in order to prevent them from developing into chicks, you will need to collect all of the eggs daily to avoid embryo development while sitting under a warm chicken. If you want baby chicks, you can either pull fertilized eggs out and put them in an incubator, or you can stick the eggs under a

broody hen. You can tell a hen is broody because she won't leave her nesting box and is irritable or squawks when you approach. Broody hens will sit in their box warming whatever eggs are beneath them for twenty-one days until they hatch, only leaving for brief periods to eat, drink and poop. If you don't want baby chicks, you can try to break the broodiness out of your hen by isolating her and removing her from the coop for a few days. Here are some other ways to grow your flock without needing to add a rooster:

1. *Buy fertilized eggs and hatch them in an incubator or put them under a broody hen (you don't need a rooster for hens to get broody)*
2. *Buy baby chicks from a local breeder or online*
3. *Rescue or purchase full-grown or adolescent chickens (important to know that sometimes new birds can go through a hazing period where the flock will pick on the new arrival)*

MISC. POULTRY

Here are a few quick tips for other types of popular poultry. Many people I've interviewed started with chickens and slowly added other types of poultry and livestock to the equation.

Ducks and geese: They still need to be locked up in a shed at night to keep predators away. Since these are both waterfowl, they prefer warmer temperatures and ideally should be raised in a place with a pond or water source.

Guinea hens: The best tick eaters! If you have a tick problem in your area, consider getting a few guinea hens. You can also raise them for eggs and meat. They are noisy, they fly and they are difficult to maintain. It takes time to train them to stay near their coop and sometimes they will decide to nest instead in nearby trees.

Turkeys: You can stick turkey eggs in an incubator or under a broody hen. If you use a broody hen, you will want to separate the turkeys from the chickens once they have hatched to prevent disease. Turkeys need more space than chickens and do best raised free-range or in a large fenced pen.

GOATS

WHY GOATS?

People raise goats for a multitude of reasons—for milk, meat, fiber and companionship. Lots of people who can't drink cow milk can digest goat milk, and goat milk can be used to make cheese, soap, caramels and a myriad of other things. These friendly, playful creatures are curious, devious and hilarious in their antics. After touring many working and hobby farms, I have fallen in love with goats. To me, their personalities are the most like dogs. They are very social. They love their owners and are excited to receive human attention. They also love getting into trouble, breaking out of their pens, climbing on the roof of your car and eating your entire vegetable or flower garden. Even when they are testing your nerves, it is hard to stay mad at them for long. Goats are hardy creatures and can live happily in many different environments. If you are interested in getting a goat, know that they are social creatures and while they don't necessary need a goat buddy, they will want a four-legged companion like a sheep, cow or horse. Uncastrated male "billie" goats can be aggressive and charge or butt at their owners. Depending on what you are raising them for, they can be a ton of work, so it is best to research ahead of time and know what you are getting into before buying the first cute goat you see.

GOAT BREEDS

Goats are divided into six species that are classified by their horn shape and place of origin. There are breeds that are best suited for milk production, fiber and for meat. Certain climates are better suited for specific breeds or cross-breeds, so consult your local goat experts to find out what breeds do best in your area.

Here are the commonly raised breeds for each category:

Dairy Goats: Alpine, Nubian, La Mancha, Oberhasli, Saanen and Toggenburg
Meat Goats: Boet, San Clemente, Spanish (a lot of dairy goats are also harvested for meat)
Fiber Goats: Angora, Cashmere
Companions Goats: Any breeds could be raised as pets, but Pygmy and Nigerian Dwarf goats are popular companion breeds

SPACE REQUIRED

Goats need both a house or shed for shelter, an outside exercise area and ideally a fenced rotating range for grazing. In their shelter, each goat needs ten to fifteen square feet (1 m²) of bedding space and in their play area they need at least 25 to 30 square feet (2 to 3 m²) each. Goats prefer to roam on pasture, so if you plan on raising more than a couple goats, you should have several fields available that you can rotate them through to graze. Rotational grazing will not only keep your grass down, but it will save on feed costs. Goats prefer to be outside, even when it is cold, and will continue to graze during the day even when there is light snow on the ground. For colder months, hot summers and kidding season, goats need shelter. Goats also don't like wind or rain and will run for cover during rainstorms.

Goats range in price from around $75 to $300, depending on the breed, age and sex. Goats have upfront costs to build their shelters, pens and fences, but they also have recurring costs for food, bedding, medication and de-worming. Many goat and sheep owners invest in purebred guard dogs to watch over their flocks and protect against predators, which can remove the need to lock your goats up in a barn or enclosure every night.

Housing: Goats do not need fancy enclosures—simply a place that is dry, well-ventilated and has clean bedding. Many people repurpose old barns or sheds for their goats. You can also build a goat shed using up-cycled building materials. Outside of your goat shelter you should have a fenced play and exercise area. Goats are amazing escape artists, so it is important that you build a sturdy fence to keep them from making a quick getaway.

Food: Goats are grazers and spend a majority of their days eating and foraging. Although goats get lots of nutrients from grazing, especially in the late spring and early summer, owners still need to provide them with good-quality hay to aid in their digestion and goat feed concentrate for growing, pregnant and milking goats. The amount of feed totally depends on the goat, the type of feed and the goat's current exertion (e.g., a milker will need around three to four pounds (1–2 kg) of feed a day, while a young dairy goat might only need a pound or so). Goats also need fresh water available throughout the day and a mineral lick. Secure any water containers as goats love tipping them over and trampling through them.

Gear: Goats need an elevated hayrack, a sturdy and protected waterer and secure fencing. Portable/moveable electric fencing proves very handy for rotating grazing pastures, and goats are less inclined to try and break out of electric fences. You will also need hoof trimmers and de-worming medications to keep them healthy. If you plan on milking your goats, you will need a milking bucket and a milking stand, which will make your life a lot easier and keep you from getting a crick in your back.

TIME INVESTMENT

All goats require daily monitoring, including feeding and watering. Repairing fences, chasing escapees, changing their bedding and moving grazing areas are usually weekly tasks. Goats need to be de-wormed two to six times a year, depending on the area (warm, humid places require more frequent de-worming). Goats' hooves need to be trimmed every month or so, depending on their environment and how much time they spend outside. Your goats also may need to be deloused from time to time and be treated with antibiotics. A deep clean of their shelter should be done at least monthly. If you are raising goats for milk you will have to breed your goats, monitor and help deliver their babies and, after kidding, mama goats have to be milked twice daily, seven days a week. How does that fresh goat milk sound now? If it's still appealing, then you are a good candidate for raising dairy goats. Breeding goats also usually involves bottle-feeding, weaning, castrating and dehorning. Meat goats, fiber goats and companion goats are a bit easier because they don't need to be milked. Meat goats are generally harvested between eight and twelve months of age. Angora fiber goats should be sheared twice a year (in order to get the most fiber). March and September are the most common months for shearing. Cashmere goats aren't to be sheared—their fiber should be plucked or combed out of their fleece. The average cashmere goat produces only four ounces of fiber annually; now it finally makes sense why cashmere is so insanely expensive. Companion goats just want food, water, exercise and your daily company. I have a friend that routinely takes his Nigerian Dwarf goats for walks in their woods.

SEASONAL NEEDS

In the winter, goats need a steady supply of hay, water and feed. In colder areas goats won't be able to graze as much as in the warmer months, so they will consume higher quantities of hay and feed in the winter. Goats need fresh bedding for warmth and also to prevent disease and parasites. It's important to clean their shelter and replace their bedding frequently in the winter months because they spend more time inside.

BREEDING

Breeding your goats is essential for milk production in dairy goats. Male and female goats should be separated except when you are actively breeding them. This way you will know roughly how far along they are in their pregnancy. A female goat (doe) can only produce milk after she has had a baby. Goats have a short gestation period of 150 days. Typically, people breed their goats in the fall and babies arrive in the spring. After a goat has her babies, her milk production kicks into high gear—this is called "freshening." At first a doe has a lot of milk, but production decreases steadily and pitters out after a year. Goats typically give birth to one to three kids at a time. Most dairy goat owners will separate the kids from their moms to bottle-feed them several times a day. This ensures the milkers produce a lot of milk and ensures that kids get enough individual attention. The castration of male goats can be done just days after birth by slipping a rubber ring over their testicles. Most goat owners, if they want to keep their male goats, will castrate them and leave just one or two uncastrated to breed with their does. As uncastrated males (billies) mature they often get aggressive and can butt and cause harm to their owners and other goats. Uncastrated males also give off a particularly offensive and pungent odor that intensifies during mating season.

GOATUCCINO

A recipe for the best dang country cappuccino, created by the first-time farmers behind Little Seed Farm, served fresh from a goat's teat. Goat milk is warm, frothy and naturally homogenized (the cream doesn't rise to the top) making it the perfect milk for your morning cappuccino. In order to enjoy this recipe, you have to be fine with drinking non-pasteurized goat milk fresh from the teat. In some rare cases people who drink raw goat milk get E.coli or Salmonella so it is important you practice good hygiene when milking and clean your goat's udder and teat thoroughly before you milk them. I wouldn't recommend consuming this goatuccino if you are pregnant.

Step 1: Start out with a great cup of dark roast coffee (you can do lighter roast if you like, but the dark roast blends great with the goat milk). Fill the coffee about ¾ to the top (or less if you prefer more milk). Add sweetener of your choice if you desire.

Step 2: Spray and clean your goat's udder and teat with teat spray.

Step 3: Squeeze milk directly into your coffee cup until foam reaches the top.

Step 4: Enjoy.

SHEEP

WHY SHEEP?

Happy bleating sheep roaming free on a pasture are a lovely sight. Sheep have the unique ability to be incredibly charming and sweet one minute and absolutely stubborn and difficult to manage the next. I raised a Romney Ewe when I was seven and although she often let me pet her and was calm when I was in her pasture, it was nearly impossible to catch her when I needed to trim her hooves or shear her wool. It was like she knew when I was in there for business and when I was just there to say hello. Like goats, sheep can be raised for fiber, meat, milk or cute lawnmowers. Sheep's milk makes incredible cheese—Greek Feta and French Roquefort are made with milk from sheep. They are hardy creatures that winter well in cold environments. Also, lambs are adorable.

SHEEP BREEDS

There are many breeds of sheep to suit different terrains, temperatures and needs. Choose a breed that works well in your environment and has a temperament that jives with you. Here are some of the most popular breeds for fiber, meat and milk. Many milking sheep breeds are also good fiber sheep and fiber sheep can also be bred for meat, so you will see some overlap here.

Meat Breeds: Mule, Suffolk, Corriedale, Hampshire, Icelandic

Fiber/Fleece Breeds: Jacob, Dorset, Romney, Icelandic, Merino, Lincoln, Corriedale, Suffolk

Dairy Breeds: East Friesian, Assaf, Awassi, Icelandic, Lacaune, Dorset

SPACE REQUIRED

Sheep can be kept in a barn or dirt lot year round but it's better for them (and much cheaper for you) if you keep them on rotational grazing pastures. Each sheep needs at least .2 acres of space, so if you have five sheep, you will need around three acres, divided into three pastures that you rotate them through. Sheep also need a draft-free, well-ventilated shed or barn for shelter with fifteen to twenty square feet (1–2 m²) of space each. Sheep can be kept on pasture with goats and cows, just make sure each animal has enough space and forage available.

EXPENSE

Sheep cost varies based on breed and age but usually are $250 to $300. The start-up costs include housing and fencing, and reccurring costs include de-worming, fresh straw for shelter and feed. Start with a smaller flock to test the waters before making a larger investment. Fiber sheep need to be sheared at least once a year, and you may want to hire someone to do it for you or at least help you. If you are raising sheep for meat, you should also factor in the cost of slaughter. Many people also invest in herding dogs when getting sheep as it makes them much easier to move and handle. Some also invest in purebred livestock guard dogs like Maremmas or Great Pyrenees.

These dogs can help ensure that your flock doesn't fall prey to predators. The cost of purchasing and training sheepherders and livestock guard dogs should be factored in when considering whether or not to keep sheep.

Housing: Sheep need a barn or open front three-sided shed for wet and winter weather and lambing. Their shelter should be routinely cleaned and fresh straw spread. Sheep shelters don't need to be fancy, but they should be waterproof, draft-free and well ventilated.

Food: Sheep can be raised mostly on pasture. In the winter, when pasture is insufficient, they will need to be fed hay. Sheep eat about four pounds (2 kg) of hay a day. Some sheep owners will also feed their sheep one pound (450 g) of grain concentrate. Sheep also need mineral salt licks to stay healthy and fresh water.

Gear: All sheep need their hooves regularly trimmed, so hoof trimmers are a necessity. Sheep need strong water troughs and hay racks for the winter. You will also need permanent or movable fencing for rotational grazing. Fiber sheep need to be sheared, so it is worth investing in good shears or electric clippers. If you plan to card and spin the wool yourself, you will need to invest in a carder and spinning wheel. Milking sheep need a milking stand and a milk bucket, and you will likely want to invest in cheese-making equipment.

TIME INVESTMENT

Sheep need to be watered every day and if they aren't on pasture they need to be fed hay. Every week or so they should be moved to a new pasture to allow that pasture time to recover and help prevent parasite infestation. Inspect your sheep's hooves every couple of months and do regular trimming to prevent hoof rot and lameness. Some breeds have hardier hooves and don't need to be trimmed as frequently. Hooves generally require more maintenance in wetter, muddier areas versus rockier, dryer locations. Sheep are susceptible to parasites and should be de-wormed once or twice a year. Many sheep owners will time de-worming with shearing and lambing season. Sheep are sheared in the beginning of summer, before temperatures get hot, allowing their fleece time to grow back before the winter cold. Dairy and fiber sheep require much more time investment than goats raised for meat. Dairy sheep need to be milked twice a day, every day.

SEASONAL NEEDS

In the winter, sheep require a steady supply of hay and water. If you are breeding your ewes, you should avoid feeding them grain in the winter so they don't get too fat for lambing season. In colder areas sheep won't be able eat their full ration of food on pasture grazing alone, so they will consume higher quantities of hay in the winter. Sheep need fresh straw bedding in their shelter all winter long to prevent parasites and to keep your flock healthy and dry.

BREEDING

The normal gestation period for sheep is 152 days. Lambs don't like cold so as a result many people breed their sheep so they will deliver in the spring when the grass is sweet and ready to eat and the temperatures are warmer. Artificial insemination is more common and infinitely easier than naturally mating your ewes with a ram. Different breeds of sheep reach sexual maturity at different times (it ranges from about nine months to two years of age). Pregnant ewes can be nearly as wide as they are tall and sometime lose their footing, roll onto their backs and can't get themselves up. It is important to keep ewes at a healthy weight so they don't have problems with being too large during lambing season. Sheep typically have two lambs, but first timers usually have only one. Build shelters early for your pregnant ewes, as it is common to have premature births. If it is still cold outside, build these shelters indoors. They should have separate pens for each ewe and plenty of clean straw to lay on. If you are raising sheep for their milk, you can start weaning lambs after the first week, but many keep the lambs with their mamas for sixty days before weaning them so they don't have to bottle feed the lambs until they can digest grass. It takes fifty to sixty days for lambs to develop the rumen necessary to digest feeds and forage.

PIGS

WHY PIGS?

Pigs have been a staple on small-scale and hobby farms for generations. They will happily eat your kitchen scraps and garden waste and easily clear overgrown land to prep for future garden expansions. And, to all carnivores out there, let's be honest, their meat is delicious. Pigs have gotten a bad reputation for being dumb and filthy, but the truth is, pigs are quite the opposite. They are hardy creatures that are intelligent, clean and can be quite charming. If given adequate space, pigs will never poop near where they sleep and they wallow in mud to prevent overheating and sunburns. Pigs grow quickly and domestic farm pigs average ten piglets per litter, making it easy to keep a continuous sounder of pigs on your property.

PIG BREEDS

There are quite a few breeds of pigs available. Some industrially bred hybrids are created specifically for food manufacturers and can barely hold themselves upright and fatten quickly for early slaughter. Hybrids aren't recommended for backyard operations, especially if you intend to try and breed your pigs. For small-scale operations, research the available breeds and inquire with local pig owners to see what breeds they've tried and which they like best for your area specifics. Usually hardier breeds are the older, rarer and less-developed varieties. Some of the most popular pig breeds are Berkshire, British Lop, Saddleback, Gloucestershire Old Spot, Large Black, Duroc, Landrace, Yorkshire, Chester White and the Tamworth. After you've selected a breed for your area and purposes, it is important to find a reputable breeder. There are many online associations and societies for specific pig breeds that can help connect you to a good breeder.

SPACE REQUIRED

Pigs can either be kept in a sty, which includes an indoor sleeping area and a yard for exercise, or they can be kept free-range in fenced areas with moveable shelters or arks to provide shade and a place to sleep. If you plan on raising more than a couple of pigs, free-range is the way to go. Each pig in a free-range environment needs a minimum of 50 square feet (4.6 m²) of roaming space. Because pigs are expert rooters, they can quickly clear thick and overgrown areas, so you might want to rotate their pastures to ensure their roaming spaces have time to recover and aren't completely stripped.

EXPENSE

Pigs range in price based on age, genetics and stock. Young feeder pigs (raised for meat) range in price between $20 to $100. A good breeding pig can cost anywhere from $300 to several thousand dollars (yeah…woah!). The expense for raising pigs can vary, depending on whether or not you have a garden or other animals. Pigs are happily raised on a range or in a sty and if you have extra dairy from goats, sheep or cows (or lots of garden and kitchen scraps), you can minimize the continual cost to feed them. A main reason some decide not to raise pigs after a year or two of trying is that the expense to feed them outweighs the ultimate cost of the meat they produce.

Housing: Pigs need shelter consisting of a clean, dry place off of the ground with bedding to lie on where they can be protected from the weather. This can be a moveable ark for free-range pigs or a sty with a pen for exercise. You can either buy a pre-built structure or build one yourself. Many moveable pig arks are lightweight with wheels to ease moving them to new pastures. Pigs will also need plenty of fresh straw to sleep on and it should be replaced frequently. Lastly, pigs need fencing to keep them from escaping. Electric fencing is the most widely used. Fences only need to be a couple of feet (60 cm) off the ground to deter pigs from trying to get out.

Food: Pigs consume a lot of water. An ample supply of fresh drinking water should always be on hand. Pigs love kitchen and garden scraps and roots, but in order to grow quickly they need to be consistently fed some grain-based feed. Two of the best things to feed pigs are wheat bran and barley meal. Never feed pigs meat products! If pigs are allowed to root in the soil you won't need to add additional minerals to their diet.

Gear: Aside from fencing and shelter, pigs require very little in the way of gear. You will need a sturdy water trough that is either very heavy or bolted to the ground to keep their water fresh and keep them from wallowing in it and a heavy food trough to keep pigs from overturning it. A wood or cement wallow that you can fill with water will keep pigs cool and happy in warmer temperatures.

TIME INVESTMENT

Pigs don't require a lot of time and attention, other than daily feeding and watering. In the summer months, you will need to ensure pigs have enough water to cool off in and their roaming area has plenty of shade. Pigs raised for meat are generally harvested between four and twelve months of age. Most male piglets are castrated, unless they are being raised to be a breeding boar.

SEASONAL NEEDS

Pigs continue to roam and venture outdoors in colder temperatures. Blocking wind from their shelters and keeping them out of the snow so they stay dry are two of the most important things you can do to keep your pigs warm and healthy in the winter. Lots of clean straw to bed down in is also important. In very cold conditions, you might want to use a heat lamp.

BREEDING

A sow (female pig) giving birth to piglets is called farrowing. Boars (uncastrated male pigs) impregnate sows by artificial insemination. Sows are usually first mated when they are six to eight months old. The gestation period is roughly three months, three weeks and three days (or 114 days). In colder places, people usually wait until later in the winter to breed so piglets won't be born when it is still freezing out. Farrowing pens create a warm, safe and clean place for your sow to give birth. They should have plenty of fresh straw and be no smaller than four by five feet (1–1.5 m). A railway across the pen creates a safe area for new piglets to sleep so their sleeping mama won't crush them, and a heat lamp should be turned on if the weather is cold. New piglets should suckle for the first hour after being born and runts should be bottle-fed if they aren't getting udder time. On average, sows deliver ten to twelve babies. After three days, if it's not too cold, piglets can venture outside. Piglets naturally wean themselves over time, as they immediately start to be interested in solid food.

COWS

WHY COWS?

There are many benefits to keeping a cow but the main reason people get cows is to have a steady supply of fresh milk and cream. Imagine, being able to make your own butter, cheese and yogurt fresh from your own cow's milk. Cows are also incredible lawnmowers and can keep grass growth down. Cows can be raised for meat or serve a dual purpose as a dairy cow that's eventually harvested for meat when her milking days are done.

I have a personal fondness for cows that stems from my childhood. My first furry friend, at the age of five, was a black Dexter heifer that my parents got to keep the fields mowed. I named her Mooey (I know, very creative) and we had a special bond. Whenever I would come out of the house Mooey would moo happily at me—she didn't do this for anyone else in my family. I would walk along the top of the rickety wooden fence around her field and she would walk alongside me as I went, there to brace me if I lost my balance. Mooey escaped one day and wasn't found for over a week. Eventually she was discovered in a neighbor's bull pen down the road. She had broken out to find a fella. After she gave birth to a bull calf, my parents decided they were done keeping cows. A month or two after she had her bull calf I came home from school and Mooey was being loaded into a tractor-trailer. My parents had sold my pet cow to the butcher and my older sister happily informed me a few weeks later that I was eating Mooey while midway through my burger. I didn't eat meat for many years after that night. This isn't a happy story, but it's a reality of raising animals. You have to deal with life and death. Even if you aren't raising animals for meat, some will get sick and die, and some will be attacked by predators or attacked by their own kind. You can't raise animals and avoid dealing with death. If you have young children and you are raising animals for meat, it is important that you explain that they will eventually become dinner. The finding-out-later or shock approach is not a good way to go.

COW BREEDS

There are quite a few different breeds of cows well suited for small-scale farms, including some mini varieties. The Jersey cow is a popular breed because they are docile, on the smaller side and good milkers. There is even a Mini-Jersey variety that is much smaller than the standard Jersey. Be aware that mini breeds are about double the price of the standard size cows and produce about a $^1/_3$ of the milk (one to one and a half gallons [4–5.5 L] from a Mini-Jersey per milking vs. six to ten gallons [23–38 L] from a regular Jersey). Do your research and go meet the cow you are planning to buy before going through with the sale. A cow's temperament is very important if you plan on milking them. Some cows are unruly and can kick or stomp on a foot during their milkings. If you aren't familiar with what to look for in a healthy, easy-to-handle cow, bring a friend who keeps cows with you to look at the cow you are considering. You don't want to get stuck with a difficult, stubborn or crazed cow. The most popular cow breeds for small-scale operations that serve dual purposes are Jersey, Holstein (also has a mini version), Milking Shorthorn, Dexter, Simmental, Ayrshire, Brown Swiss and Guernsey. The most popular mini cows are Jersey (milk), Dexters (milk and meat), Lowlines (mini Angus beef cows), Herefords (meat), and Zebu (meat, humped Brahman suited for hot/dry environments).

SPACE REQUIRED

Zoning laws can be very specific about keeping cows so before looking online at breeders, check the regulations for your property first. You might find that you need a certain number of acres in order to keep a cow and that they need to be located a certain distance from your house. Each cow requires at least an acre of land, divided into three pastures for rotational grazing. Cows are not a good choice for small parcels of land, especially if you are keeping other animals. If your main reason for wanting a cow is fresh milk and you don't have a large plot, consider getting goats, as they require less space. You will need a draft-free barn with a minimum of 75 square feet (7 m²) of space per cow. For personal milk consumption (and maybe a little extra to sell), a family really only needs one or two cows. Start with one and add on if you want more milk. You will also need space in your barn to store hay and grain for the winter months.

EXPENSE

Cows aren't cheap. They are expensive to purchase—an average dairy cow costs anywhere from $900 to $3,000, and will continue to cost you money to keep them fed, healthy and happy. If you are keeping a cow for milk, you will need to buy milking equipment and will likely want to invest in tools to make dairy products from your milk. If you are raising a beef cow, you should factor in the cost of slaughtering. Before you buy a cow, do the math and make sure you can afford keeping one long term.

Housing: Cows will need a draft-free barn with a window, a designated milking area and sleeping area for the winter season. This barn can be an open-front three-sided barn, a free-stall or an enclosed stanchion barn. If you live in an area with hot summers, your cow will also appreciate a shelter or lean-to in their pasture for shade.

Food: Rotational pasture grazing is the most economical way to keep a cow. You can feed a cow year round but it is going to be much more expensive than feeding them a combo of pasture, hay and grain. A cow needs at least one to two acres and three grazing fields. A cow consumes about two pounds (900 g) of hay each day for every 100 pounds (45 kg) of their body weight (a general rule is 30 to 40 pounds [13.5–18 kg] of hay per day for a standard size cow). Grain helps boost dairy cow production; a pound (450 g) of grain a day for every three gallons (11 L) of milk produced is standard.

In the winter months, you will need to keep a steady stock of hay for daily feedings. In months where they can eat primarily pasture, you should still have some hay available. You also need a salt lick readily available. You don't have to feed your cow grain but they sure do love it. If your cow gets loose, an easy way to coax them home is a bucket of grain. A ruminant-formulated mineral and salt mix is also recommended if your pasture does not have ample minerals.

Gear: For both dairy and meat cows you will need water troughs for their barn and their pastures, a hay rack, manure shovel, a steady supply of clean hay for bedding in the winter, hay forks and a wheelbarrow for transporting manure. For dairy cows, you will need a milk pail, water pail, milking stool, udder washcloths, milk scale, halter and rope, a brush for cleaning and barn thermometer. You might also want to invest in cheese-making equipment and a churn to make butter.

TIME INVESTMENT

Cows aren't low maintenance—they require daily watering, feeding and if you are primarily pasture feeding your cows, a week to every couple of days you should move your cow to a new pasture. Rotating pastures helps reduce the chances of your cows getting parasites and gives that pasture a chance to regrow. Dairy cows need to be milked twice a day, ten to fourteen hours apart for ten months out of the year. You have to be good about the schedule because it is incredibly painful for cows if they aren't milked on time. Talk about being tethered to your farm. Are you okay forgoing evening plans with friends so you can milk your cow? Milking a cow in the summer months can feel romantic,

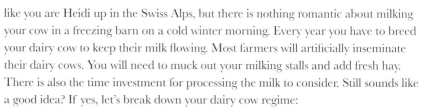

like you are Heidi up in the Swiss Alps, but there is nothing romantic about milking your cow in a freezing barn on a cold winter morning. Every year you have to breed your dairy cow to keep their milk flowing. Most farmers will artificially inseminate their dairy cows. You will need to muck out your milking stalls and add fresh hay. There is also the time investment for processing the milk to consider. Still sounds like a good idea? If yes, let's break down your dairy cow regime:

Feeding: 20 minutes (10 in the morning, 10 at night)
Milking: 40 minutes (20 in the morning, 20 at night)
Straining/Cooling Milk and Cleaning Up: 30 to 40 minutes
Removing Manure and Brushing the Cow: 15 to 20 minutes

That's over an hour and a half of work every day to keep a dairy cow, not even factoring in the time it takes to make dairy products from their milk and the labor involved in calving season. You can also opt to grow your own hay for winter, so if you plan on doing that, factor it into your overall time investment.

SEASONAL NEEDS

Cows need shelter in the winter, although they will still venture outside on occasion. Their barn should be shoveled out regularly and fresh straw spread out for sleeping. If cows can't graze on pasture in the winter, they will need to be fed hay. It's much cheaper to buy hay in bulk, so it's ideal to have a dry place to store a winter supply. To keep cows healthy and their milk production steady, you should also add some grain to their diet in the winter. If you live in a particularly cold place with brutal winters, research hardier breeds like the Ayrshire, Belted Galloway, Canadienne and the shaggy Highland.

BREEDING

Both beef and dairy cows have a nine-month gestation period. As mentioned earlier, in order to continue milking your cow, she will need to be bred every year. Dairy cows begin producing milk once they give birth to a calf. Most cows are then milked for ten months and then have a two-month dry period until they give birth to their next calf. Many people breed their cows in the late summer so they deliver in the early spring, timing their dry period for the colder winter months. No one likes milking in the freezing cold! Heifers (female cows) reach sexual maturity age at nine months, but people usually wait until they are at least thirteen to fifteen months old before breeding. Beef farmers usually use a bull (uncastrated male) to naturally breed their cows, while most dairy farmers use artificial insemination. Calves need to drink from their mom's udder in the beginning and can start being weaned after the first week. Start by separating the cow from her calf for just a few hours every day. Keep them where they can see one another but not where the calf can feed. Mix three parts of milk to one-part water and feed the calf from a bottle or bucket (you might need to teach them how to drink from a bucket).

KEEPING ANIMALS: A SUMMARY
(AND A NOTE ON "HOBBY FARMING")

To summarize, keeping animals isn't something that should be rushed into. Tour your local farms and talk to people who have been raising the animals and breeds you're interested in, bonus points for volunteering to care for, milk, feed or help with breeding season. Learn as much as you can before you invest in your own animals. There are many advantages to raising your own animals and for lots of ex-urbanites those benefits are worth the time and expense. If you moved with a partner, it's important you both are committed to raising animals. If only one of you is excited about the prospect of keeping animals, it could cause problems in your relationship down the road. My advice for new transplants is always the same: start small. Dip your toes into animal ownership with a few chickens, but don't jump in headfirst and buy a few cows. If you like raising chickens and are ready for a bigger challenge, maybe your next step is a couple of rabbits, some goats or a turkey or two.

If the notion of a "hobby farm" seems appealing, remember that you'll need a flexible work schedule and plenty of time available every single day to keep your operation going seven days a week, 365 days a year. Many hobby farmers I've interviewed say they feel very tethered to their farms. Even taking the afternoon off to swim in the river during the hot days of summer requires extra planning and work to ensure all of the farm chores are done. It takes several years to get a hobby farm set up and running smoothly. A majority of first-time farmers don't take vacations, can't go to family functions, weddings or plan trips for the first few years. Ultimately, farming can be incredibly rewarding but it takes time to get the formula right. From time to time, you will inevitably throw your hands up in the air and wish you'd never embarked on this journey, but that is just part of the process. There will be breeds of animals that don't work for you, varieties of crops that don't grow well and a long to-do list that will never come to an end. But if you're up for the time it takes to build it, there is nothing quite as wonderful and rewarding as growing and raising your own food.

MEETING YOUR MATES

Making friends and dating

"I think there is a misconception that you might be lonely or bored. For everyone I know, country living is busier and more social than their previous life in the city. It seems by having fewer options you do more and actually see your friends more often."

– Cig Harvey, Photographer

Many people worry that moving away from a city to a small town means that they won't have nearly as many friends and that finding friends will be more difficult. While it certainly can feel that way in the beginning, don't despair, your rural posse is waiting for you somewhere—you just have to find them. In the country you have to be much more proactive when it comes to forging relationships—both with friends and romantic partners. It's important to know that making friends and dating in the country isn't like making friends and dating in the city. You no longer have endless options or the nagging thought that there is something better waiting just around the corner. It's more like going to school with the same fifty kids for the rest of your life. You will have times where you are closer to some more than others. The same people will annoy you and charm you at various intervals over the course of your years together. Because rural areas have a much higher retention rate than the city, there won't be a steady flow or influx of new faces. People don't move much; they tend to stay put. Those you meet your first few years living in your new area will likely continue be a part of your life in one way or another. It's important to remember this because first impressions in the country are very important. You should be kind to everyone you meet; don't lose your temper and don't burn bridges. Friendships in the country are not about choosing who to be friends with, they're about making peace with everyone and leaving the door open for friendship to grow.

For anyone who made the move single, never fear. Although the dating pool will be smaller in your new locale, if you want to meet someone, as long as you make a concerted effort to put yourself out there, you will. Much of the advice for making friends applies directly to dating—don't skip ahead and just read the dating section, because making friends should be your first priority when moving. You'll never meet Mr. or Ms. Right without building a social circle first. Don't put unnecessary pressure on yourself to find love right away. Focus first on building quality friendships and relationships within your community. Many of the people I've interviewed who moved single, or became single shortly after moving, were only able to find love after they built themselves a strong network of friends. Plus, if you don't have friends first, who are you going to gush or complain to about your most recent date?

Small towns can feel closed off to outsiders. With a sense of community pride comes a wariness of folks from elsewhere. It's an underlying of rite of passage to becoming a local. How to get past it? Be open and generous. Offer to watch someone's dog when they are out of town, lend a hand setting up an event or share your pears if you have an abundance on your tree. Be eager to support the efforts of the people you meet by attending their cooking class or art exhibit. Be unafraid to try new things when invited for an outing. Don't worry about being clumsy at cross-country skiing, out of breath on a hike or lousy at the open studio drawing class. Just showing up brings you closer to friendship. Don't be shy about sharing your own talents. In a small community, people are always looking to learn from one another. If you have a law degree, help a friend understand the deed to her property. If you know about wine, teach your friends the joy of a good rosé in the summer sun. If you know graphic design from your city life, offer to help a friend with their logo. Think about what you have to offer and share generously.

BE PROACTIVE ABOUT SOCIALIZING & GET INVOLVED

You will never make friends sitting in your house; you have to get up and do stuff. Volunteer for a non-profit, help organize a public event or attend some local town meetings. Not only will you learn a lot more about your new community, but you will also begin to meet the movers and shakers who help make things work in your area. Join a gym or, better yet, a running club or mountain biking team where you can socialize while you work out. Go to local events like craft fairs, school fundraisers, holiday parties and church services. Every time you leave the house challenge yourself to talk to at least one new person before coming home. I know this isn't easy for some people, myself included, but I guarantee that it will help you make friends and build community. Sign up for anything that interests you—talks at the library, art shows, garden tours—and introduce yourself to everyone you meet at those events.

OPPOSITES ATTRACT

Many city dwellers develop subconscious (or sometimes conscious) parameters for potential friends. With so many options to choose from, creating stipulations makes it easier to hone in and establish your social circle. In the country, fewer options mean that you can no longer be as knit-picky or stubborn when it comes to making and keeping friends. The person who initially rubs you the wrong way might end up being a friend down the road, so don't do anything to sabotage that potential. I met a woman when I first moved whom I didn't initially connect with, but after spending time with her and getting to know her better, she ended up being one of my closest friends. If you have a conflict with a friend or acquaintance it is important that you work it out, even if that means having to swallow

your pride and be the bigger person. There is no way to avoid your problems in a small town; you will inevitably see the person you are having issues with at the market or the next dinner party, and ignoring them is only going to make the situation worse.

One of the funny things I noticed when moving to the country was the number of old men whose long-standing conflicts had flourished into friendships. Their animosity had grown into familiar sparring. They began to disagree with one another for sport, looking forward to each encounter with a grin. Time together will do this; it will bring a softness and an understanding to any relationship. Let go of any subconscious or conscious "friendship parameters" you've developed and don't rely entirely on your first impressions of someone. In the country, friendships grow and evolve over time. Keep your friends close and any potential enemies closer—those enemies might just end up being your best friends later on.

CREATE YOUR OWN SOCIAL GATHERINGS

If you feel like there aren't many community social gatherings that are of interest to you, create one! A great way to find and make new friends is to start a weekly or monthly group event. A book club, craft night, music jam, writer's sharing session—whatever you're excited about and want to share with others. When a young storyteller moved to our community from the city, he started a Moth-inspired monthly story night based around specific themes. People would write three-minute pieces on the monthly topic and present them to the group. The story night took off and is now a treasured gathering that many in our community attend. He very quickly was able to make friends and get settled, all just by starting something in his new community. A group of ladies and I started a bi-monthly art night that travels from one house to the next during the desolate stretches of winter. Everyone brings an art or craft project to work on and a bottle of wine or spiked cider. The night is filled with laughter and it helps keep spirits high and inspiration flowing. Art night has grown as new friends are made and added to the mix. Creating a gathering or group that feeds your particular interests is a great way to build community, make new friends and nurture existing relationships.

AGE AIN'T NOTHING BUT A NUMBER

Gone are the days where all your friends will be pretty much the same as you. I remember watching bar-hopping packs of women and men huddled in tight groups in the city dressed in pretty much the same outfits, same hairdos, same everything. In urban metropolises it is easy to only hang out with people that are relatively the same age and on the same page of life as you because the places you like to hang out at are the places like-minded individuals tend to frequent. Colleagues, work mentors and friends' parents were the only people older than me I regularly hung out with in the city. In the country, there are fewer people, fewer places and fewer individuals in your specific age group. The people you meet and hit it off with aren't necessarily going to be same age as you, but that doesn't mean that you can't form a lasting friendship with them. It didn't take long to realize that I would be severely limiting my friend options if I continued to only hang out with people in my same age bracket. I started hanging out with my mother-in-law's friends and made friends both with women decades older and younger than me. I treasure these new friendships because I finally realize how important it is to be friends with people of all ages. Not only can you learn volumes from people who have lived longer than you but you can also help guide and inspire those who haven't. Being able to communicate and form relationships with people of all different ages and from different walks of life offers you a much richer existence in the country. Don't limit yourself by only trying to find friends that are the same as you. Challenge yourself and make friends with people of all ages and all walks of life. I guarantee you will create a better country experience by making friends with all different kinds of folks.

DON'T PARTAKE IN GOSSIP

Remember the saying, "If you don't have anything nice to say, don't say anything at all"? Well, that saying was likely created by someone living in a rural area. If you hear others gossiping, don't join in, even if you are tempted. Word gets around in small towns and nothing is kept secret long. Abstaining from gossip will keep you out of any potential conflicts and will help you build a trustworthy and kind reputation in your community. If someone asks your opinion of someone, even if it is someone you don't particularly like, find something nice to say about them. Don't focus on negative attributes and try to find the silver linings in everyone you meet, even the difficult ones. The longer you live in a community, the more you will learn about the people that live there, and you might find out that the reason the woman who lives down the road is grumpy is because her son passed away in his teens or because her husband walked out on her. Don't rush to quick judgment and air your grievances or speculations to others. Staying on the up and up will make it easier to be accepted, as people will see you as a positive addition to the community and not just another town gossip.

KIDS, THE ULTIMATE ICE BREAKER

Having kids is an instant way to make friends rurally, as kids require you to go out and meet people, whether you want to or not. If you are thinking about moving rurally because you want a better life for your children or because you want to start a family, take comfort in knowing that your children will help serve as your friendship ambassadors. Even if you are introverted and have a hard time making friends, arranging play dates with area children will give you one-on-one time with their parents. Every ex-urbanite I've met who has moved with kids has had a relatively easy time building a social circle.

Get involved in your child's school, volunteer to coach their sports team or run their scout troop—these are all great ways to meet other couples with children. Sure, you might not like all of your children's friends' parents, but remember, it's not about instant friendship—it's about building relationships over time. You won't be able to avoid them, so try to look for good qualities rather than focus on any bad ones. One thing to be aware of moving to the country is people tend to have children a bit earlier in rural areas, so if you waited until your thirties or forties to have children don't be surprised if you are one of the older moms or dads in your child's grade. Remind yourself that age is no longer a pre-requisite for lasting friendship to blossom. There are lots of things to learn from people of all ages, both young and old.

DINNER PARTIES

Throwing a dinner party is an excellent way to bring people together and make new friends in the country. Dinner parties are the country equivalent of a wild night out with friends. Some city dwellers have experience hosting dinner parties, while many others rely on meeting friends at restaurants or bars on the weekend. If you are a dinner party host newbie you don't need to be intimidated. Stick to something you feel confident cooking, and don't be shy about making the same thing each time. I have a friend who is a genius with her spaghetti Bolognese and makes a mean roast chicken—these are her signature dinner party fares. Both meals feed a multitude of people, and friends can supply a big green salad, wine and baguettes, and the evening is made. There is something nice about knowing just what a delicious cozy meal you're in for. For the host, having a few signature dishes to lean on makes prepping and cooking easier and gives you more time to relax and enjoy socializing with your friends. Another dinner party favorite is "activity food" that requires the guests to get interactive. Make your own pizza, tacos or sushi night is instantly fun and gets the party animated quickly. Activity food is easy for the host because all you have to do is prep the ingredients and your guests do the rest. Have some light snacks and drinks ready to go when people arrive so everyone can chat and relax before dinner starts (pour yourself one while you cook to really start the evening off right). Put some music on in the background to make any quiet lulls in the conversation less awkward. It is nice to leave your guests with something sweet after dinner, but unless it's a birthday, I don't usually like the pressure of a hot baked dessert that hurries the dinner course or prolongs the evening if people need to get home. A scoop of ice cream, a fancy cookie and some fruit compote is an easy, quick and well-received low-pressure dessert. Have coffee or tea available for the dessert course, especially if people have longer drives ahead of them.

FOOLPROOF DINNER PARTY

How many people do you invite?

The number of people depends entirely on how many you can accommodate. The best and liveliest dinner parties have at least six people; any less and it categorizes as a meal with friends.

How do you choose the guest list?

Invite some people you are close with and some that you would like to get to know better. Try to create a list of folks with overlapping hobbies or professions so people can easily find common ground (e.g., creatives, people who love the outdoors, travelers, farmers, sports enthusiasts, etc.). Everyone doesn't have to have the exact same interests, but it is nice if there are some commonalities so no one feels like the odd one out. If you are inviting single folks and couples, don't just invite one single person or the dreaded "set-up" scenario where you invite only two single people that you are attempting to play matchmaker to (unless of course you tell them both ahead of time and they okay it).

What do you listen to?

Music helps prevent the dreaded lulls in conversation. Cater to your audience and if you are going with a theme for the night try to find music that fits that theme.

What do you serve?

Pre-dinner: Have snacks and drinks waiting (nuts, olives, cheeses, cut veggies and meats are great options for pre-dinner socializing). Drinks can be as easy as beer or wine or you can have a few bottles with mixers. For extra credit, create a seasonal cocktail.

Food: Annemarie's kale salad with garlicky caper dressing, Cig's Magic Bolognese and a seasonal fruit crumble.

CIG'S MAGIC BOLOGNESE

This is my friend Cig's dinner party dish. Everyone looks forward to eating this magic Bolognese. This recipe simmers in a pot for two hours, allowing time for the host to relax before dinnertime.

Serves 5–7 people

INGREDIENTS

½ cup (118 ml) heavy cream
1 (12-oz [340-g]) packet of bacon, chopped
1½ (227 g) cups chopped onions
1 cup (151 g) chopped celery
2 cups (302 g) chopped carrots
1 pound (450 g) ground beef
Salt and pepper to taste
1 cup of (240 ml) bold red wine (I like Malbec.)
2 tbsp (19 g) minced garlic
3 tbsp (46 g) tomato paste
2 tbsp (10 g) Worcestershire sauce
2 cups (480 ml) beef stock
1 cup (240 ml) milk

DIRECTIONS

In a small pot simmer the cream, reducing it by half before removing from the heat (be careful not to overcook or curdle the cream). Cook the bacon pieces in a large pot and when the fat is fully rendered, add the onions, celery and carrots. Cook for a few minutes until the onions and celery are translucent. Add the ground beef, cooking it until it browns. Add salt and pepper to taste. Stir in the wine, garlic, tomato paste, Worcestershire sauce and stock; mix well. Reduce the heat to simmer. Cook with the lid askew for 1½ to 2 hours. After 30 minutes or so, stir in the cream. After another 30 minutes or so, stir in the milk. Season with salt and pepper. Serve over the al dente pasta of your choosing.

RAW KALE SALAD

This is my friend Annemarie's famous salad. It is so beloved she has requests at nearly every dinner party she attends to bring along this flavorful and healthy salad. Unlike most salads it still tastes great on day two, although I doubt you'll have leftovers.

Serves 5–7 people

INGREDIENTS
2 large bunches of kale

Salt and pepper to taste

GARLICKY CAPER DRESSING
½ yellow onion

1 large bunch parsley

4 cloves garlic

2 tbsp (23 g) capers

Zest of 1 lemon

Juice of 2 lemons

⅓ cup (79 ml) sherry vinegar

1 cup (240 ml) olive oil

1 tbsp (16 g) Dijon mustard

½ tsp kosher salt

¼ tsp red pepper flakes

¼ tsp fresh ground pepper

½ cup (90 g) Parmesan cheese, grated

DIRECTIONS
Massage the kale and toss with salt and pepper. This will begin to break down the cell walls of the kale, making it more delicious and digestible. Thirty minutes before serving the kale salad, toss with the dressing.

GARLICKY CAPER DRESSING
Place all the ingredients except for the Parmesan in a blender. Puree for 30 seconds. Fold in the Parmesan.

EASY SEASONAL FRUIT CRUMBLE

You can use any seasonal fruit for this the recipe or a combo of several. I love using pear with a tablespoon (14 g) of ginger; or ½ blackberry and ½ apple; strawberry and rhubarb; or blueberry and peach.

Serves 6–10 people

INGREDIENTS

6 cups (908 g) of seasonal fruit, washed, peeled, cut
¼ cup (48 g) granulated sugar or 2 tbsp (30 ml) of maple syrup or 2 tbsp (30 ml) honey
1½ cups (241 g) oats
½ cup (50 g) flour
⅔ cup (96 g) brown sugar
Pinch of salt
½ cup (115 g) cold butter (cut into small cubes)
Sliced almonds (optional)

DIRECTIONS

Set oven to 350°F (176°C). Add the fruit to a 9 x 9-inch (23 x 23-cm) baking pan and evenly coat with the sugar, maple syrup or honey. If you are using apples or pears, squeeze a bit of lemon juice if you have it. In a separate bowl, combine the remaining ingredients. Using a fork or clean hands, mash up the dry ingredients and the butter into a crumble consistency. Pour the dry crumble evenly over the fruit. If you like, add a handful of sliced almonds to the top. Cook for 45 minutes or until the top browns. Set out to cool for 10 to 15 minutes before eating. Serve with vanilla ice cream for ultimate decadence.

GIVE IT TIME

Friendships may not happen quickly. In the country it is an incremental collection of moments together, building memories and history steadily, that forms a friendship. After living in the fast and furious city, you may have to remind yourself of this slower pace. Don't get discouraged! Friendships will come; developing them in the country can just take a bit more patience. Maybe you're having a grand time with a friend and they start flaking on your plans. Realize they may be preoccupied with a broken septic tank, family commitments or just simply need some time to themselves. Give them space. They'll be back before you know it. In the county, it's the long game that counts.

FINDING A MATE

THE COUNTRY DATING DILEMMA

One of the main reasons single urbanites dreaming of leaving the city delay their move is the worry that they will never meet a partner in the country. As we briefly discussed in the first chapter, if you are single and are interested in finding a partner, you don't want to move to an area without first checking out the singles scene. Small towns with universities, craft schools or tourist seasons are great options because they will have a steadier flow of new faces. If the scene in the town you want to move to leaves something to be desired, consider other areas before locking in your decision. If you are dead set on a place but there aren't many available singles, try it out for a year and see if you can make some romantic headway before considering other locales. Looking for a mate in the country requires one to be proactive, positive and willing to develop a plan of action. Sitting on your laurels and waiting for people to come to you isn't going to yield results. Let's be honest, trying to find a mate in a small town can be challenging, but so can finding a mate in a big city. Friends in New York City are constantly complaining to me about how difficult the dating scene is there. Really, it's all about perspective. Destiny can happen anywhere. Just ask happily married couples how they met—it runs the gamut. Focusing on your own journey, actively participating in life, following your passions and being open to new possibilities are the best ways to both attract and find a mate. If your life's journey is pulling you to the country, go for it. Love can find you anywhere.

FINDING A MATE ISN'T KEY FOR HAPPINESS

I feel obliged to say, first things first, you don't need a significant other to have a happy and rewarding life in the country—or anywhere for that matter. Not everyone is actively looking for, or wanting, a mate. Companionship takes many forms. I have many happily single friends in the country that aren't actively searching for that someone. They have flexibility in their lives to go wherever the wind takes them and can actively pursue their passions. Certainly there are some tasks required of you in the country that are made easier by an extra set of hands, but those could be the hands of friends or neighbors—they don't have to be those of a romantic partner. I don't want anyone to think that you need to find love in order to find joy in a rural environment, because that simply is not the case.

Moving to a rural area with a partner comes with its own set of obstacles. Depending on your mannerisms, it can be easy to take refuge in one another and not actively venture out to build a life for you collectively and individually. Moving to a rural area without a partner is liberating—the world is your oyster. Necessity breeds courage, and moving alone you are much more likely to take risks and put yourself out there to meet friends and find community. Those of you who aren't looking for dating advice, skip the next couple of pages. Everyone else, keep reading.

PUT YOURSELF OUT THERE

Very few people met their significant others by sitting around their house, unless of course they happen to fall for the repairman who comes to fix their dryer. The best way to improve your odds of meeting someone in the country is to get your butt off the couch and be proactive. Frequent the local watering hole or coffee shop, go on hikes, take long walks through town and strike up conversations along the way. Volunteer at community organizations, go to town meetings and attend events and local festivals. If there are things that have always interested you but you never had much time to explore, pursue them in the country. Sign up for white water rafting trips, pottery or writing classes or join a local YMCA or exercise club. You might just hit it off with someone on your excursion or in your class or meet someone that will end up introducing you to someone special. By attending things that are of interest to you, you not only will have a chance to meet potential new friends, but you also might meet prospective partners with similar hobbies.

FEWER OPTIONS ISN'T ALWAYS A NEGATIVE

If you look in your closet and there are a hundred things to choose from, it's easy to get stuck. You might keep trying on the pants that don't fit, or the awkward dress that your friends and family hate, or the overly stylish and ultimately silly hat. Lots of options make it difficult to commit to an outfit, as there is always the possibility that there is a better ensemble right around the corner. Fewer options make getting dressed easier and provide you with clarity; it's the same with dating. Fewer options make it easier to not get distracted and spend more time getting to know someone before dismissing them. Online dating in cities offers people a never-ending pool of eligible singles…but how lucky in love have you been thus far with those odds? You will never get to fully know a potential match if you only spend thirty minutes drinking coffee with them before writing them off for some small thing they said or did. How many couples do you know that were friends before they became involved? Just because the spark wasn't there initially doesn't mean it can't develop over time. The lack of available choices in rural areas makes you put a little more time in and really get to know someone before deciding whether or not they have partner potential. You take the time to polish a friendship or relationship as opposed to looking for the perfect polished piece right out of the gate.

GO AHEAD, GET SET UP

Being the new single guy or gal in a small town isn't always terrible. You might be shocked at how excited community members are to set you up with other singles in your area. New single arrivals are exciting in a small town; they can get the whole town buzzing. Whenever a new single person moves to our community people immediately start brainstorming who they would be a good match with—we can't help it. If you aren't interested in being set up, just politely tell your friends that you need some time to get a lay of the land before trying to date anyone. They might still force the issue, but at least anyone they are trying to set you up with will be aware that you aren't actively looking. Several country singletons I've interviewed met their spouses via the "set up" scenario. Some were set up with local eligible people; others were set up with people who grew up in the area but now live away. This is a clever way town folk attempt to lure their children or childhood friends home. Just like getting set up in the city, your friends or acquaintances might not have a good idea of what you consider desirable in a potential mate. If someone is anxious to set you up, give them a bit more information about what you are looking for. Do you want someone creative, athletic, funny, outdoorsy? Are there any physical traits you gravitate towards more than others? Giving them a bit more information about what you're looking for can help lead to more successful set-ups.

TAKE THE RUMOR MILL WITH A GRAIN OF SALT

A tricky part of dating rurally is the inevitable stories you'll hear about potential mates—especially those that have lived in your community for quite some time. Imagine if the intimate details of your relationship record followed you wherever you went. Most of us are guilty of breaking someone's heart or, at the very least, hurting someone's feelings. There are two sides to every story and if you are interested in someone that grew up in the area where you are living or has lived there for a while, take any rumors that you hear about them with a grain of salt. Listen to what others have to say but don't let rumors scare you away. Sometimes relationships and marriages don't work out, sometimes temptation gains the upper hand and sometimes people change—either for the better or for the worse. Perfectly nice and undeserving people can be deemed unsuitable in the town gossip chain for one thing or another, so don't rush to judgment and write someone off because of things you've heard about them.

The best way to approach this predicament is to face it head on. If you are interested in someone, and they are interested in you, but you've heard some bad rumors, ask them about it. Chances are they already know what's being said about them and, at the very least, they can explain their side of things. If you catch them off-guard, don't divulge whom you heard the rumors from, as that can put you in hot water, just tell them you heard through the grapevine and see how they respond. Hearing any stories from their point of view might dissolve any trepidation you have or they could uphold your suspicions. Either way, don't let the rumor mill deter you from making a meaningful match—everyone has a history and there are at least two sides to every story.

DON'T BURN BRIDGES & NO GHOSTING

Moving from the city and its endless digital dating options can make it difficult to understand the rules of the dating game in the country. You can't hop around from person to person without building a reputation for yourself. I've seen young single people come to town and date with the same voracity as they did in the city and lose their chances of making a meaningful match because word quickly gets around that they are not serious and not worth wasting your time on. Dating around is totally fine, but communication is key. If you are dating several people at the same time, it is important that you tell everyone you are seeing that you are still going out with other people. You can't hide in the country. You might run into someone you're casually dating while on another date; give that person a heads-up ahead of time so they don't feel like they're being played.

You also can't "ghost" someone in the country (just completely cutting off communication with them). If you've met someone else or have decided they aren't "it" you have to put on your big kid pants and tell them the truth. It sucks; it's hard to have to have difficult adult conversations, but it's necessary. Think of dating more like making friends and testing out if that person is a good match for a romantic relationship. Just because the romance isn't there doesn't mean they can't be a friend or, at the very least, an amicable acquaintance. Burning bridges while looking for a mate can prove devastating if you meet someone who's perfect only to discover they are the best friend, brother or co-worker of someone you burned. In the country, fewer options mean more intermingling. In the city, friends and siblings of exes are usually considered off-limits but in the country, as long as you give it some time and make sure the ex knows your intention—anyone available is fair game.

THERE'S AN APP FOR THAT

Even if you poo-pooed online dating in the city, don't snub your nose at meeting people online rurally. You can cast a wider net—beyond your immediate social circle—and it's not just a way to meet possible mates but also a way to make friends. Hiding behind the thin veil of anonymity on dating sites still requires you to be on your best behavior, so don't burn any unnecessary bridges. Online dating sites and apps are just digital aides to help you get out of your comfort zone and meet people you might not normally encounter in your day-to-day rhythms. It is important that you use these tools to your best advantage and create a profile that is authentic, honest and considered. Don't post any photos that you wouldn't like everyone in your small community seeing, as it is a possibility that those images could go locally viral. Avoid profile photos that show lots of skin, photos of you with exes (or people that could be exes) and group shots that don't immediately make it obvious whose profile it is. If your main priority is casual sex, only create profiles on sites that are geared towards casual encounters and shy away from the more mainstream dating and relationship sites that more people in your area will be privy to. OKCupid, Match, Farmersonly, Westernmatch and Tinder are some widely used dating sites and apps that people living rurally use. If you are using a location-based app that finds available singles in your area, take notice if you all of sudden see a surge of new available people in your zip code. Tourism surges are common in areas that attract a lot of people in certain seasons or on the weekends. If you find someone of interest that you match with, don't waste a clean shirt or lipstick without first inquiring if they live in your area or are just visiting. Just because they are visiting doesn't mean they might not be open to relocating, but it helps weed out people just looking for a good time on their trip.

GOING THE EXTRA MILE

If you have exhausted your local dating options, or prefer to keep your personal life low profile, dating people within driving distance, but outside of your immediate community, is a good option. Online dating sites prove the most helpful when searching for available singles outside of your community. Be a bit more diligent when it comes to vetting though, as you will no longer have the background story on potential mates readily available (this can be a welcomed thing though, as people can build bad reputations that aren't accurate). It might annoy you that you have to drive forty-five minutes to see them, but think about how long it took you to go on dates in the city—factoring in drive times, parking or riding public transit can put things in perspective.

If you are searching for potential mates in surrounding communities, the no ghosting and no burning bridges rules still apply. Just because you're dating someone an hour or two away doesn't mean that if you break up you won't ever see them again. Fewer people, more spread out, means more chances for accidental run-ins. It also doesn't mean that people in other small communities near you aren't connected in some way to people where you live. You could end up dating the cousin or brother of a friend without even knowing it. If things don't work out, keep it amicable. If you decide they aren't a good fit for you after a couple of dates, be honest and let them know, in a kind way, that you aren't interested in pursuing things with them anymore. You don't want to leave things in a bad place as it will make it difficult to date anyone else in the town they live in—crossing town after town off your list to avoid exes will not make it easy to find that someone special.

DON'T STEAL YOUR MATE FROM ANOTHER

If you meet someone you hit it off with but find out they aren't currently on the market, don't be devious. It's not worth trying to sabotage an existing relationship to land your mate. Nothing rocks a small town like infidelity. Stealing another person's partner is a quick and foolproof way to lose the respect and friendships you've developed in your community. If it is meant to be, it will happen, but make sure you take the straight and narrow approach. Don't sneak around. Before you act on any impulses, make sure the person they were with is no longer in the picture and that a suitable amount of time has passed. If they were dating someone for a while, give it a month or two for the dust to settle and for their ex-partner to heal and move on before being seen around town together. If they were married, wait a few months until after the divorce is finalized before seeing one another. If they have kids, it is even more important to be respectful as their ex will likely remain living in close proximity and be intimately connected to you for the duration of your relationship. Living in a small community makes it difficult to keep your personal life private so it's important to stay on the up and up. Plenty of people living rurally get divorced and remarried, but it's crucial to be respectful. If you're tempted away from your current mate or tempting away the mate of another, don't do permanent damage—be an adult and either end things with your partner or have the person you're interested in end things with theirs before embarking on your journey together.

IMPORTING A MATE

If after a year or two everything else in your new country life is falling into place, but you still are having trouble finding a mate, it might be time to consider importing one. Just like you were dreaming of country living before making the move solo, there are plenty of city people who share the dream of leaving their urban existence behind but aren't brave enough to make the leap alone. Meeting someone already based rurally that has developed a network and planted roots is appealing to any single person looking for a partner and a way out of the city. Everything has already been set up for them, all they need to do is figure out how to make a living and move. Start looking for people online in nearby major metropolitan areas and change your profile to specifically say that you are looking for someone who would be open to relocating. Reach out to friends and family members outside of your community to see if they have any suggestions on people who would be a good fit for you that are open to moving rurally. I myself am an "import" as my husband met me the day he signed papers on the house we now live in in Maine. I met him while on a work trip to New York and had never even visited Maine before meeting him.

Many new transplants consider the import route if they have exhausted available options in their area. Importing a mate has worked well for many people I've interviewed, but it's not without its potential problems. Before encouraging someone you're seeing to leave their current location and move to your small community you should be absolutely certain they are a good fit for you and have real potential for a long-term lasting relationship. A woman I met had invited a man from the city that she'd been dating to come live with her to see if he was interested in relocating and building a life with her. He ended up cheating on her with a married friend and breaking up a local marriage. Now she constantly runs into him in town because he decided to stay, just not with her. Of course you never know what the future holds, but before deciding to import a mate, make sure you are confident they are a good fit and that they are respectful enough to play nice if things should go south at some point.

MEETING YOUR MATES: IN CONCLUSION

When it comes to meeting your mates rurally—both friends and romantic interests—the main advice is the same: be proactive, be kind, be respectful, don't burn bridges and give it time. In the country everything is a bit slower paced so don't try to rush or force things. Just put yourself out there, make friends with your neighbors and the people you run into during your daily rhythms and get involved in your community. Even if you move to an area where you already have friends and history, don't just lean on those relationships—forge new ones as well. If you move with a significant other, don't just stay home and hang out with them all the time. It's important that you build a social network outside of your home, as there will inevitably be a time when you need a friend to talk to. The majority of people I've interviewed who decided to move back to the city after a short stint living rurally were those that didn't make an effort to make friends and become part of their community. Loving where you are goes hand-in-hand with loving the community you are in.

My social life in the country is much richer than my social life ever was in the city. Although I may have fewer friends and acquaintances than I did before, the friendships I've found in the country are stronger and more enduring than those I had in the city. I know I can call on my friends here when I am in a bind and they will come to my aid. I also spend so much more quality time nurturing my friendships here. In the city, everyone is so busy with their own lives that it's hard to carve out time to see friends. I have friends of all ages and no longer have unconscious "friendship parameters" that I apply to forging new relationships. Although I moved to the country with a significant other, I have witnessed many of my single friends meet their mates in the country. The city me of four years ago would've never been brave enough to move to the country single, but now after witnessing the successes of so many looking for their partners rurally (and watching my single city friends struggle to find someone special), I know that more options do not necessarily lead to better results. Relationships make life richer and meeting your mates is an essential step in making a smooth and happy transition to rural life.

EMBRACING THE SEASONS

Finding your rhythm in winter, spring, summer and fall

"The country is a feast for the senses. Whether it's the fresh scent of blossoms and earth in spring and summer, the warm scent of cider and wood smoke in autumn and winter, the arctic chill of a February breeze, or the vigorous heat of an August afternoon, one is made to feel and move with the earth, through the seasons and harvests, the slow times and the quick. I find my senses are most at ease here. In contrast, the city is a rough overdose for the senses, leaving one numb to the kind touch of the wild."

— Misha Johnson, Free Verse Farm

Living in the city, it is easy for entire seasons to pass one by without much notice. When snow and leaves fall, the city takes care of their removal. When the muddy and wet days of spring appear, the storm drains quickly whisk the water away from busy feet hitting the pavement. The hot days of summer are only endured on sticky subway platforms and when traveling from one air-conditioned building to another. Produce sections in grocery stores are stocked with anything and everything you might ever want to eat—blueberries, summer squash and watermelons in the dead of winter, yes please! The harbingers of seasons in the city are fall pumpkin patches in vacant lots, replaced by winter's Christmas trees being sold on street corners, followed by the wetter days of spring with daffodils popping up in cement planters, followed by my favorite season, the hot garbage and pee smell days of summer. Ah, seasons in the city, how lovely.

In the country, you are intimately connected to the seasons and the passage of time. Finally, you can witness the beauty of powdery white snow. You can sit on your back porch in the early spring and hear the crescendo song of birds returning from warmer reaches. You can understand the concept of eating "in season" in a whole new way, as you are immersed in harvest time. It is important in the country to come to terms with and enjoy the rhythms of all four seasons. Sure, you can still have your favorites, but solace and happiness throughout the year requires an acceptance of everything Mother Nature sends your way, even when you're raking what feels like an Everest-sized mass of leaves, coping with a blizzard, trudging through ankle-deep mud or being chased by a black cloud of summer's biting insects.

After almost five years of living in a rural area, I can finally say that I have learned to embrace and love all four seasons. I appreciate both the merits and hardships of every season. Sure, the winters in Maine can still feel oppressively long and dark, but I've learned to wear the right clothes to spend more time outdoors, found activities to partake in, and have created fun things to do that make me look forward to the shorter days and colder nights. If you dread a certain season and can't find contentment during those months, your country life will not be as full or happy as it could be. Now, I have to preface here, seasons are different throughout the country—in warmer areas snow isn't part of the winter equation and fall doesn't mean constant leaf cleanup for all, but for the purpose of this book, we will be covering the stereotypical "seasons." If you live in a place that is warmer in the winter, you can still partake in a number of the activities and rhythms of the season that we cover. In this chapter, we will go through each season and give you tips on tools and skills you'll need, fun things to do, things to make, the best things to wear and some helpful tips to make each impending season one that you look forward to. So, let's break down and learn how to find a rhythm in winter, spring, summer and fall!

WINTER

The quiet peaceful slowness of frosty winter mornings. Bright fleeting days followed by long dark nights. The pure white blanket of undisturbed freshly fallen snow. Layers, mittens, woolen socks, and thermoses filled with hot beverages. Holiday parties, twinkling lights, craft fairs and entryways crammed with boots and coats. Rainstorms, snowstorms, ice storms followed by the romantic glow of candlelight when your power goes out. Winter is a time of rest; animals hibernate and birds migrate to warmer reaches. Mother Nature stretches her arms and lays down for a well-deserved nap. For many, winter is a difficult season to embrace as it brings with it darkness, fewer fresh things to eat, higher heating bills, endless snow shoveling and a slowdown of the myriad of social and outdoor activities of warmer months. For some, winter is their favorite time of year, a time when they aren't being chased by bugs, constantly cutting the lawn or working non-stop. Winter gives you a natural break to recharge, work on hobbies and spend quality time with yourself, your family and your friends.

For me, winter was the most difficult season to learn to love. Growing up in a small town on the coast of the northernmost part of California, I never had to deal with snow but we were still very in tune with the changes that winter ushered in. The shorter days, bare trees, colder conditions, a layer of heavy sparkling frost every morning and black ice on the roads. Winter is not without its difficulties—

even in warmer places. When I moved to Seattle, I didn't have to deal with winter much. I lived in an apartment where heat was included, parked in a garage where I didn't have to defrost my car every morning and the temperatures or conditions were never severe enough to prevent me from still walking everywhere I wanted, even in useless, stylish clothing. Moving to Maine in February was like getting punched in the stomach, hard. First, I didn't know how to drive in snow, so I white knuckled my way through many a trip to town. Second, I had no clue how to dress and didn't have any clothing suitable for snow and negative temperatures. Third, my dislike of winter and lack of willingness to find ways to embrace it made my first two winters in Maine completely unbearable. Winter was winning and I needed to play a better hand; I needed to figure out how to love this season and appreciate both its positive attributes and hardships.

TOOLS & SKILLS YOU'LL NEED

Winter is a season of rest, but also one that requires some skills and tools to ensure you don't end up sliding all over country roads, falling off your roof while trying to fix an ice dam or getting stuck in your house during a blizzard without proper supplies and a way to get out.

Vehicle prep: Living rurally, in most instances, means being much more reliant on your car. Unless you live in the village center and can walk to most of your amenities, you will inevitably spend significantly more time driving. Safely driving in the winter months means preparing your car for the colder temperatures and icy conditions. Living in most cities, you can get away with all-season tires, but country road conditions usually demand winter or studded snow tires. All-season tires harden in cold weather, offering less traction on icy roads. Winter tires use a special rubber that stays pliable so both traction and braking are better. In areas with lots of snowfall, studded snow tires are the way to go. Studded tires are winter tires with metal studs in them that are designed to dig into the ice and provide even more traction in icy winter conditions. Studded tires are noisier than winter tires and in most places there is a required removal date to switch to summer or all-seasons because the studs can wreak havoc on roads without snow and ice. Winter tires, both with studs and without, generally last five to seven years of standard winter season use. Each fall, check your winter tires to make sure they still have adequate tread; balding tires in snowy or icy conditions are extremely dangerous. You also should check your antifreeze and make sure there is a 50/50 mix of water and antifreeze (you can buy a tester at an auto parts store). Lastly, windshield wipers are essential for safe winter driving. Take it from me, getting stuck behind a semi-truck in freezing rain with old wiper blades or no washer fluid is terrifying. Replace your blades in the late fall and refill your washer fluid with winter washer fluid that won't freeze. When your car is parked outside and it's snowing or snow is in the forecast, flip your blades up to prevent them from freezing to your windshield. Contrary to popular belief, you shouldn't let your car "warm up" for longer than a minute or two in the morning. Older cars might need a little more time, but according to most mechanics, newer cars shouldn't be left idling longer than thirty seconds before starting your drive. Start your drive by moving a bit slower than usual and work your way up to normal speeds.

SNOW REMOVAL

If you're living in an area with a snowy winter, welcome to snow removal. Get acquainted because it is going to be the bane of your existence. Staying on top of snow removal is incredibly important both to protect your house and your person. If you let it pile up, removal will be much more difficult and dangerous than if you regularly chip away at it during snowstorms.

Walkways and driveways: For short driveways and walkways, snow shoveling is a great way to stay fit and keep warm in the winter. There are many different models of snow shovels in both plastic and metal. Buy a durable model that isn't too long, short or heavy for your comfort level. If you have a long walkway, multiple entrances, a parking area or a bad back, a snow blower is the way to go. Snow blowers can be bought in single-stage, two-stage or three-stage. The single-stage blowers come in both electric and gas models, are lighter weight, capable of handling smaller areas and less than eight inches (20 cm) of snow at a time. The two-stage and three-stage are gas powered and can handle deeper snow and larger areas. Electric blowers start at the press of a button, while gas blowers need to be pull started. Be aware that snow blower hand injuries are common. Snow blowers get stuck or clogged with snow and people will use their hands to try to remove the clog without turning the machine off first. Even if you turn the machine off, you should still use an object other than your hand to remove any obstructions. If you have a long driveway, you're going to want to invest in a plow or pay a snowplow driver to plow it for you. A plow attachment is a costly investment and they can only really go on a vehicle with 4x4 capability. You can get a plow for your tractor and even some 4x4 lawnmowers, but depending on the frequency of snow and the length of your driveway, hiring a plow truck driver in the winter might be your easiest and cheapest option short term. It costs $45 to plow and sand our 150-foot (46-m) driveway each time. During blizzards, the driveway needs to be plowed every couple of hours. It can get expensive fast. After our third year in Maine, we decided to buy an old beater Bronco with a plow already attached. The cost for the vehicle was less than the cost of a year's worth of plowing. Now that automobile is our winter plow truck and it hauls all our trash to the dump the rest of the year. If you live in a snowy place with a long driveway and you plan on living there for at least the next ten years, it might be worth the investment to get a plow attachment for your truck or buy a beater 4x4 that you can use in the winter to plow your drive. Adding sand to your driveway when you plow will help improve traction and give your tires something to grip onto.

Roof and eaves: I had never heard of an ice dam until I moved rurally. Ice dams are caused by snow and ice buildup on roofs that cause water leaks through the roof. Ice dams happen when melted snow and ice collects at the eaves of a sloping roof and the melting snow above cannot properly drain through the dam. The melt water has nowhere to go and causes leaks through the roof, causing ceiling, wall and structural damage. To avoid ice dams and keep your roof structurally sound, invest in a good roof rake. There are lots of different kinds of roof rakes at different lengths. You should get one long enough that you can safely remove snow from your roof without it hitting you when it comes off. Start at the bottom of the roof and work your way up to the top. Pitched metal roofs typically do not have issues with ice damming as snow is shed off of metal roofs quickly. Metal roofs also last much longer than shingle and asphalt roofs but they tend to cost more to install. If you need a new roof and you have had issues with ice damming, it might be worth the extra investment to get a metal roof. If you have a metal roof it is important to be cautious and not stand too close if there is collected snow as it could be shed off in a big quick dump. Icicles should be knocked down over entryways, but you shouldn't try to remove them in other places. Icicles are natural drainage paths for snowmelt and removing them could damage your gutters (if you have them).

HOW TO WALK ON ICE

First things first, after shoveling or blowing your walkways, sprinkle salt or chemical deicers to keep your walkways and stairs from getting icy. I've had three friends break their wrists just from walking outside in front of their house on the ice. When walking on slippery surfaces, either shuffle or take small steps to keep yourself stable. Keep your hands out of pockets, be prepared to fall and bend slightly forward—keeping your center of gravity as directly over your feet as possible. If you love to walk and want to continue walking at a similar pace as you did in warmer months, invest in some crampons. These are metal spiked nets that go over your shoes and dig into ice to provide traction.

FUN THINGS TO DO

Silently gliding through a pristine snowy wonderland, drinking whiskey in a warm little hut waiting for fish to bite or bombing down a mountain through fresh powder—winter is a special season because there are so many entertaining activities you can partake in that you can't do any other time of year. Snowmobiling, skiing, snowboarding, cross country skiing, snowshoeing, ice fishing, ice skating and sledding are all fun outdoor activities that will help keep you moving and your spirits bright. Staying active in the winter is essential for overall health and happiness. Across the country there are hut-to-hut (or lodge-to-lodge) treks that you can do on skis or snowshoes. There are also thousands of miles of snowmobile trails to explore. Before investing money in purchasing the gear required for these various outdoor winter activities, rent a few times first to determine if that particular outdoor activity is right for you. You can even rent an ice fishing house by the hour or by the day in areas where lakes freeze over. Don't let being worried about looking stupid or clumsy get in the way of finding an outdoor activity that gets you excited to embrace winter every season. Cross-country skiing and snowshoeing have ended up being my go-to winter activities. Having not learned downhill skiing or snowboarding as a child, I found these sports too fast and the risk of injury too great. I didn't like the gasoline fumes and frozen hands of snowmobiling, ice skating on untended ponds and lakes is only possible during very specific conditions, and I never cared for sitting around waiting for fish to bite. The important thing is that I tried a bunch of outdoor activities before settling on a couple that make me giddy when the snow starts to fall.

Beyond outdoor activities, there are tons of social activities you can look forward to in the winter season. Even if you aren't religious or don't celebrate Christmas, it's still common in most small towns to say "Merry Christmas" instead of "Happy Holidays." It's easy to feel a little left out in rural areas if you belong to a faith that doesn't celebrate Christmas. A good way to cope and build community is to throw a dinner party for your friends that celebrates and highlights your religious beliefs. A Jewish friend has a holiday party every year in the small community they live in where they serve traditional Jewish food and recite the Hanukkah blessings while lighting a candle on their menorah. Small communities, especially those with long winters, celebrate the holiday season with gusto, as the holidays help keep spirits bright through the colder early months of winter. Craft fairs, tree lighting ceremonies, Christmas festivals, multi-denomination midnight masses, caroling, holiday get-togethers, winter solstice parties and New Year's Eve celebrations are all common early-winter social activities to be a part of. Small towns buzz during the winter holiday season with lots of activities and things to do. Don't get cooped up in your house—go out and attend some of these community events. It is a great way to make friends, become a welcomed face in your community and fill your long dark nights with fun.

Beyond community events, there are many things you can do around your house during the longer nights of winter to fully embrace and enjoy the season. Throwing dinner parties, game nights, movie nights, book clubs, quilting circles and the like are great nighttime activities to keep you engaged and excited. If you aren't getting invited to these activities, don't get discouraged, throw them at your house and eventually you will inspire others to do the same. We live for our themed dinner parties and art nights in the winter. Themed dinner parties or potlucks are a fun way to gather with friends and experiment with cuisine you might not normally attempt to make—Mexican, Russian, Thai, Indian, Greek, etc. Potlucks take the pressure off the host and it is fun to try all of the food triumphs and inevitable flops (usually my dishes). For art nights we gather at rotating friends' homes, bring a fun snack or dinner potluck item to share and we either have a specific collective project to work on like making a necklace or sketching the person sitting across from us, or we bring projects that we are working on and use the night to both be productive and laugh with friends. Mystery dinner theatre, movie nights with themed snacks—any number of things can be a good excuse to gather with friends and have a casual and fun night in the winter. Believe me, being more intentional about your socializing in the winter months will help you get through any difficult patches and it will give you something to look forward to when the days get shorter.

THINGS TO MAKE

A simmering pot on the stove filling your home with lovely aromas—there's nothing like cooking to get you excited for winter. Standing over a hot stove in warmer seasons isn't nearly as fun. Spending more time indoors makes delicious aromas of spiced ciders and stews even more appreciated. The slower pace of winter and drawn out evening hours give you a wonderful opportunity to experiment in the kitchen, learn new skills and work on projects. For me, winter is all about getting creative in the kitchen and working on a multitude of other more sedentary endeavors. Honestly, I now look forward to the prospect of getting snowed in because that means I have ample time to drink tea or hot toddies and get lost in a recipe or project. Each winter I like to draft a list of different kinds of food I want to experiment with and perfect—pulled pork sandwiches, meat stews, seafood chowder, making bread, etc. I also like to challenge myself to do a daily creative project, like writing for thirty minutes each morning or doing a daily drawing, watercolor or collage. Lastly, I like to choose a project or two to work on in the winter months that requires me to learn a new skill, like rebuilding my motorcycle's carburetor, knitting a scarf, making an outfit from a pattern, constructing a snow fort or building a piece of furniture. Imagine if every winter you were able to master, or at the very least attempt, a new skill. Acquiring new skills in the country not only helps you embrace the season but they also make you more self-sufficient and your life richer. So go ahead, use winter to practice baking by trying out a new recipe every weekend or start/join a quilting circle and challenge yourself to finish a new quilt every winter. Instead of filling your evening hours with Netflix marathons and screen time, use some of those extra hours of darkness to make delicious meals, learn new skills and work on projects.

HOT TODDY

Nothing cuts the cold like a delicious warm cocktail. Some doctors actually recommend drinking a hot toddy to combat sore throats and coughs. So here you go, a doctor recommended, delicious, warming winter cocktail recipe.

Serves 2 people (two mugs)

INGREDIENTS
1½ cups (355 ml) hot water
Juice from ½ a lemon
3 tbsp (45 ml) honey (you can add more or less depending on how sweet you like your toddy to be)
1 shot whiskey/bourbon of your choice (I love Maker's Mark or Bulleit Bourbon)

DIRECTIONS
Mix the hot water with honey and lemon until the honey is dissolved. Add shot of whiskey/bourbon and mix well. Enjoy!

PERFECT BEEF STEW

In a lot of small towns with long winters, grocery shopping can be pretty depressing. Produce sections are picked over and root vegetables are the last surviving heroes. I pretty much survive off of stews and soups in the winter. They cook throughout the day, fill my house with delicious aromas and warm bodies and stomachs after a day's worth of outdoor activities. Here is my favorite winter stew recipe, experimented with and adapted over time. It uses frozen peas from the garden, root vegetables and beef—all ingredients are readily available in the colder months. This is also a winter dinner party favorite.

Serves 8–10

INGREDIENTS

2 tbsp (30 ml) olive oil

3 lbs (1.4 kg) stew beef, cut into
¾" (2-cm) cubes (shoulder or rump)

Flour for dredging meat

6 carrots, sliced

2 large onions, diced

4 cloves garlic, minced

2 tbsp (29 g) tomato paste

A bouquet garni, made by tying together one large sprig of thyme, one sprig of rosemary, parsley stems and one bay leaf

8 cups (2 L) beef stock

1 tbsp (15 g) Worcestershire sauce

½ cup (118 ml) of red wine (I like Malbec)

8–10 medium yellow potatoes, peeled
(1 lb [454 g] total)

Kosher salt and fresh ground pepper, to taste

1 cup (151 g) frozen green peas

2 tbsp (29 g) unsalted butter

¼ cup (10 g) chopped fresh parsley

DIRECTIONS

Start by preheating the oven to 350°F (176°C). Heat the olive oil over medium heat in a large oven-safe stewing pot. Season the beef, dredge it in flour and brown it in batches, transferring each piece with a slotted spoon to a plate when done. Add the carrots and onions and cook until they are soft and transparent. Add the garlic and continue cooking until the vegetables start to gain color. Add the tomato paste and mush into the vegetables. Cook for 2 to 3 minutes or until it begins to gain color. Return the meat to the pot, add the bouquet garni, stock, Worcestershire sauce and red wine. Cover and bring to a boil. Reduce to a simmer and cook for 1 hour. Add the potatoes and bake the stew for 45 minutes or until the meat and potatoes are tender. Taste and season with salt and pepper. Discard the bouquet garni. Add the peas and cook for 2 minutes just to heat them through. To finish the stew, swirl the remaining 2 tablespoons (29 g) of butter into the sauce and sprinkle each bowl with parsley.

There is no such thing as bad weather, just bad clothing. I had heard people say that before moving rurally but it never stuck because it didn't have to. In the city, I could easily wear a wool coat on a snowy day without getting soaked and chilled to the bone. Fully appreciating and enjoying the winter season means learning to embrace practical clothing. First things first, put your cotton away! If you've got some great cotton sweaters, wear them in the spring or fall—they aren't going to be an asset in the winter months. Thin long underwear worn under your clothes is a first step in staying warm and comfortable. Merino wool and blends aren't as itchy as regular wool but if you are still sensitive to wool, go for silk or synthetic long under-layers. There are three different weights of long underwear—lightweight, mid-weight and heavyweight. Socks are another game changer; wool and synthetic socks made for cold weather conditions will keep your feet from freezing even when doing outdoor activities in the snow. Tall waterproof insulated boots are great for snow adventures. Shorter boots work well in cities where snow removal is done for you, but if you have to go outside to clean up snow, you will want tall boots so you don't get snow packed around the top and melting into your boots making your feet freeze. Also don't buy boots without traction, or you will be sliding all over the place. Vibram soles and tough treads are your best bet. You can also add crampons for added traction. Wearing a coat that isn't waterproof in the snow is going to make for a soggy, miserable excursion. Invest in some waterproof outer layers. If you primarily are doing activities outside that make you sweat, buy waterproof shells (with minimal to no insulation) and adjust layers underneath for proper warmth. If you don't tend to work up a sweat outdoors, a waterproof insulated jacket will work with minimal layers underneath. At the beginning of fall, I go through my entire closet and pull out all my warm weather clothes—cotton socks, light jackets, open-toed shoes, etc.—and put them in a plastic Tupperware. It makes getting dressed in the winter easier, as I only have the clothes available that work for the weather. Before I moved rurally, I never stored away winter or summer clothes, but living rurally in an area with a cold winter, it doesn't make sense to keep summer clothes out because there literally is no reason I would consider wearing a cotton dress in the depths of winter.

HELPFUL TIPS

1. *Put your clothes in the dryer for a few minutes before putting them on in the morning—it's like giving yourself a warm hug.*

2. *Put a small space heater in your bathroom to make the dry off after your morning or evening showers more enjoyable.*

3. *Make jam out of summer's frozen berries—you have more time in the winter, and you will appreciate the heat and labor of canning more. The taste of summer's bounty is so much better when fresh fruit is hard to come by.*

4. *In the dark of winter, string twinkly lights and/or light candles to make your home feel cozy and inviting.*

5. *Smells are also important since you are stuck inside more—get a rosemary tree, hang evergreen boughs, light scented candles, simmer stews, soups, mulled wine or apple cider on the stovetop.*

6. *Watch summer camp movies towards the end of winter to remind you that warmer days are ahead.*

7. *Peruse and order from seed catalogs to get you excited for spring planting season.*

8. *Throw an outdoor movie indoors. If a friend has a big heated space or workshop, borrow a projector, have people bring lawn chairs, make popcorn and pretend you're at an outdoor movie.*

9. *Take a mini-vacation. Sometimes just an overnight trip to a city or nearby town can be a nice break from the winter routine. If you can manage it, a trip to a warmer destination during the harshest time of winter can be something to look forward to.*

SPRING

The welcomed and sweet songs of returning birds. Daylight advances as the darkness retreats. The thaw commences and the forests and streams begin breathing again. Rain and mud boots come out and heavy jackets are stored away. Spring flowers shoot up from the softening ground and the neon shock of new leaves unfurl from their buds. Planting season begins and winter's hibernation ends. Spring is a time of rebirth; the natural world re-awakens. It is a time for fresh starts and new beginnings. For some, spring is a joyous time of year when color returns, people come out of hiding, spring cleaning starts and windows are finally opened to let the fresh air in. For others, the muddy thawing ground, swarms of newly hatched biting insects, quickly growing lawns and endless rainstorms make spring's awakening less enjoyable.

For me, spring in the city was wonderful. Cherry blossoms bursting from trees, tulips and daffodils popping up everywhere, and the opening season for bicycle rides. Moving to a rural area with a long winter and short spring was extremely challenging. By the time March rolled around I was ready for flowers to start blooming, but the snow kept falling. Once the snow finally started to melt in mid-April, the ground became a flooded soup of mud that lasted until mid-May when the leaves finally made their debut. I had no experience with mud season before moving and it caught me completely off-guard. I was also overly anxious to get my garden planted and put everything in the ground immediately following the last estimated frost date, only to have an early May snow kill all my seedlings. I realized that in order to enjoy the season, I had to embrace the slower pace of spring's renewal, find ways to have fun in the mud and rain, hang out with spring's newly arrived baby animals and partake in the outdoor activities spring ushers in.

TOOLS & SKILLS YOU'LL NEED

Spring is a time for new beginnings—a time to clean up, get organized and ready your land, home and yourself for longer, warmer days ahead. Both winter and the spring thaw can wreak havoc on your home and property. Being diligent about cleanup early will give you more time when the leaves pop and the weather heats up to enjoy a little time for yourself. First, as soon as snow is no longer in the forecast, get the underbelly of your car deep cleaned (ideally, every month in the winter you should clean your car's underbelly to help prevent salt and chemical deicer from rusting away the bottom of your car). At the beginning of spring, get one final deep clean to wash away any build-ups—this will prolong the life of your car.

Outdoor spring cleanup is no joke. There will inevitably be fallen branches, remnants of fall leaves, gravel or asphalt kicked up on your lawn from plowing, etc. Before the grass starts growing, get all of winter's debris cleared. Running over a giant rock or a stick hidden in the grass can destroy your lawnmower blades. Before you mow, do a walking survey of your yard to make sure there aren't any obstructions in the way. Lawn mowing is kicked into overdrive in the wetter, warmer spring months. Some weeks in spring require two cuttings. The general rule of thumb for a healthy lawn is to cut long first and then lower your blades after the first few cuttings. This will allow your lawn to grow together and not stunt patches of it that are slower growers. Don't cut your lawn until the ground solidifies and never cut it when it's wet. Wet grass is heavy and can easily get clogged in your mower. Cut later in the day on dry days. Self-propelled push mowers are great for properties smaller than an acre; anything more than an acre and you should look into a riding mower. If your property is uneven, a 4x4 riding mower might be required to make it up steeping runs. If you have more than five acres that you want to keep cleared, investing in grazing livestock or a tractor with a mowing attachment is your best bet. If you have a lot of property to manage and no livestock, you might also want to invest in a brush clearer, weed whacker and chainsaw. It's amazing how quickly brush, weeds and saplings can sneak up on you. If you want to keep your fields clear, you need to keep up on your maintenance or you can quickly lose the battle. You can avoid routine mowing by plowing your field and throwing wildflower seed. This is a great way to attract butterflies and other pollinators.

WHAT'S THE POINT OF CUTTING THE LAWN?

Cutting the lawn and keeping brush down in areas with ticks and poisonous snakes deter them from hanging out close to your house. In the spring, newly hatched ticks are in their nymph stage and are tiny and barely visible to the human eye. In areas with lots of ticks be vigilant and make sure you check yourself every night before you go to bed. If you come inside from doing yard work, throw all your clothes in the dryer for twenty to thirty minutes before putting them back on. Ninety percent of snakebites happen on the legs; if snakes are a problem where you live, be sure to work outside in tall boots to prevent snakes from breaking the skin if they attack you.

Spring also means garden preparation time—turning and testing the soil, adding necessary amendments, planting seeds and pruning all of your fruit trees and shrubs. In the gardening chapter (page 69), I discussed in greater detail how to prepare for the growing season—including how to prune fruit trees, how to plant seeds, and how to best test and amend your soil. One thing to be aware of when prepping your garden for the season is that soil compaction is bad. Water retention, root growth and nutrient absorption are all affected. When working on your garden beds, try to keep your feet out of them. If this can't be avoided, create specific pathways to follow where you aren't planning on planting. Pruning fruit trees can be a tiresome and difficult job, especially if they are tall and require a ladder. Investing in a pole saw (small chainsaw at the end of a long pole), a pair of extendable loppers, a three-legged ladder for uneven ground and a pruning saw will make your life a lot easier.

Water build-up and flooding is common during the spring thaw. Flooded basements are one of the most common spring annoyances in my area. Digging out drainage ditches, installing French drains and knowing how to pump out your basement safely are all skills you will need to acquire or hire out if spring flooding becomes a consistent problem.

HOW TO DEAL WITH A FLOODED BASEMENT

1. Shut off all electricity to the flood areas of your home (as an extra precaution, if you have a generator, cut off power to your entire home and run the water pump off of your generator).

2. Rent a water pump (you might want to buy one if it's a frequent problem), or if you just have a little water build up, a wet shop vac will work. Position in the lowest point of the basement to pump out as much water as possible.

3. Mop up remaining water, open all the windows and turn on some industrial fans to help dry things out for the next couple of days.

4. Close windows and run a dehumidifier for a couple of days to remove remaining water from the air.

5. Cut out any insulation, drywall or carpeting that was soaked to prevent mold from spreading.

FUN THINGS TO DO

Despite the laundry list of yard work and cleanup, spring is a season filled with many fun things to do. Snowmelt makes late spring rivers prime for river rafting and kayaking. Muddy fields and woods make 4-wheel off-roading a thrilling and dirty adventure. Spring also kicks off mountain and road bike season and people begin taking their inaugural motorcycle and scooter rides. One thing to keep in mind for all road cycling and biking activities is that sand and grit build up on country roads after the spring thaw. This grit can be dangerous, as it makes it easy to lose traction around turns and when braking. In our area, they sweep the grit off of the roads in mid-May, while other areas just let it wash away naturally in spring showers. Before heading out on your bike, just make note of the road conditions. If there is a lot of silt and sand on the roads, take it slow around corners and leave yourself plenty of room to brake when vehicles are in front of you.

Spring also means baby animals and the beginning of bulb flower season. Many livestock owners breed their animals to arrive in the spring. Keep on the lookout for open farm days where you can visit area farms and see the new arrivals. It is a great way to meet area food producers and also get to hang out with frolicking baby animals—win win. If you love flowers, check in your area for bulb farms to visit in the spring. Touring vibrant, fragrant fields of tulips and daffodils can be a welcomed jolt for the senses after a long monochrome winter season.

This might seem crazy to put in the fun things to do category, but spring cleaning is one of my favorite activities. I never felt the need to de-clutter when living in the city, as I spent very little time cooped up at home in the winter months. It's difficult to not start collecting things when you move rurally, as you need more tools than before and you suddenly have more space that you can fill with whatever you want. Spring cleaning is a time to throw open all of your windows, remove the stale dry air of winter and reevaluate if you really need all the things you have. I start by packing away all of my winter clothes and pulling out my spring/summer wardrobe. Before I put my spring/summer clothes in my closet, I try them all on and give away all the pieces that I no longer want or need. Then, I love to go through the freezer and pantry to make sure there aren't any remnants of the fall harvest that need to be eaten right away or composted. Then we move on to the basement and workshop to tidy up the tools, and replace winter outdoor gear with spring and summer gear. Finally, we go through the cupboards and linen closet, taking anything we don't use anymore to the local thrift store. There's nothing that helps transition you into the spring season like cleaning and organizing your space.

Going hand-in-hand with spring cleaning are late spring yard sales and flea markets. One person's trash is another's treasure. In rural areas, people don't like to waste things. There is always someone who would appreciate and use your old bicycle, pile of scrap wood or dresser. My treat for cleaning and de-cluttering my house is getting to go to yard sales. In order to not just re-fill my house with clutter, I try to make a list of specific things I need. It not only helps me avoid buying impulse things but it also makes it feel more like a fun scavenger hunt. If I'm looking for furniture, I pre-measure the locations where they will live so I don't end up buying something that doesn't work. You can also find some great things at thrift stores in the late spring. Many of the items in our home were bought at flea markets, thrift stores and yard sales. One thing to be aware of—yard sales in the country are no joke. People wake up super early to get the best stuff. Develop a Saturday plan of action by checking your local newspaper for yard sale listings and make note of any yard sale signs you see a few days prior. Make a plan of attack and don't get out later than 9:00 a.m. or you will miss out on the best items.

THINGS TO MAKE

Spring gives eager stomachs tired of winter's root vegetables a first taste of the delicious bounty heading their way. Spring's early crops are welcomed with open arms—asparagus, peas, tender greens, rhubarb and strawberries. The early months of spring still have longer nights allowing more time for preparing meals to celebrate the new fresh produce of the season. The warmer days of spring also mean brushing off and cleaning the grill for summer. I love throwing some olive oil and salt drizzled asparagus on the grill for its first fire up of the season. To finally celebrate the return of fruit's hottest couple, I make strawberry rhubarb syrup to put in sparkling water, cocktails, ice cream and snow cones.

STRAWBERRY RHUBARD SYRUP

This syrup is an easy way to bottle your early spring rhubarb and starwberry harvests. It's amazing in cocktails, champagne (in place of OJ), on ice cream, you name it!

Makes about 2 cups (475 ml) of syrup

INGREDIENTS

*4 cups (719 g) rhubarb, chopped into
½" (1-cm) pieces (about 6–8 stems)*

*4 cups (606 g) chopped strawberries (stem
and core removed)*

1½ cups (360 ml) water

*¾ cup (144 g) sweetener (raw sugar is what
I use, but you can substitute with honey or
maple syrup if you prefer)*

1 lemon

DIRECTIONS

Add the fruit, water, sweetener (sugar, honey or maple syrup) and a 2-inch (5-cm) strip of lemon rind to a large saucepan. Bring to a boil and then reduce the heat to simmer until the mixture has thickened. Break down the fruit with the back of a wooden spoon as it cooks. After about 20 minutes, remove from the heat, add a few squeezes of lemon juice to taste and run the mixture through a fine mesh strainer. You can freeze the syrup or it will keep in the refrigerator for two weeks. The solids left over in the strainer are amazing on toast, ice cream or mixed into morning oatmeal. Save them for a little delicious spring fruit infusion.

HOW TO MAKE A FLOWER CROWN

With all of the spring blooms popping up everywhere, making flower crowns is a fun springtime activity. All you need are some basic supplies to make an incredible flower crown. I include floral-specific materials but I've also made MacGyver-esque crowns with mint dental floss, thread and dried grasses.

MATERIALS
Measuring tape
Green floral wire
Wire cutters and scissors
Greenery (ferns, leaves, ivy, grasses)
Green floral tape (you can just use wire if you can't get tape)
Flowers!

DIRECTIONS
Start by measuring the head it is going to go on and create a ring using several rings of the floral wire. Add leaves and greenery to the wire and wrap it with the floral tape or wire to create a base. Once you have a good greenery base, add your flowers. Leave a 3 to 5 inch (8 to 13 cm) stem on your flowers so you can wrap with floral tape or wire at least 4 to 5 times. You can cut off the excess stem once it feels secure to the crown. Keep adding flowers until you get your desired look. Store wrapped in a moist napkin in the fridge for several hours if you aren't planning on wearing it right away.

THINGS TO WEAR

The rebirth of spring, sadly also means the rebirth of biting insects. Newly hatched bugs have particularly voracious appetites and can make spring's outdoor chores miserable. Investing in a beekeeping hat or face net, long sleeved work shirts and gloves will help keep you bug bite free. Muddy conditions, heavy spring showers and warming temperatures require waterproof shells with hoods, rain boots and boots made for working in mud. Muck boots, although leaving something to be desired in the style category, are my saving grace in the spring. Working and walking in regular rain boots can be difficult. Muck boots have an amazing tread; they don't feel as clumsy as rain boots and some have a steel toe for doing heavy yard work jobs. More time outdoors means sun exposure. You can get a sunburn even on overcast days. A wide-brim hat and sunscreen will help protect delicate post-winter skin. As spring warms, the rain dissipates and the ground solidifies, and you can finally pull out your cottons, open-toed shoes and warmer weather clothes.

HELPFUL TIPS

1. *Order your firewood for winter or chop your own. You can save money by ordering "green" firewood (meaning not fully dry) and season it yourself. Just make sure you have a dry place out of the weather to store and season it. Waiting until summer or fall means that prices will increase, supplies will be lower and you'll have to order already seasoned wood, which is more expensive. Usually if you order your firewood in the spring, they will deliver your firewood in the summer.*

2. *If you get your car stuck in the mud, add some traction by putting sticks, boughs, brush, etc. behind/under your tire and let a little air out of your tire. If that doesn't work, call a neighbor to help.*

3. *If you find yourself battling allergies during the spring bloom, try local honey. Ingesting local pollen-based honey over time may help reduce your allergy symptoms.*

4. *If you live in an area with ticks and will be spending a lot of time outside, investing in some Permethrin pre-treated clothes will kill ticks on contact. You can also treat your clothes yourself by buying a Permethrin kit or you can send your favorite outdoor clothes to www.insectshield.com and they will treat them for you.*

SUMMER

The growing crescendo of crickets. Long hot days followed by short sticky nights. Sunday drives with the windows down and the music up. Watermelon juice running down your chin. Picnics, backyard BBQs and roasting marshmallows over a twinkling campfire. The recognizable scent of sunscreen, playful shrieks of children free from school and the pops of fireworks. Summer is a fast-paced time of year that can feel crammed with too many things to do—yard work, social activities, camping trips, festivals, etc. For some, summer is difficult to embrace because of its heat, humidity, swarms of biting insects and endless yard work. For others, summertime feels fleeting—passing by much too quickly to fully be enjoyed. There are beds to be weeded, tomatoes to be processed, decks to be painted and parties to attend. The faster pace and longer 'to do' list can make it hard to slow down, take a rest and make the most of the summer season. It's important to learn to embrace the frenzied beat of summer, along with learning to carve out time to pause, stop working and enjoy these hotter, more social months.

For me, summer wasn't hard to learn to love; I've always enjoyed longer days and warmer nights. The thing that was difficult to adjust to living rurally was learning to take time to appreciate summer and not just frantically working right through it. I live in a town that has a touristy summer season. People come from cities all over to enjoy the natural beauty and small-town quaintness this wonderful little community has to offer. That means heavier traffic, difficulty parking in the village and endless social activities on the docket. Many of my friends, myself included, make a majority of our yearly income in the summer, so days are crammed with work and nights are filled with social gatherings. Summer also means needing to mow the lawn at least once a week, tending to the garden, doing yard work, making outdoor home repairs, harvesting and processing produce, teaching workshops and taking on heavier workloads for my home business. My first summer I totally missed it—I was too busy working and crossing things off of my 'to do' list to actually enjoy the season. My second summer, I still bit off more than I could comfortably chew. I realized that by not taking time to balance relaxation and quiet time with work and social obligations, I was making summer feel rushed and it didn't set me up for a happy or seamless transition into fall because all I wanted was more time to enjoy summer.

TOOLS & SKILLS YOU'LL NEED

Summer season is a busy time of year, both socially and work wise. Summer's yard work is a continuation of spring's chores—weekly lawn mowing, brush clearing and hacking back weeds. In dryer areas, you will need to mow less than regions with heavier summer rainfall. If you're growing your own food or flowers, you will need to keep up with weeding, watering and feeding your garden. Summer is also the ideal time for home improvement projects. Painting the exterior of your house, building decks or taking on any complex renovation projects in the summertime is ideal because you won't have to battle weather conditions as much. Paint is the ultimate makeover. If your home's paint is chipping and flaking, it is time to consider repainting. Hiring a professional painter can be expensive but painting your own home is time consuming—so price it out and consider your options before making a decision. We painted the exterior of our house ourselves when we first moved. It took us almost a full month and honestly when we need to do it again, I might hire someone to at least help next time.

HOW TO PAINT YOUR HOUSE

1. *Clean your house using a pressure washer and a mildew removing solution or bleach mix. You don't want any pre-existing mold left to rest under new paint. Once you've applied the mix, wash it again with clean water and let it dry thoroughly.*

2. *Scrape away all chipping paint, even if it means exposing the wood underneath. Leaving old paint will cause the new coat of paint to bubble and chip sooner.*

3. *Add an exterior surface repair compound to uneven areas and sand smooth.*

4. *If the door and window trim caulk is in poor condition, scrape it off and add new paintable exterior caulk. Remove damaged window putty and replace with new glazing.*

5. *Prime all bare wood and areas where the repair compound was added.*

6. *Paint two coats of paint—one coat won't hold up nearly as long or cover as well. Paint from the top to the bottom to reduce drips.*

7. *Paint the trim and door with two coats after you finish the exterior siding.*

FUN THINGS TO DO

The summertime is action packed with entertaining things to do and see. Summertime is when people spend as much time outside as possible and socializing is at its peak. If you live near a water source (river, lake, pond or ocean), experimenting with water sports is a great way to embrace the summer season. Floating down a river on an inner tube, water skiing or wakeboarding, windsailing, kiteboarding, canoeing, fishing, stand-up paddle boarding, kayaking, etc.—there are many water activities to choose from. Just like winter outdoor activity equipment, summer water sport equipment can be an expensive investment. Rent equipment first or borrow from friends to make sure you really want to purchase your own. Several of my friends have pooled their resources and bought kayaks and stand-up paddleboards that they share throughout the summer and fall.

The summertime also means loads of community and social events—outdoor movie nights, block parties and town BBQs, music festivals, county fairs, rodeos and demolition derbies. Attending and volunteering at community events in the summer is a great way to meet people, be immersed in your town's cultural offerings and become a familiar face in your town. A lot of small towns produce a summer activity guide that lists out all of the things to do in the summertime. Summer in rural areas, especially those with long winters, is a time of celebration. In addition to community-run events, there are also farm dinners hosted in the later summer months to celebrate the bounty of the season, day and overnight summer camps for kids and plenty of BBQs and parties to attend. If you aren't getting invited to many activities or parties, throw some yourself. Organize a picnic at an outdoor destination, arrange a "floatilla" party down a river, throw a laid-back BBQ or host an outdoor movie. The best way to get invited to events is to expand your social circle and include others in your summer activities.

THINGS TO MAKE

Embrace the fresh and delicious bounty of summertime by making simple meals that don't require much preparation or cooking. Delicious salads, popsicles made with fresh fruit, grilled meats, veggies and fish are all great options. Sweating over a hot stove isn't enjoyable, so take your cooking outside to the grill. Experiment with different grilling techniques, and incorporate a pizza stone to make pizzas on the grill. Challenge yourself to spend as much time cooking outside as you do inside.

My favorite way to eat the first few harvests of treasured summer tomatoes is to cut them into thin slices and sprinkle with salt and pepper. Add a drizzle of oil, balsamic reduction, some small mozzarella balls and basil leaves to turn that summer snack into a more substantial side dish.

My favorite DIY summer project is an adult slip n' slide. You can build this on a steep hillside, small slope or even a flat stretch (just add extra dish soap lubricant to keep people moving down the slide on flatter surfaces). Sure you can pick up a pre-made one at most stores, but they aren't very durable or long enough for adults. Measure how long a slide your yard can accommodate and head to the hardware store. Here's what you need:

-6 Mil. Plastic Sheet: 10' (3 m) by however long you want your slide to be (choose something thick so it won't tear)

-Shovel and scrap wood or large rocks

-Pool noodles (optional)

-Industrial Velcro tape (optional)

-Sprinkler (two are ideal)

-Eco-friendly dish soap

Spread your plastic out in the desired area. Dig a 12-inch (30-cm) wide, 12-inch (30-cm) deep, 10-foot (3-m) wide trench at the top. Wrap the top of the plastic evenly over scrap wood or rocks several times before burying in the trench. Try to replace the sod to keep it from becoming a mud pit. Apply noodle bumpers down the sides using the Velcro tape (optional). Position the sprinklers on either side of the top of the slide. Add eco-friendly dish soap or tear-free shampoo to reduce friction.

THINGS TO WEAR

In the summer, staying cool and comfortable is the name of the game. Wide-brimmed hats to keep sun off of your face, SPF and Permethrin treated clothing to deflect sun and deter bugs, a comfortable pair of hiking boots and some water shoes for river, ocean and lake exploring. Sounds super fashionable, right? Lucky for you, lots of clothing companies have realized there is a real demand for both attractive and functional clothes. Cotton, linen and synthetic fibers that wick away moisture are all good bets for staying cool and comfortable. It is a fallacy that wearing less clothing keeps you cooler; wearing light-colored, lightweight, breathable clothing that covers and protects your skin is the best way to go, especially when working outside.

HELPFUL TIPS

1. Apply sunscreen throughout the day—one application is not enough. If you are swimming, reapply every time you get out of the water.

2. Schedule a staycation during the summer so you can actually take time to enjoy it. You can just stay at home or you can take a little mini-trip to a nearby town or cabin to have some time to yourself to relax.

3. Throw a "floatilla" party on a nearby waterway. Bring some drinks, snacks, floatation devices and rope to tether the floating party together.

4. A lot of repair shops are willing to sell pre-inflated inner tubes. If you want an amazing monster inner tube, find a repair shop willing to sell you a tractor-trailer inner tube.

5. Yard games are a great addition to any BBQ or outdoor party. Build your own cornhole set or horse shoe pit, or invest in a bocce, croquet or badminton set up.

6. If it's brutally hot out and you aren't close to a body of water or swimming pool to dip in, take a cold shower or fill your bathtub or a plastic mini swimming pool with ice cubes and water and take a refreshing plunge. Or relive your childhood and run through the sprinklers.

7. Host an outdoor movie screening—rent or buy a projector, hang a sheet on the side of your house and pop some popcorn for an unforgettable summer gathering.

FALL

The crisp coolness and crunch of leaves underfoot on a fall morning stroll. The amber hued skies ushering in the waning hours of daylight. The roar of summer's orchestra begins to quiet to a murmur. Nature is slowly retreating back to earth for its approaching winter slumber. Scarves, flannel, sweaters and mugs of warm apple cider. Harvest season, costume parties, pumpkin patches and the smell of the woodstove's inaugural debut. Fall is both a welcomed slowdown from the frenzy of summer and a time of return—children head back to school, crops are harvested and people begin to put things to bed for the winter. For some, fall's winter preparation is overwhelming—the pruning, the raking, the chopping and stacking of wood and the impending doom of winter leaves little to look forward to. For others, fall is a welcomed season, a time when they can finally get relief from the scorching heat of summer, when they can get back into routine, enjoy cooking over a hot stove again and carve out some more time for themselves.

For me, fall has always been a beloved season, although even when I lived in the city, it felt like it arrived a little too soon. In Seattle, the leaves would change, the pace would slow and I would find more time to spend time outdoors before the chill of winter hit. The main things that were difficult to get used to living away from the city were the fall cleanup, preparation for winter and the hunting season. I had literally no concept of how many leaves would fall from just one tree. In the city, most leaves are blown and raked away for you. Our front yard is home to two maple trees, and in the fall we need to rake and haul at least five truckloads of leaves away. Nearly every weekend has a few hours of leaf removal. I also didn't realize how much was involved in gearing up for winter—stacking wood, canning food, checking to make sure the furnace is working, putting storm windows on and putting the garden to bed. My first fall in Maine I was excited to slow down, but quickly realized that there were many things on the agenda that wouldn't allow me to rest anytime soon. I finally finished all of my fall chores, laced up my hiking boots and headed outside only to hear the ring of the first (of many) gunshots; hunting season had begun. By the end of hunting season, the ground had frozen and winter was weeks away. I realized that staggering fall chores throughout the season and leaving time for fun fall activities was necessary in order to fully embrace the season.

TOOLS & SKILLS YOU'LL NEED

When I think fall, I think leaves…endless falling leaves. If you are asking if you have to remove leaves the answer is…do you like your lawn in the spring? If yes, then you must remove leaves in the fall. Leaving leaves to overwinter in your yard will make them difficult to remove in the spring and they will destroy your lawn in places where they get frozen and can't be removed. There are a bunch of ways to remove leaves from your yard. You can take the old fashion approach and rake them, leaf blow them, attach a bag to your mower and mow over them or use a leaf vacuum. We've tried most of these

techniques, minus the leaf vacuum (which is quite expensive) and found, for us, raking is the easiest. We rake leaves onto a giant tarp and then haul that tarp into the woods after we're done raking up the yard. A leaf blower is tricky to master, loud, heavy and the gas fumes aren't a bonus. Bagging with the mower requires frequent passes and has clogged our mower several times. A wide plastic rake is great for dry leaves and metal fan rakes are very effective for wet and frozen leaves (bow rakes are best used in the garden or for very frozen or heavy piles). Wear gloves when raking or suffer blisters on your hands. Ticks love hiding in leaf piles so take precaution when clearing or playing in fall leaves.

Fall is a great time to remove any broken limbs from nearby trees to prevent them from damaging your home or automobiles in the winter. Cutting saplings back and clearing brush is also easier to do in the fall, after the leaves have fallen but before the freezing temperatures hit. Late fall is also the time to put your garden to bed for the winter. Removing all plants, vines and weeds, turning or tilling the soil to deter pests from wintering in your bed and adding straw or row covers to root vegetables that you plan to continue harvesting. If you want to help rebuild the integrity of your soil, plant a cover crop like rye or clover that you can turn into the soil in the spring. If your beds are riddled with weeds, cover them with black plastic for the winter, so it will prevent weed growth in the spring.

Fall also means the beginning of wood burning season. Before you start your first fire, have your chimney inspected and cleaned to prevent creosote build-up from starting a chimney fire. If you have a fireplace or woodstove in your home, it's important to locate your woodpile as close to your home as possible. Hauling loads of wood in the fall is no problem, but having to trudge through the snow with armloads of wood throughout the winter is no fun. Each fall we pull our seasoned firewood out of the basement of our barn and haul loads of it to our front porch to stack. You just want to make sure that wherever you place your woodpile it is out of the weather. Wet wood won't burn properly, so if you don't have a dry place near your house you might want to build a shelter or shed to house your firewood.

FUN THINGS TO DO

There are loads of activities to do in the fall. Fall's cooler temperatures and fewer bugs make it extra enjoyable to go out hiking, mountain and road biking, kayaking and fishing. Harvest season brings with it its share of festivals and town events. Halloween means pumpkin patches, corn mazes and costume parties. In our small village, trick-or-treaters congregate on one main street in town. The community pools resources to provide extra candy to the homeowners on that street to pass out because otherwise they would get eaten out of candy and home. Even those that don't have youngsters with them congregate to see the costumes and be a part of the merriment. Check out the community and school event listings for the fall season and join in on the fun. Our favorite party of the year is the Halloween costume party that a local art center throws in our town every October. Fall also means celebrating Thanksgiving. If you are far away from family and are going to be spending Thanksgiving locally, invite over friends and neighbors to join in the festivities.

Later fall, in most rural areas, is the beginning of hunting season. Hunting season supplies some of my friends with all their meat for the winter. Hunting is by no means easy and it isn't for the faint of heart. In our area there are different seasons for bow hunting and for rifle hunting. Both types require practice and patience. If you are interested in trying your hand at hunting, first consult your local town office to get the appropriate permits and learn the rules. It's best to go out with experienced hunters to avoid accidentally trespassing on private land and learn the areas where the animals you are hunting tend to congregate. Many areas have hunting inspection locations where you need to take your kill to be inspected. Be aware of the hunting laws or you could receive a heavy fine.

THINGS TO MAKE

Fall's bountiful harvest and chillier temperatures make it the perfect time to start simmering soups and sauces on your stovetop. I love apples. I love picking them, eating them and making things with them. In the fall, I try to collect the apples and pears off of our trees before the deer, turkeys, porcupines and crows get them all. I make baked apples, crumbles, pies and homemade applesauce. I can't get enough of homemade applesauce. It is so easy to make and tastes so much better than store bought. I substitute my applesauce for butter in recipes to make baking recipes healthier, and I mix it with my morning oatmeal. Because we have both apple and pear trees, I tend to make a combo pear/apple sauce and add some ginger to spice things up a bit.

APPLE AND PEAR SAUCE

Those early crisp fall mornings feel much warmer and more inviting with this delicious sauce. You'll never want to buy apple sauce again once you realize how easy and delicious it is when you make it from scratch.

Makes 4–4.5 cups (1–1.2 kg) of sauce, serves 4 people

INGREDIENTS

8 cups (1.4 kg) apples and pears (doesn't have to be an even split) peeled, cored and skinned

1 cup (240 ml) water

1 tbsp (21 g) maple syrup

1 tsp (3 g) cinnamon

¼ tsp nutmeg

1½ tbsp (11 g) freshly grated ginger

DIRECTIONS

Add all the ingredients into large pot or Dutch oven. Cook on medium heat and then reduce to simmer after it starts steaming. Keep checking to make sure there is enough liquid; if it looks like it's drying out, add a tablespoon (15 ml) of water or juice at a time. Use an immersion blender or heavy whisking to turn into a sauce. Store in the fridge for up to two weeks or freeze for later use.

MAKE A SCARECROW

Here's a festive fall project that also helps scare away birds and deer from your garden and orchards.

MATERIALS

Hammer and nails

Tall wooden stick (about 5–6 feet (1.5–2 m) tall, this will be the head and the base for the body)

Wooden cross stick (this will be the arms)

Old clothes

Rope or twine

Hay, straw or plastic bags for stuffing (as long as the bags can't escape to injure wildlife)

Rubber gloves or gardening gloves

Safety pins

Sharpie pens

Old pillowcase

Wig and hat (optional)

DIRECTIONS

Hammer the cross stick into the tall wooden base, about a foot down from the top. Put the shirt on the stick and tie the bottom with rope or twine. Fill the shirt with stuffing. Add stuffed gloves to the arms if you would like hands and secure with safety pins. Add the pants or overalls, cutting a small hole in the crotch to fit over the wooden support stick. Tie the bottom of the pant legs with twine, fill with stuffing and secure to the shirt with safety pins. Add socks or lightweight boots by stuffing tightly around the pant legs. Hammer the tall wood base into the ground. Draw a face on a pillowcase, adding stuffing, and place over the top of the support stick. Secure the head by tying it with twine and tuck the pillowcase into the neck of the shirt. Add a wig and hat if desired.

THINGS TO WEAR

Fall means layers. Chilly temperatures will have you abandon your summer wardrobe and replace it with flannel, wool sweaters, hats and mittens. For pre-winter cleanup, invest in a pair of insulated leather work gloves. These will keep your hands warm and protected when hacking back trees and removing brush. A signature hue of fall attire in most rural areas is hunter orange. Neon orange hats and vests prevent outdoor enthusiasts from being confused for a deer or other large game animal by a hunter. If your community has an active hunting season, be sure to add a hunter orange collar, bandana or vest to your pets as well.

HELPFUL TIPS

1. *Set baited mousetraps outside of the foundation of your house in the fall to ward off vermin looking for a warm place to winter.*

2. *Simmer apple juice on your stove with cinnamon sticks, cloves and orange slices for delicious cider that fills your home with lovely fall aromas.*

3. *If you don't want trick-or-treaters at your door, keep your porch light off.*

4. *Some landscaping businesses will take your fall leaves and cleared brush off your hands to turn into woodchips and mulch. Inquire with local landscapers to see if there are any in your area accepting yard waste.*

5. *Dig up and bring some of your garden's plants indoors for the winter months—most herbs, peppers and lavender do well being transplanted in pots and brought indoors.*

IN CONCLUSION

Embracing and enjoying all four seasons is a foolproof way of seamlessly transitioning to country life. Sure, you will still have your favorite seasons (those might change based on the area you move), but it's important to find things to love about every season and get into a rhythm to help you more efficiently conquer the tasks that each season brings. There should always be a good balance of enjoyment and work. Keep reminding yourself, even in busy seasons, to take time for yourself. Spend time outdoors (even in harsh weather), attend community events, throw gatherings, make stuff and experiment in the kitchen. With enough time and practice, a wonderful rhythm to the seasons will develop and you will find yourself looking forward to the quiet months of winter, the spring awakening, the buzz of summer and the slowing pace of fall.

STAYING ALIVE

*Preparing for natural disasters, animals attacks
and the unexpected*

*"I like being self-sufficient. If the power goes out, we're fine. We have food, water and warmth.
This winter we had a lot of really rough, cold weather. I called my mother after one bad snowstorm
and I expected her to be worried. She said, 'Oh, I worry less about you out there than anybody.'
That made me feel good."*

– Jesse Frost, Farmer and Homesteader

Living in a city is like being wrapped in a warm cozy blanket of convenience. Sure, you are competing for resources, it's expensive and you have to wait in line for everything, but you basically never have to leave your apartment if you don't want to. You can order all of your daily essentials and extravagances online and have them delivered directly to your door. For many transplants, this level of dependence on the conveniences of city life is one of the reasons they decided to leave. Moving rurally gives you the opportunity to become more self-reliant—both by practice and by necessity. Self-reliance breeds confidence and an immense feeling of satisfaction. Knowing how to take care of yourself, making things as opposed to buying, doing more with less, growing and raising your own food and not becoming complacent in modern day conveniences. Not to say living in the country in the digital age is not without its many accessibilities, but learning to be more self-sufficient will inevitably come in handy in your new rural life.

In the country, it might feel like you are much more on your own, but the reality is that successful rural dwellers are both self-sufficient and dependent on one another. Becoming a part of your community and learning some basic survival skills is a step towards joining a network of others who will be there for you when hard times come. It's hard to ignore that we are living in a time of extremes. Temperatures and water levels are rising and natural disasters are increasing in frequency and strength. Not to go overly doomsday, but times they are a'changing. In the city, although help responds quicker in natural disasters and emergency situations, there are more people competing for the resources and help available. In the country, you take care of your neighbors and friends, instead of competing with them. That said, you can't rely entirely on help from neighbors and friends; you need to learn to take care of yourself first. As pioneer Back-to-the-Lander Eliot Coleman said in his Urban Exodus interview, "You have to learn to look after yourself. There is a wonderful community in the country, but all participants in the community must know how to survive on their own first. When you each put in as much as you take, then you have a community that will work."

Staying alive and self-sufficiency—they may seem separate but they are one and the same living rurally. If you get snowed in, the roads are blocked and you don't have supplies readily available, your neighbors and friends might not be physically able to come to your aid. Living outside of a major metropolitan area, there are fewer hands, and although you will have a community rallied behind you, it is important to be prepared ahead of time for emergency situations and know what to do. Living immersed in nature and further away from a hospital means you should learn how to respond and react when you encounter a wild or rabid animal or are bitten by a snake, spider or tick. Ready for this? Let's learn some of the basics of how to survive when the worst happens.

NATURAL DISASTERS

Knowing how to prepare and respond in natural disasters is essential for survival in the country. Even if you live in an area that hasn't had a flood in over 100 years, that doesn't mean one won't happen while you are living there. We are going to go through the fundamentals of what to do before and during natural disaster situations. If you are moving, or have moved to an area prone to certain natural disasters, do your homework and learn everything there is to know about how to prepare, respond and recover. Learning the hard way during an actual natural disaster is no way to go.

EXTREME COLD

Before: In areas where extreme cold, blizzards and ice storms are possible, always pay close attention to weather reports. If foul weather is predicted in the forecast, make sure you have a stocked fridge, gas for your generator (more on that later in the section) and bring firewood reserves inside if you have a woodstove or fireplace. Severe winter storms can mean long power outages and blocked country roads. You should also prepare your home to weather these extreme cold conditions, preferably in the early fall before the winter season hits. Make sure your walls and attic are insulated, cover windows with plastic from the inside or install storm windows, weatherstrip doors and windows and insulate water lines or replace old lines with PEX (PEX will still freeze but is a lot less likely to burst in extreme cold). Cut away branches that hang out over your home to prevent them from breaking and falling on your roof. If you have a woodstove or fireplace, have the chimney and flue inspected regularly to prevent chimney fires and blockages.

During: Hunker down with a good book, board games or a movie. Don't go outside unless it is absolutely necessary. Cook a good hardy meal to keep you warm. Have candles and/or flashlights handy if the power goes out. Fill your sink/bathtub/empty containers with water if your pump stops working. Open your water taps slightly so they drip to help prevent your pipes from freezing. Test your carbon monoxide detector to make sure it is working. Close your curtains and blinds to keep as much heat in your home as possible and light your fireplace or woodstove (if you have one). If the power goes out, closely monitor your home's temperature; try to keep it above freezing by feeding your woodstove or running a heater off your generator. Later in the chapter we will discuss ways of keeping your home warm if you don't have a generator or alternative heat source available.

EARTHQUAKES

Before: Create an evacuation plan with your family. Have one for home and for school/work. It should outline where supplies are, where you will all meet, the best places to ride out the shaking, etc. Secure appliances, heavy furniture, bookcases, shelves, etc. to the wall using "L" brackets. Move heavy objects to the bottom of shelves and bookcases. Learn how to shut off your utilities and have your home inspected to ensure it is structurally sound and capable of withstanding an earthquake.

During: Drop to your knees, cover your head and neck and crawl towards shelter. Shelter can be a heavy table, desk, etc. Try to stay away from windows. The standard "hide under a doorway" isn't the most structurally sound place in most modern houses. Don't run to find a doorway or try to go outside. Best to brace yourself and wait out the shaking. If you're outside, stay there and move yourself away from hazards like buildings, utility wires, etc. If you are in your car, pull over to the side of the road away from utility wires, poles or overpasses, put your e-brake on and wait it out. After the shaking stops, check and treat yourself and others around you for injuries. Second, go to your meeting location and retrieve your emergency preparedness kit (more on that later in the chapter). If you are at home, check your water/power/gas lines to make sure they haven't been damaged. If they have, turn them off. Stay away from damaged buildings; go outside if the structure of your house has been compromised. Stay away from beaches and expect that there will be aftershocks.

FLOODS

Before: First, if your town and/or home is located in a flood zone, learn about emergency evacuation routes, shelters and warning signals. Establish an out-of-area contact that all your family members can reach out to should you get separated. Make sure everyone memorizes their phone number and address. When a flood warning happens, fill your car's tank with gas, retrieve your preparedness kit and listen to the radio or television for updates. Fill your bathtub, sinks and empty bottles with clean water. Secure outdoor items (like BBQs and furniture) and bring them inside or tie them down. If an evacuation is called, turn off all your utilities and close the main gas valve to your house.

During: If evacuated, follow the designated routes, take only essential items with you and don't try to drive across flooded roads. Don't return to your home until emergency officials have given you the okay. Downed power lines, gas leaks, structural damages, etc. can make re-entering your home dangerous. Wait until you are green-lighted to return and assess the damage. If evacuation is not called, move yourself to the highest point in your home, continue to monitor activities on your radio and prepare to evacuate to a shelter or a neighbor's house should flood waters damage your home or emergency personnel tell you to do so. Don't venture outside unless you are instructed to do so and wait for the all clear from emergency personnel on your radio before going out to survey the damage.

HURRICANES

Before: Determine if you are located in an area where hurricanes can cause damage. Just because you don't live in a coastal area, doesn't mean you are immune from hurricane damage. Go to your town office and get information on evacuation routes, shelter locations, warning signals and what you should do to prepare. If a hurricane watch is called, go fill up your car's gas tank, move indoors or secure all outdoor items, fill sinks/bathtubs/empty containers with fresh water and cover windows and doors with nailed up plywood or storm shutters. A hurricane watch means weather conditions could cause one—these are announced usually forty-eight hours before a hurricane warning. A hurricane warning is serious; it means that a hurricane is imminent and has either started or is about to start.

During: If you hear an order to evacuate your home, do not ignore it, even if your neighbors aren't planning on leaving. Only take what you need with you, bring your emergency car preparedness kit, turn off the gas/water/electricity and follow the instructed evacuation route. If you are told to stay home (sometimes this is safer than leaving), stay inside and keep listening to the radio for updates. The most common injuries in hurricanes are from flying debris, so shelter yourself in a room without windows—preferably a closet that can protect you from glass and other flying objects. Don't venture outside unless you are instructed to do so; wait for the all clear from emergency personnel on your radio before going out to survey the damage.

TORNADOS

Before: People often compare tornadoes to hurricanes, but the fact of the matter is they couldn't be more different. Tornadoes advanced warnings are often fifteen to thirty minutes before they touch down, compared to several days for hurricanes. Tornadoes are usually no more than a quarter of a mile wide (hurricanes can be hundreds of miles wide), last less than an hour and winds can reach 300 mph (hurricanes are usually less than 180 mph). If you live in an area that has tornadoes, a key to preparing for a tornado means being vigilant about monitoring the weather. Most areas with tornadoes have sirens (both for a tornado warning and for a tornado watch), so it's important to know the difference between the two sirens. A tornado watch is issued when severe thunderstorms and weather conditions favor tornado formations. During a watch, track progress on a radio or television, monitor the weather, fill your bathtub/sinks/empty bottles with water, make sure your emergency preparedness kit is located in your shelter area and get ready to take cover.

During: A tornado warning is issued when a funnel comes up on the weather radar or has been sighted. When a tornado warning has been issued you should immediately take shelter. Like hurricanes, the number one cause of injury is flying debris. The safest place to be during a tornado is in an underground tornado shelter or the interior part of a basement. For added protection, go under a sturdy table, desk or mattress; cover yourself in a blanket or sleeping bag; and protect your head with your arms. If you are outside or living in a mobile home without a tornado shelter, find low ground away from areas with lots of trees, a culvert, ditch or ravine; cover yourself in a thick blanket or sleeping bag; and protect your head with your hands. Wait until the tornado has passed before coming out of your shelter. Be cautious, as there might be significant damage waiting for you outside the door to your basement or shelter.

TSUNAMIS

Before: Tsunamis are caused by rapid displacements of a large volume of water. Earthquakes are the most common cause, but volcanic eruptions, icebergs, meteor hits and landslides can also cause a tsunami. If you live in a coastal area, learn your tsunami evacuation route and make sure you have an emergency preparedness kit in all of your vehicles. If you have children in school, make sure you are familiar with the school's tsunami evacuation plan. Because earthquakes can happen without warning, tsunamis often also happen without much warning. After an earthquake, tsunami watches or warnings can be issued to areas that might be affected by a tsunami.

During: If a tsunami watch or warning is issued, use your town's emergency evacuation route to get to high ground. After an earthquake hits your coastal community, head for high ground if you can. If you are at or near the ocean and notice unusual ocean behavior (water receding exposing reefs/fish, or a wall of water that sounds like a jet engine), immediately head as fast as you can to your designated evacuation route. Listen to your radio for updates and don't return to the coast until it's been deemed safe—often there's more than one large wave that hits.

VOLCANOES

Before: Volcanoes can produce toxic gases, ash, lava flows and flash floods. Sometimes volcanic activity can be predicted ahead of time but they can also erupt without any warning. If you live in an area with dormant or active volcanoes, consult your town office to determine what risk zone you live in. The risk zones range from extreme, high, medium, low and safe zones. Each volcano is unique; consult with local experts to determine what your best course of action should be if volcanic activity commences. If a volcano warning is issued, immediately turn on your radio for updates, fill your bathtub/sinks/empty bottles with water, fill up your gas tank and put your emergency preparedness kit in your car. Move cars into the garage or under shelters, enclose any livestock in their shelters and provide them with food/water and adjust your fridge/refrigerator to a colder setting to keep food fresh longer.

During: If an eruption happens and you are told to evacuate, follow the route they have instructed you to go, and, if you have time, turn off your gas/electricity/water and disconnect your appliances. If you are told to stay put, keep listening to your radio for updates (your area might be required to evacuate after other more at-risk areas have been evacuated), close and lock windows and doors, close your fireplace damper, turn off central air, move to a room without windows above the ground level and have a hard-wired phone close by to call emergency officials in case you get stuck. Don't venture outside until safety officials give the okay. Wear goggles and an n95 breathing mask to protect you from poisonous gas.

Before: Wildfires can happen anywhere and without notice. In some areas, wildfires are common, but know that they can happen anywhere. All it takes are dry conditions and a cigarette tossed from a car window. The best thing you can do to prepare for possible wildfires is to maintain a clear area around your home of 30 to 100 feet (9–30 m). Keep the lawn regularly mowed, remove brush, woodpiles and other flamable materials in your clear area. Regularly clean your roof, gutters and remove trees or branches that hang out over your house. Installing a pool or man-made pond or having a water source on your property is an asset should a wildfire head your way. Keep long hoses and sprinklers handy to douse your home and clear area. If a wildfire is reported nearby, listen to the radio or television for updates.

During: If you aren't ordered to evacuate and have time to prepare your home, close all blinds, shutters, attic/basement vents, windows, doors (to prevent draft), pet doors and remove drapes and curtains. Shut off all fuel lines at their source (propane, natural gas, etc.). Before going outside, put on protective clothing: sturdy shoes, cotton clothes, long sleeves/pants, gloves, an n95 mask and goggles. Hook up sprinklers and put them on the roof of your house and near any fuel source tanks to douse them with water. Fill any large containers outside with water—hot tubs, pools, garbage cans, tubs, etc. Gather fire tools (rake, axe, chainsaw, bucket and shovel). Hose down your clear zone around your house, saturating the ground as much as possible. If asked to evacuate, make sure your emergency kit and supplies are in your car and quickly collect any mementos and valuables you can't live without. Don't spend too much time collecting things; it's important to be prompt. Make sure all of your pets are with you. Leave all of your lights on so it is more visible to firefighters in thick smoke. Drive safely and slowly on the designated evacuation route, and keep your car vents turned off to prevent smoke inhalation. Only return home when authorities have given the green light.

EMERGENCY PREPAREDNESS KIT

Regardless of what natural disasters are most common in your area, the most important thing to prepare is an emergency preparedness kit. Putting this kit together should be at the top of your 'to do' list when you move. Don't delay; you never know when disaster might strike. If you get caught off-guard and have yet to meet friends or neighbors to come to your rescue, you could be up S#%& Creek without a paddle. I am going to give you the basic run-down on what you need in a robust emergency preparedness kit that will help get you through most natural disasters. You might not need all of these things, but it is better to be overprepared rather than underprepared. If you live in an area prone to natural disasters, consult local experts to make sure there aren't any specific additions you should add. Keep supplies in waterproof containers that are easy to move and carry. Store your kit in an accessible place, ideally in your main shelter or area you plan on congregating should a disaster strike.

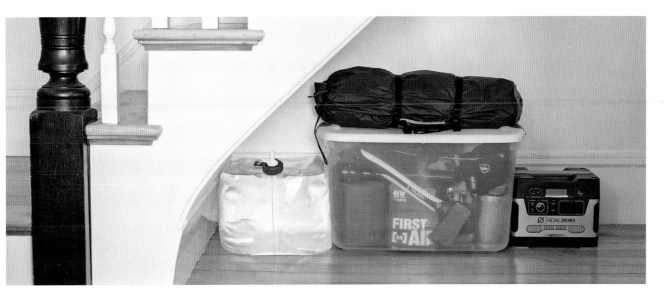

HOME SUPPLIES

At a minimum, your kit should have enough food and water (five gallons [19 L], per person, per day) for each person in your home for five to seven days. Food supplies should be non-perishable (canned, freeze dried, etc.). See the food section (on page 170) for more information on storing and using emergency food supplies. Your home preparedness kit should also include the following:

- *Pocketknife and non-electric can opener*

- *Food and water for pets (five to seven day supply)*

- *Disposable or lightweight reusable cups, plates, utensils, heavy-duty aluminum foil and cooking implements (kitchen camping gear works great)*

- *Portland gas or charcoal grill and necessary fuel for cooking*

- *Paper towels and toilet paper*

- *Water purification supplies (see the water purification section on page 169)*

- *Baby food, diapers, etc. if you have a baby*

- *Changes of clothes (protective clothing like long pants, warm coats, etc.)*

- *Heavy-duty shoes, protective gloves, rubber boots and protective eye goggles*

- *Breathing protection—n95 respirator masks*

- *A large 100 + piece first aid kit, first aid book, prescription medications and eyeglasses and any special medical needs (EpiPen, asthma inhaler, knee brace, etc.)*

- *Scissors, tweezers, thermometer, safety pins, needle and thread*

- *Insect repellent and sunscreen*

- *Personal hygiene products, disposable hand wipes, soap, toothpaste, tampons/pads, etc.*

- *Tent, sleeping bags/extra blankets*

- *Fire extinguisher*

- *Waterproof matches, lighters and candles*

- *Flashlights and camping lamps with extra batteries*

- *Battery powered radio with extra batteries*

- *Plastic bags of various sizes*

- *Ax, broom, shovel, pliers, adjustable wrench, hammer, screwdriver with interchangeable heads, 100 feet (30 m) of rope, plastic sheeting, garden hose and duct tape*

- *Knife and flare gun*

You should also have a plastic waterproof folder containing copies of your driver's licenses, passports, front/back of your credit cards, list of emergency contact numbers, homeowner's or renter's insurance, auto/life/health insurance cards and some emergency cash should you need to make purchases before the banks reopen.

CAR SUPPLIES

Having a smaller kit for your car is an essential step for anyone living in an area with natural disasters that may require a quick emergency evacuation. Car kits are also great to have should you be traveling and get stuck in a blizzard or other crisis. Every time you check your oil levels on your car, do a routine check to make sure your spare tire, jack and tire changing tools are in good condition. Keep this car preparedness kit in a backpack so you can easily carry it should you need to continue on foot.

Here's a list of what you should include: sleeping bag or blankets, bottled water, non-perishable food (energy bars, trail mix, etc.), change of clothes, emergency cash, small multipurpose fire extinguisher, first aid kit and manual, flares, reflector, flashlight with extra batteries, battery-operated radio with extra batteries, gloves, warm jacket, loud whistle, compass, rope for towing and rescue, pocketknife, small tool kit, jumper cables, weeklong supply of prescription medicine, toilet paper, disposable hand wipes and duct tape.

GENERATORS—I'VE GOT THE POWER!

Power outages in rural areas are more common than in the city and can last much longer. Last winter our power was out for nearly two weeks and we only live about seven minutes from our town center. Investing in a generator is definitely going to come in handy at some point. Generators can keep your fridge and freezer running so your perishable food supplies won't go bad, your heat on so your pipes don't freeze, your electric water pump working so you have water and your lights on. It is important to use your generator safely to prevent carbon monoxide poisoning, never use it indoors or in the garage, basement, near open windows or air intakes outside of your home. A waterproof shed or covered area near your house is the best place to run a generator; use outdoor-rated extension cords to run the electricity into your house safely. Have back-up fuel available if you run out. Buying a home generator can be confusing, as there are many different models, sizes and wattages available—ranging from 3,000 up to 15,000 watts. Think about what appliances and devices you will want to run from the generator, factoring the wattages for each. Here's a rough wattage guide—these fluctuate based on model:

Fridge (600), Freezer (600), Water Pump (1900), Water Heater (5,000), Sump Pump (600), Space Heater (1800), Heat Pump (4700), Microwave (1,500), Electric Oven (3,500), TV (200), Computer (250)

STAYING WARM WITHOUT ELECTRICITY OR AN ALTERNATE HEAT SOURCE

If you are trapped in your house during a blackout in extreme cold weather and you don't have a backup generator or woodstove to heat your home, there are alternative ways to stay warm. Don't run a cook stove or burn charcoal indoors, as they could produce deadly smoke and gas. Start by creating a "warm" room; choose the smallest room in your home, preferably with the fewest windows. Cover all windows and doors with blankets and strip all beds and linen closets of blankets and sandwich yourself in them. Wear warm layers and huddle together for warmth. If you still feel cold, erect a tent or fort and layer blankets over the top and bottom of it to capture body heat.

WATER PURIFICIATION

There are lots of things on the market now that will help you purify water and make it potable. Go online or to an outdoor store and look at all the options out there. Keeping water purification supplies in your emergency preparedness kits will make it possible to make collected water drinkable, even if your water storage supplies run out. You should always have at least two water purification methods available, should one fail. Collected water can be melted snow, creeks, lakes, ponds, etc. Always try to source the cleanest water you can find. Water with lots of particles in it will clog filters. You can "pre-filter" dirty water by running it through a handkerchief or other piece of fabric. If murky water is all you can find, let it sit for at least a few hours so the particles can settle at the bottom. Here are some different ways to help purify your drinking water.

Boiling: This is the tried and true, some would say, "old fashioned" option. A five-minute roaring boil will kill most bacteria, parasites and pathogens. If you are located at a higher elevation, boil a little longer. Boiling will not remove heavy metals or chemicals from water, so be wary of collecting from areas with agriculture run-off.

UV Light: There are many UV light purifiers available. Most take only about 90 seconds to purify 32 fluid ounces (950 ml) of water and you can drink the water immediately after it's purified. UV light works best with clearer water; if the water you are purifying is murky, treat it twice.

Iodine Tablets and Drops: Iodine tablets and drops kill viruses, bacteria and giardia in water. Pregnant women, people with shellfish allergies or with thyroid problems should avoid using these tablets. They are effective at removing bacteria and usually take about an hour to work before the water is drinkable. Something to note: iodine tablets are known for making water taste foul. Tablets and drops usually only have a one- to two-year shelf life and are ineffective after they expire.

Survival Straws: These straws can be used just like a normal drinking straw. Most have a carbon filter, which removes larger bacteria, pathogens, odors and foul tastes from the water.

Chlorine Bleach or Chlorine Tablets: Bleach or chlorine tablets can be used to disinfect water. For tablets, follow the directions on the packet. For bleach, the amount you use will depend on the quality of the water. Clear room temperature water needs two drops per quart, while cold and/or murky water should get four drops. Put the drops in the water, shake vigorously and let stand for thirty minutes. The water should have a slight bleach odor; if it doesn't, add another drop and let sit for another fifteen to thirty minutes before drinking.

Filters: There are loads of portable gravity-powered and pump water filters available. These filters, depending on their size, can treat gallons of water per day. If you live in an area that is remote, it is worth investing in a larger filter and a small pump that you can use should you need to mobilize to find help.

FOOD STORAGE & EXPIRATION DATES

Storing rations for food supply disruptions is crucial for survival when disaster strikes. Plan on having a five-to seven-day supply of non-perishable food. Storing food in a cool (40–60°F [4–16°C]), dry, dark place will help enhance the shelf life. Store food in containers that rodents and insects cannot get into. Date all food and replace if and when it reaches its expiration date. Discard any cans that are leaking or bulging. Canned foods and dry mixes generally last about two years. When using emergency food, first use the food in your refrigerator and then move on to the food in your freezer. Once perishable refrigerated food has been room temperature for over two hours, discard it. If you have a generator, keep your freezer running if you have extra food supplies in there. Here is a handy guide for the shelf life of freezer food:

Beef/lamb: 4–12 months

Pork: 6–8 months

Poultry: 9–12 months

Ground meats: 3–4 months

Stews and soups: 2–3 months

Vegetables: 8–10 months

Fruit: 6–12 months

Sauces: 6–12 months

FORAGING FOR FOOD

There are lots of edible and medicinal plants growing all over the country. Growing up in northern California, my mother and I would forage watercress from the banks of the stream by our house and dandelion greens from our yard. There is something amazing about foraging for free food and medicine. The only effort required is the time spent hunting, gathering and preparing. It is always best to execute extreme caution when foraging. Take a local foraging class with an experienced forager before collecting things on your own. This is especially important when foraging mushrooms as there are some poisonous look-alike mushrooms out there that could make you sick or even kill you. Learning how to safely forage edible and medicinal plants in your area is enjoyable and makes you more self-reliant. Extra bonus, if a natural disaster or emergency situation strikes, you have the skills necessary to collect nature's bounty and to supplement the reserves you've put away in your preparedness kit. Here are just a couple of my favorite, easy to identify, widespread wild plants known for both their edible and medicinal qualities. Again, take a class or check with local experts before ingesting anything you forage.

Blackberries: Blackberries grow all over and they are delicious either raw or baked into desserts, made into jam or included in a myriad of recipes. They usually ripen in mid-summer to early fall. A favorite childhood activity was blackberry picking with my sisters. We would reward our labors by making "purple cows"—a milkshake made with blackberries, vanilla ice cream and almond milk. Medicinally, the root of the blackberry is known for its astringent qualities. Blackberry root tinctures and tea are used to treat diarrhea, hemorrhoids, intestinal problems and dysentery.

Burdock: You know that giant plant that takes over and creates annoying brown Velcro-balls that get stuck in your clothes and on your pets? Well, now you can actually reap the benefits of this plant by eating it and using it medicinally. While the entire burdock plant is edible, most people eat the long carrot-like root and harvest the flower stalks before the Velcro seed balls arrive. They can be slow roasted, boiled or eaten raw. Medicinally, burdock is used as a blood purifier, a mild diuretic and can be used to treat gout, indigestion and filter impurities out of your kidneys.

Dandelions: Many people consider dandelions a nuisance weed, but dandelions are incredible, totally edible plants. Dandelions were my "gateway" foraging plant. They got me excited about the prospect of collecting my own food and medicine. They pack a nutritional punch with high levels of vitamins A, K, C and E. The yellow flowers can be made into tea or wine. The leaves are best eaten when young, before the plant flowers, to avoid a bitter taste. Dandelion leaves can be used in a salad, put in soups, sautéed, etc. The root can be dried and roasted to create a convincing coffee substitute. Medicinally, dandelions help alleviate an upset stomach, intestinal gas, bruises, muscle and joint pain and eczema.

Rose hips: Rose hips are the fruit of the rose plant. They ripen to a rich red color in the late summer through to the fall. Fresh rose hips are deliciously tart and have high levels of vitamin C and antioxidants. Drying rose hips destroys most of the vitamin C content, so consuming fresh rose hips is the best way to receive the maximum vitamin C benefits. Rose hips are used in a number of culinary recipes, including making jams, soups and teas. Medicinally, rose hips are used to treat numerous stomach disorders, sciatica, diarrhea, fever, high blood pressure and many other medicinal applications.

Stinging nettle: You pay excessive amounts for foraged nettles in fancy urban restaurants; now you can harvest them yourself. You can find nettles in the spring through the end of summer. Harvest the leaves using gloves because, as the name suggests, they sting! Cooking or soaking in water removes the sting. Nettle is a forager's super food, with high levels of calcium, magnesium, manganese and iron. You can make a fresh nettle tea or find a bunch of cooking recipes using nettles. Medicinally, stinging nettles are used to help relieve allergies, reduce joint pain and arthritis, and treat eczema and a number of other ailments.

Yarrow: This is a wild herb with feathery leaves and small white clustered flowers. It can be found just about everywhere in the Northern Hemisphere. You can use the young leaves in salads, soups or substitute for tarragon in recipes. Medicinally, the leaves are made into a poultice to apply on wounds and rashes. It is also made into teas and tinctures to help reduce fevers, fight colds, seasonal allergies and menstrual cramps.

WHEN LIGHTNING STRIKES

Head indoors with your pets if you can, and don't use electrical equipment like computers and corded phones. Unplug devices that aren't on a surge protector and could be short-circuited. Don't come in contact with water coming out of your pipes—no showers, hand washing or doing dishes. Stay away from windows and doors. Don't lie or lean on concrete floors or walls, as lightning can travel through the rebar in concrete structures. If you can't go indoors, get in a car with a roof and roll up the windows (make sure you aren't touching anything metal in the car). If you are stuck in an open area, move away from tall structures and trees and crouch low to the ground (don't lie on the ground—you want to make as little contact with the ground and be as low as possible). If you are with a group of people, spread out and crouch down to avoid multiple injuries from a single strike.

HOW TO PERFORM CPR

Knowing CPR could definitely come in handy in the country. First responders can take a long time to arrive, so knowing how to resuscitate someone if they aren't responsive could end up saving their life. First, if the person is not responsive, not breathing or not breathing normally, call 911 and put your phone on speakerphone next to the victim. Second, begin chest compressions in the center of the chest. Pump hard and fast 30 times at the rate of 100 to 120 per minute. Third, tilt their head back, lift their chin and pinch their nose closed. Cover their mouth with yours and blow two breaths (blow with enough force that their chest rises). Fourth, repeat thirty reps of pumping with two breaths until help arrives or they become responsive and start breathing normally.

MOUNTAIN LIONS, TIGERS AND BEARS—OH MY!

Okay, so chances are you will never encounter a tiger living in a rural area, unless you stumble across a depressing "wild cat" tourist trap, but you are leaving the concrete jungle and reconnecting with the natural world—you can't be naïve to the fact that you will be living amongst insects and creatures that could cause you harm. Knowing what to do and how to react will help you keep your cool, no matter what animal, serpent or arachnid encounter you may have in the natural world.

HOW TO TELL IF AN ANIMAL HAS RABIES

Sadly, you can't tell if an animal has rabies just by looking at it. A test is the only way to know for sure. Animals with rabies often foam at the mouth because rabies causes them to make more saliva than they normally produce. Another warning sign of rabies is an animal acting strangely. The most common behavior of an animal with rabies is being overly docile or tame, allowing you to get closer to it than you would normally be able. Other rabid animal symptoms are hostility and aggression. The best course of action if you think you have encountered a rabid animal is to go inside and immediately call your local animal control officer. They may even be able to tell you if there have been any other rabies outbreaks nearby. If your pets aren't up to date with their rabies shots, take them immediately into the vet and get them checked out. If you are bitten or scratched by an animal that might be rabid, clean the wound with soap and water, douse with rubbing alcohol and seek immediate medical attention.

WHAT TO DO IF YOU RUN INTO A MOUNTAIN LION

Mountain lions (also known as cougars) can be found all over North America. They mainly prey on deer, coyotes and raccoons, but they also love to snag a juicy sheep or goat from time to time so they are considered a dangerous menace to livestock farmers. The first time I saw a mountain lion in the wild I was shocked at how muscular and large it was. While human cougar attacks and deaths are rare, it is important to know how to respond if you encounter one of these giant cats. First, do not run, as cougars like to ambush prey from behind and will consider you an easy target. Stand your ground, maintain eye contact, make yourself look as big as possible and make loud noises. Open your arms and wave them above your head, spread your legs, yell firmly and loudly and clap your hands. Look around to make sure you aren't between the cougar and its cubs or prey. Back away slowly but continue to make eye contact, be loud, throw things and take up space. If you are attacked, fight back with all you've got. Use sticks, rocks, backpacks, etc.—whatever you have available—and try to protect your throat and neck.

WHAT TO DO IF YOU RUN INTO A BEAR

Bears attack fatalities are extremely rare. For the 750,000 black bears in the U.S., less than one person a year dies from a bear attack (black bears, brown bears and grizzlies). So just chill; chances are even if you run into a bear you are going to survive your encounter. Bears can be menaces; if you live in bear country, get ready to have your garbage cans rummaged through and strewn about. When I was growing up we had a problem with a black bear that would grab our trash can and tear up the mountain with it, leaving a path of mess behind her. Moving our garbage bins inside and getting a dog solved our bear problem. It is important to learn some bear mannerisms in order to be better prepared should you encounter a bear in the woods or on your property. First, bears generally want to avoid confrontation; although they might posture and pretend to be aggressive to avoid a fight (just like some of the loud mouth bullies you went to high school with), they are all talk. A bear standing on its hind legs is a sign of curiosity, not anger. It is important to stay calm and, whatever you do, don't run! Bears are fast and they can and will outrun you.

When walking in the woods, make noise—talk, sing or carry a "bear bell" that will warn bears you are around so they can leave the area. Bears aren't always super aware, so it is important you make noise so they can be alerted of your presence instead of surprising them. If you encounter a bear, quiet your tone and speak to them in a calm manner. Stand tall, put your hands above your head to look as large as possible and hold your ground. They might growl and do a couple of bluff charges to try and get you to run, but stay calm and stay in one place. Do not scream or run. The most dangerous place you could be is between a momma bear and her cubs so calmly look around to make sure there aren't any cubs around you. If there are, slowly move in a direction away from them. If the bear stays stationary, move slowly sideways and maintain eye contact with the bear until you have reached a safe distance. If a bear charges and makes physical contact, how you should respond depends on the type of bear you are dealing with. Black bears are timid and you should fight back by hitting them in their nose and face. You should only play dead when being attacked by a brown or grizzly bear.

SNAKEBITES

There were under 20 causalities in the roughly 7,000 snake bites reported in the U.S. last year. I'm telling you this because it is important to remain calm if a snake bites you or someone you know. Chances are they/you will be just fine. If a snake bites you and you aren't sure if it is venomous, you should still follow these instructions. First, try to make note of what the snake looked like and don't try to catch it. All poisonous snakes in the U.S., with the exception of the coral snake, are pit vipers. Pit vipers generally have a wide triangular head with an elliptical pupil. Not that you are going to gaze longingly into the snake's eyes but there you go. Coral snakes are colorful with red, yellow and black bands. If you are bitten by a snake and are unsure what kind it is, call 911 or have someone rush you to the hospital (don't drive yourself as the venom might make you dizzy or impair your eyesight). Immediately take off all tight clothing and jewelry before swelling starts. Try to keep the bite below your heart and stay calm (slow your heart beat down) to prevent venom from moving quicker through your body. Wrap the wound in a clean, untreated bandage. Do not try to suck the wound. Do not use a tourniquet. Do not apply ice. Do not try to cut the venom out of the wound. These are all widely spread myths about how to treat a venomous bite. Antivenin is the only way to treat venomous snakebites. Snakebite kits can help give you more time to get to a hospital but they can't fully treat a bite. Get yourself to a hospital.

SPIDER BITES

Let's be honest, for most of us spiders are scary. I once put my foot in my shoe only to feel something large crawling around and when I pulled my foot out there was a giant wolf spider on my sock. Needless to say, I tend to shake my shoes out now before putting them on. Spider bite symptoms range from very minor to severe. They can cause pain, itchy rashes, muscle pain and cramping, nausea, vomiting, chills, fever, difficulty breathing and blistering. Spider bites are common, but dying from a spider bite is very rare. In the U.S., the brown recluse (brown spider with fiddle on its abdomen) and the black widow (black or brown spider with a red/brown hourglass on its abdomen) are the two main spiders you have to worry about. If you get a bite and are able to identify one of these two spiders as the culprit, follow these instructions and seek immediate medical attention. If you don't know what type of spider it was, follow these instructions and seek medical attention if your systems worsen. First, clean the bite with soap and water. Second, ice the wound or apply a cool washcloth compress. If you suspect that a poisonous spider bit you, elevate the bite area and seek medical help.

EMBEDDED TICKS

Ticks can be found all over the world. They range from the size of a pin to sunflower seed. Their bites are often harmless, but they can spread both debilitating and deadly diseases so it is important to take ticks seriously. Ticks love to hide in tall grass, piles of leaves and in trees. Living rurally, it is nearly impossible to avoid them. You most certainly will need to remove your share of ticks if you have pets. Although ticks can be found year-round, they typically reproduce in the spring (+ 40°F [4°C]). Tick nymphs can be tiny and very difficult to see. In the U.S., there are five main types of ticks: black-legged or deer tick, American dog tick, brown dog tick, lone star tick and the Rocky Mountain woods tick. All of these ticks can spread various diseases to humans but the deer tick is the only tick known to spread Lyme disease. If you live in an area with ticks, get in the habit of doing a tick check before you go to bed. Inspect all crevices and in your hair, as ticks like to go to dark places to feast. If you find an embedded tick, use fine-tipped tweezers to grasp the tick close to the skin's surface. Pull with slow, even pressure because you want to try and get the whole tick and not leave the head of the tick behind. Leaving the head may cause infection, so if it gets separated, try to grab it with the tweezers after you remove the body. Put the tick in a plastic bag and save it for the next two weeks (if you develop any symptoms, you can have the tick tested for disease, which will make diagnosis and treatment easier). Clean the wound site with soap and water and then rub with rubbing alcohol. A black-legged/deer tick needs to be embedded for 24 hours before they can give you Lyme disease but scientists don't know how long they need to be embedded to transmit other diseases. The most important thing you can do after removing a tick is to save it and monitor your health for the next month. If you begin to develop a rash, lesions or a bullseye red target around the bite, or if you experience chills, fever or joint pain, seek immediate medical attention.

SKUNKED REMEDY

If yourself, your children or your pets get sprayed by a skunk it is definitely not life threatening but it can certainly ruin your day. It is at least a yearly event at our house to de-skunk our dog and I have had a few close calls myself. Skunks love living in crawl spaces and under sheds, which can make surprise encounters a routine occurrence. Forget what you heard about tomato baths, they are messy, smelly and the smell continues to linger afterwards. The best remedy to cure a skunking is to use this recipe, originally given to us by our vet for our dog but used by our friends successfully after their own personal encounters, to kill the stink for good.

INGREDIENTS
1 bottle feminine douche (the smelliest kind they have)

1–2 cups (240–480 ml) blue liquid Dawn (to remove the oil)

1–2 cups (240–480 ml) the smelliest shampoo you can find (Garnier Fructis works well)

1 package baking soda

DIRECTIONS
Combine all the ingredients in a bowl and make a thin paste. Coat all over sprayed area and work into a lather. Rinse with warm water. Repeat one to three times if smell is still there.

IN CONCLUSION

So there you go. I hope you now have a much better understanding of how to stay alive in the country, no matter what is thrown at you. Making a plan and being prepared for natural disasters is a step towards being more self-reliant. Living rurally, you never know when disaster might strike or how long you will need to survive on your own before help arrives. Knowing you have the skills and tools necessary to take care of yourself and your family gives you piece of mind, even when the skies darken or the earth begins to shake. Becoming self-sufficient and developing survival skills will help you weather any storm, disaster, animal attack or unexpected crisis thrown your way. Even though small communities rally together in emergency situations, first you need to know how to protect and take care of yourself because you can't rely on your town to take care of you.

MAKING THAT MONEY

Earning a living in the country

"Finding sustaining work in the countryside can be very, very hard. I tried to start a branding agency here in the beginning with some friends and everyone wanted to pay us in raw milk and chickens. You can't put those in your bank account."

— *Courtney Maum, Writer*

Perhaps one of the most important make or breaks for ex-city folks moving to the country is finding a way to make a living. There is a common misconception that living in the country is cheaper than living in the city. While in some cases this can be true, oftentimes people are shocked to find out that their basic essentials cost about the same amount as they did in the city. Chock it up to lack of competition; if there is only one grocery store and one oil provider in your area, they are able to set the prices. Don't be fooled by the promise of a mortgage or rent that is less than half of what you pay in the city, because what you save to keep a roof over your head will be absorbed by a myriad of other things, including maintenance, heating oil (or AC depending on where you live), gas for your car (you'll be driving a lot more than in the city) and many other unexpected expenses. Having a steady income is essential for anyone considering living rurally. Even homesteaders have things they have to spend money on; there is no way to live entirely off the land, especially in the beginning.

In this chapter, I'll break down the three ways to "make that money" in the country. First, telecommuting, what many consider the dream situation—keeping your city job (and city salary) and working remotely. Second, finding a position (or several) in your new locale. Third, building your business and working for yourself. We will go over the pluses and minuses for every option, along with strategies for success. The tips we'll go over are fluid and can really be applied to any of the three categories. Many ex-urbanites will go through several career changes after they relocate, so following the guidance outlined in this chapter will help no matter what direction you initially take. No route is better than the others; it really depends on the person, what your goals are for the future, what your work style is and the community you are moving into. Now, let's figure out how to make that money living rurally.

KEEPING YOUR CITY JOB OR TELECOMMUTING

TELECOMMUTING—LIVING THE DREAM, SOMETIMES

As we discussed briefly in the first chapter, one of the best ways to ensure a stable transition to country life is to take your city job with you or find a telecommuting position before you leave the city. A higher city salary can help you offset your initial start-up costs, especially if you take the leap and buy property or a house straight away. We are lucky that we live in a time where many companies give employees an option to work remotely. A *TIME* magazine study recently found that 45 percent of the U.S. workforce now has a job that is suitable for full- or part-time telecommuting. While not all industries are the same, many businesses are starting to realize that their productivity doesn't decrease when their employees telecommute and it can save them money, as they don't need to pay for additional office space. All this said—it is surprising how many people are still fearful to broach the subject of working remotely with their boss.

First, it is best if you have been working for your company for at least a year. Put the time in and make yourself invaluable. Help out on projects and work that you aren't put on, burn the midnight oil, show that you are a committed and hardworking member of the team. Second, put together a telecommuting proposal to share with your management team. Outline your day-to-day responsibilities, how your role would change (if it would), include percentages for travel, meetings, calls, etc. Detailing the specifics of your future home office, as a designated and connected workspace, is appealing to companies.

If they are hesitant, ask if they would be willing to do a trial run. Work from home for a month in the city and let your company monitor your productivity. This will also help determine whether working remotely is a good fit for you, as it isn't for everyone. Be aware that once you leave the city you might decide that the demands of your city job no longer fit your new lifestyle, but at least you'll have the security of a steady paycheck to aid your rural job search or to help fund the start-up costs for your new business. Also, know that job security is never guaranteed; make sure you still have some money saved up before making the move just in case you lose your job after you've made the leap.

If your current job isn't willing to let you work remotely, start the hunt for a telecommuting position before you make your move rurally. A city address on your resume can mean higher salary offers from potential employers. You don't have to tell them you plan on moving unless part of your position requires in-person or frequent travel, as your travel expenses may prove problematic in the future. Even if you are hired for a telecommuting position with a new company, stick it out for at least six months for the training process, to make yourself invaluable and to make sure it's a good fit for you long term.

IS YOUR JOB THE RIGHT JOB FOR TELECOMMUTING?

Before moving to a small town in Maine, I ran product launches for an international phone company in Seattle. Although my job was almost 75 percent travel, and I worked from my apartment and coffee shops the other 25 percent of the time, continuing that position living in Maine wasn't an option because the closest airport was an hour and half drive away. Leaving my job and moving without any career prospects was terrifying. Once I arrived in Maine and received a few depressingly low offers from local companies, I realized that I could have continued working for my company had I asked to transfer departments. Your location can be very important if you want to keep your city job. Even if your company allows you to work remotely, they may also require you to come for meetings or conferences every so often. If you already travel a significant amount for work, you will need to live close to an airport. Ask yourself if you would be okay leaving your new rural location for weeks at a time. Take time to think about your options and the lifestyle you want for yourself in the country. If your city job doesn't currently allow enough free time or flexibility, it might not be a good fit for you when you leave the city behind.

WORKING REMOTELY—SET YOURSELF UP FOR SUCCESS

Working remotely in the city can be much less isolating than working from a rural area. There are many benefits for urban telecommuters that rural telecommuters don't have. In a city one can attend industry events, have occasional face time with colleagues and/or clients and pop into a coffee shop and have instant community with other freelancers and remote workers. In the country, it is usually just you, a computer, Wi-Fi and a cell phone. Many new rural telecommuters feel cut off and isolated. There are several ways to help set yourself up for rural telecommuting success; get your pencil ready.

BOOKEND YOUR WORK DAY WITH A COMMUTE

This might seem like a crazy concept, after all you probably left the city for a better quality of life and one of the top things on your list is "no more traffic!" and "zero commute!" Think for a minute though what that commute offered you— uninterrupted time to gear you up for your workday and then to decompress from the workday. Immediately switching on and off work mode doesn't allow this period of transition. Lucky for you, your "commute" time can now be spent walking down your road or through the woods. Walking at the beginning and end of your workday will not only make you much more efficient but it will also help you turn-off after a hectic day. By bookending your work days with a walk, you will be feeding another ex-urbanite desire, one that is constantly stated as one of the main things people miss when moving rurally: walking! Walking is at the top of most former urbanites list of things they miss the most about city life (walking, alongside decent coffee and anonymity). You get to kill two birds with one stone!

FIND YOUR PRODUCTIVE SPACE

Create a designated, productive and organized workspace. I worked from our kitchen table the first year of our business and as a result I found myself constantly distracted. There is always a new load of laundry that needs to go in or a floor that needs to be vacuumed. Rotating your workspace in a non-designated area can drastically reduce your productivity and remove the structured observance of your workday. I would start work early in the morning, hop back and forth between work stuff and home stuff and finally close my laptop at 9:00 p.m. I felt like I was working all the time, even though I probably only logged about five to six hours of actual

work a day. My solution came by designating a room with a door for my home office. It wasn't an easy transition; it requires a forced observance of routine to develop the habit. For three weeks, I forced myself to wake up, shower, do some exercise, go to my office, work until noon, eat lunch, work until 5:00 p.m. (or earlier if I finished my work for the day), close the laptop and leave the laptop in the work space. I immediately noticed a difference both in the quality of work I was producing and also an increase in my overall happiness. I spent my lunch breaks outside eating on a blanket or weeding the garden; I would return to my office refreshed and ready to power through the rest of the workday. I'm telling this story because I got it completely wrong when I first moved rurally. I wasn't working to live; I was still living to work—old habits die hard.

If your place is too small to set aside an entire room for your office or you don't have a door, add a divider to the space and keep that area clutter free and organized. Also, as we discussed in the previous chapter, make sure where you are moving in the country has access to high-speed Internet (you would be surprised how many rural places still only have dial up or slow satellite). If you can't get decent Wi-Fi and live away from your town center, look into office rentals in-town. Many rural places have offices or shared spaces available for rent at inexpensive monthly rates. If you took your city job with you, your employer might even be willing to pay for an office rental, as it gives them the peace of mind that you have a designated work space and separation from home life and work life. Many companies even like to see photos of your set up, so it is worth asking your employer when you have the telecommuting talk if they would be open to renting an office space for you. It would be even better if you brought office rental options to the meeting so they can see how serious you are about this move. Moving rurally might not make any sense to your colleagues and some will picture you "working remotely" from a hammock, drinking lemonade in your new country locale, so it is important to dispel these ridiculous assumptions and prove you won't be any less of an asset living outside of the city.

THE POWER OF LISTS

Another productivity tool for telecommuters is to break down your tasks each day and cut out all the busy work and aimless surfing online. We are all guilty of diving into the Internet black hole and clicking through photos of an old flame on Facebook. End your day and begin your day with a task list. You can use online tools, calendar reminders, or take my preferred old-fashioned approach and just write them down. I keep a yellow notepad on my desk specifically for the day's list of tasks and meetings. Once I cross off all the tasks for the day I feel no shame in leaving work early, doing yard work, playing fetch with my dog or getting an early start on dinner. Making a list at the end of the day is key, as everything is fresh in your mind and you know what tasks still need attention the following day. By revisiting your list in the morning, after you've gone through your emails, you can quickly prioritize and hit the ground running.

QUIT MINDLESS INTERNET SURFING

If you still find yourself getting off track and surfing online, you are not alone. This is such a common problem that many online tools have been created to put people's Internet surfing in check. If you are one of those people who can eat half a cookie and save the other half for later (I do not fall into this category) give yourself an allowance or window of aimless time. Schedule fifteen to twenty minutes of time to read online news, check social media, etc. Once your surfing time is used up, close your web browser and focus on the task at hand. For those of us who lack that level of willpower, never fear, here are some awesome tools you can use to curb your mindless Internet time.

Concentrate: A site-blocker for Chrome that allows you to set a timer to block specific sites. Simply add your time-sucking sites, set the timer and then get working.

StayFocused: A simple site-blocker for Chrome that allows you to enter your tempting time-wasting sites and allocate a maximum duration of time spent on them each day. When you've used up your time, the site is blocked for the rest of the day. Also, it makes it difficult to change the amount of time you've allotted yourself by requiring you to type a long paragraph verbatim, without making any errors. If you mess up, the entire box clears and you have to start all over again.

Leechblock: This robust plugin allows you to block certain websites for periods of time. For example, you can ban looking at Facebook on weekdays until 5:00 p.m. You can also block certain sites after you have visited for a certain amount of time. If you want to avoid over thirty minutes of Facebook stalking, Leechblock will block the site after you have hit your thirty-minute quota. The drawback is that this plugin only works on Firefox, so if you are really jonesing for some Internet surf time, you can be sneaky and switch to Chrome or Safari.

GET OFF YOUR PHONE

So now that you have your Internet browsers working for you and your mindless Internet surfing is under control, you are all good right? Wrong. A smartphone is a telecommuter and small-business owner's best friend but they can also be their worst enemy. Smartphones allow you to stay connected even when you aren't actively working at your desk. For new work-from-home country transplants, this means you can answer those pressing emails from your boss or clients while sitting in the doctor's office, hiking in the woods or running errands in town. It also means you have a way to cheat by using your device to waste hours scrolling through Instagram or Reddit. Luckily, tools have been created to help curb this mindless time wasting as well. My favorite is FocusOn. This tool blocks apps and websites on your smartphone for set periods of time. Even if you haven't made the move rurally yet, these tools to curb your aimless browsing time are worth their weight in gold. Not only will you stay focused and move through tasks quicker, but honestly what is to be gained by diving into the black hole of the Internet and winding up on a site rating celebrity babies in order of hotness?

BE AVAILABLE

The anxiety managers feel about allowing employees to work remotely is that they won't be as available or quick to respond to pressing needs. You can alleviate this anxiety by answering emails promptly, volunteering for new work and opportunities and checking in with your mangers and coworkers frequently. Using collaboration tools like Skype, Basecamp, Instant Messenger, Google Docs and the like, will allow for regular interactions and collaborations throughout the day. Many remote workers start their days with a video conference with their coworkers to go over the day's tasks. Giving your colleagues "face time" throughout the day keeps you an active and valuable member of the team. Just make sure you schedule these meetings when you're in your office and your office is clean and organized (at least in plain sight). Throwing on a "Skype blazer" or "Skype tie" can go a long way to solidify your telecommuter professionalism with your colleagues while working from home. I keep a "Skype blazer" handy on the back of my chair in my office for any last-minute video conferences with remote clients.

CONTINUE TO BUILD YOUR NETWORK

Just because you are working remotely, doesn't mean you shouldn't continue to attend industry conferences and off-site trainings. Remember that finding a job in the country isn't easy and just because you have a cushy telecommuting job now, doesn't mean you'll always have it. By connecting with people locally who work in the same industry as you, you not only are growing your social circle, but you're also continuing to grow your network of potential collaborators, mentors and mentees. You never know when those local industry contacts will come in handy. By hosting a dinner, mixer or collaboration night, you can keep fresh on current trends in your industry, learn what companies employ people locally that do what you do and make friends that you can commiserate and collaborate with in the future.

DON'T FORGET TO CHILL

This is the biggest mistake that so many new country telecommuting transplants make. Yeah, it's a bit of a catch-22 with "Be Available," but it's crucial that you give yourself breaks and a lunch hour. Remember, you moved for a better quality of life and being a slave to your computer won't allow you to build the life you imagined when you decided to leave the city. A foolproof method for ensuring you take breaks throughout the day is leaving a timer in a room away from where you work that goes off every two to three hours and reminds you to take a ten to fifteen minute break for yourself. Take a walk through the woods, weed the garden or just sit outside and gaze off into the distance. This will help reduce your stress levels and give your eyes a break from screen time. Any guilt you might feel, let it go, as workplace distractions and Internet surfing would gobble up much more time if you were still working in the city. Add lunch as a reoccurring event in your calendar so you don't accidentally work through it and end up hangry (hungry + angry) on a conference call. Remember, living rurally usually requires a lot more effort than living in a city. You will likely have a lawn to mow, creatures to take care of, meals to cook and lots of things to fix and maintain. If you continue to work long hours without breaks you might as well just go back to the city because at least there you can get take out and drink your sorrows away at a bar within walking distance to your house.

BRUSH YOUR TEETH AND NO PAJAMAS

Your style will inevitably change for practicality and comfort after fully transitioning to rural life but even if you decide that suspenders are the best invention ever, freelance and telecommuting experts all agree that working from home in pajamas is not a pattern to fall into. Beyond feeling tired and cooped up in your house, failing to take care of basic needs, like brushing your hair and teeth and putting on clean clothes, can lead to depression. Combine that with feelings of isolation and you have a recipe for disaster. The best way to avoid this tempting morning routine is to lay your clothes out for the day the night before. Many freelancers base their schedule around the day's weather patterns. If it's a sunny April day, you might be more inclined to wear something to work that can double in the garden or mowing the lawn on your lunch break. It honestly doesn't matter what you wear to work, just as long as you focus on continuing to take care of yourself and not falling into a slump.

THE PERILS OF SWEATPANTS—MY OWN EXPERIENCE

The first summer and fall I worked from home, I was really good about continuing with my morning routine before plugging in for the day. Then winter arrived and I didn't have any social plans that required me to leave the house for a few months. We were hit with several ice storms in a row and could only use our basement door to come in and out of our house as our front door had been blocked by a frozen snowdrift of epic proportions. I decided that my husband's uncle's grey Fila sweatpants from the 90s (yes, you read that right—only the most amazing sweatpants pass down through families) were the only article of clothing I wanted to wear. They resembled oversized genie pants, complete with a drawstring and pockets for snacks. For almost a solid month I would sleep, work, sleep, work in them. Although my dental hygiene remained steady, I went long stints between showers. I became utterly depressed, gained ten pounds and was totally inefficient during work hours. So utterly lost in my own life, I would troll social media for hours, looking at everyone's curated perfect city lives, complete with built-in city snow management and festive holiday cocktail parties. My sister came to visit that January and was shocked to find me a shell of myself—shuffling around the house in beanbag slippers, unwashed hair and those giant Fila sweatpants. She staged an immediate intervention; we went to an outdoor store to buy some thin thermal under layers so she could entice me away from the blanketed comfort of the genie sweatpants. I signed myself up at the local YMCA so I would be forced to leave the house every day to see other humans and get some exercise and I retired my sweatpants to special weekend and evening occasions like Game of Thrones marathons and camping trips. Only a week or so after bidding a tearful adieu to my security-blanket sweatpants, I started to notice immediate changes to my mood, productivity and outlook on life. Going to the gym in the morning helped me meet new people, invigorated me for a day of pushing pixels, and I was toasty warm in my under-layers. I couldn't imagine falling back into that routine as I know how utterly hopeless it felt. Wearing pajamas while working remotely might seem like a ridiculous and trivial thing, but take it from someone who knows, it isn't a pattern worth getting sucked into.

FINDING A JOB RURALLY

DO YOUR HOMEWORK

As we covered in the first chapter, finding potential job opportunities in the area you are considering is a crucial step if you are moving without a lot in savings and don't have the ability to coast for a bit while you look for work. Look at what companies and small businesses are based in the area you want to live. Schedule informational interviews before you make the move, as this will help you get a lay of the land and meet some of the movers and shakers in the area. If you are planning on moving to a place without much industry or local job prospects, do a 100-mile radius search, as driving a couple of hours a couple of times a month might be worth a steady income and (fingers crossed) health insurance. The saying "it's not what you know, but who you know" goes even further in rural areas when it comes to finding work. Expecting to find a job without networking in your prospective country locale will make your job hunt challenging.

THERE ISN'T AN APP FOR THAT

Sure, you might be able to find something on the tried and true LinkedIn, Monster or Craigslist, but usually these services aren't widely used outside of more populated areas. Finding work in the country requires you to put feelers out there, meet people, learn new skills, be willing to start at the bottom and step outside of your comfort zone. Go to the local watering hole at happy hour and make friends with the people coming in after work. Attend community gatherings, church services or join local professional guild organizations like Rotary, the Masons or the Elks Club. Find local community groups on Facebook or you may even have an actual physical community bulletin board in your town where people post signs for open positions, rentals, etc. When it comes time to send in a resume or apply, DO NOT EMAIL IT unless you are applying for a job at a large company with over 100 employees. It is a city mentality that one should email an application. Unless the posting specifically asks people to not inquire in person, you should definitely go in to drop off your cover letter and resume. Notice that I said cover letter and resume; a cover letter goes a long way and hiring managers might pass your application by if you don't have one. The cover letter also allows you to tell your story. If you are leaving New York City and moving to a tiny town in Pennsylvania, the hiring manager is going to want to know why you are making the move, if you are planning on relocating long term and why you are interested in the particular position you are applying for. When you drop off your application, make friends with the people who receive it, ask them what they love about their jobs, the community, etc. Leaving a positive impression on whoever takes your application can go a long way in getting to the top of the stack of applicants.

Ashley, a hiring manager for a photography workshop school in a desirable small town in Maine says that snail mail is an excellent way to get her attention. Anyone who sends their cover letter, resume and samples in the mail are sure to get an interview as it shows her that they've put extra time in. Sought after positions in appealing rural areas often have many applicants of varying levels of experience. Stand out from the crowd by delivering your cover letter and resume in person or, if you are still living in the city, send it in the mail and then send a follow up email or call. Ashley hires many people based in urban areas and uses Skype in place of in-person interviews. Not sure if you interview well on video conferences? Practice with a friend or neighbor to make sure you feel comfortable and confident before your interview.

DRESS FOR SUCCESS

Do your homework before scheduling an interview with a perspective employer. Drive by your potential place of employment in the morning hours, see what time people arrive at work and observe what they are wearing. Overdressing or underdressing at an interview can be the kiss of death. If the workplace is casual, don't wear a suit and tie. If the workplace is business attire, dress accordingly.

Dressing for the position you are interviewing for might seem fickle but dressing too "city" can either entice or offend prospective employers, based on what they are looking for. Creative arts and new media positions allow more creative license for attire, while business managers and sales team openings usually require a more drawing inside the lines approach. Workplaces in rural areas, generally speaking, are more casual than their city counterparts.

BE HUMBLE

City credentials are usually enticing to rurally based companies, so you don't need to oversell yourself. Be humble about your achievements and let your work speak for itself. There are urbanite stereotypes in rural areas that everyone from the city is boastful and think they know how to do everything better than country folk. It's shocking how often this is validated by new arrivals. Don't perpetuate this stereotype, for the sake of every future country transplant; each one of us brings something new to the table. Focus on your strengths in the interview process and when you land the job be quick to lend a hand and slow to judge. Even if you were a corporate "rock star" (ugh, that term gives me the chills) in your city life, it doesn't mean your previous work methods and style will gel at your new company. Be adaptable and take time to understand the process at your new place of work before suggesting ways to streamline, improve efficiency, etc.

FLEX TIME

One strange thing about the transition of living in a city to living rurally is that very few people in the country work a standard 8:00 a.m. to 5:00 p.m. job. Changing your expectations and societal norms of what you think a career looks like is a first important step in finding and securing a job that allows for the better quality of life you are seeking. Sure, there are still people who work at banks, in retail and the like, that observe the standard forty-hour work week, but lots of folk's work schedules allow for much more flex time to attend to the many things you need to spend time on living rurally. Don't get stuck in a job that doesn't allow you time to do the things you need to do. The town dump is usually only open during business hours, many stores close by 5:00 p.m., some schools require parents to pick up/drop off and without flexibility in your day, you don't have time available to actually enjoy this new life you are creating for yourself. Even if you're interviewing with a company that observes a more structured schedule, ask about flex time and if they are open to employees working from home a day or two each week.

THE JOYS AND PITFALLS OF SEASONAL WORK

Don't be afraid to wear many hats, work many jobs and/or work seasonal jobs. Many people in rural areas work several different jobs to make ends meet. Working several jobs throughout the year can add variety to your life, introduce you to new people and give you more control of your schedule. In colder areas, a lot of the plow truck drivers work in landscaping in the spring, summer and fall. In tourist towns, people make most of their income for the year working in tourism during the busy months. Some rural residents travel part of the year for work so they can spend their favorite months of the year back home without needing to work odd jobs to pay the bills. Farmers in northern climates work part time jobs in the lean winter months to get by. This is not something to snub your nose at, as it can be really wonderful to switch things up every couple of months. The main pitfalls of seasonal and multi-job employment are usually lower wages, no benefits and lack of job security. You never know if the restaurant or ski resort will be hiring your position the following year. Staying in contact with your manager and staying in the know if your hiring manager leaves will strengthen your odds of creating a consistent schedule of seasonal work.

TWO STEPS FORWARD, I TAKE TWO STEPS BACK

It can be a difficult pill to swallow but preparing yourself to take a step back in your career or even starting from scratch is something people thinking about leaving the city should consider. Ask yourself if your current career path is fulfilling, and if you can see yourself continuing to do your existing job in the next five/ten/fifteen years. If you are unsure, exploring other options in the area you're planning on moving to is a good exercise. Many people change their careers when they leave the city—both because their existing career doesn't exist where they are moving and sometimes because they are ready for a change. You will likely be taking a pay cut when getting hired rurally, so it is a good opportunity to transition to a job that is a better fit or is more fulfilling for you long term—it also helps cut the sting when your job offer comes in lower than expected.

LEARN NEW SKILLS

If there aren't any opportunities available in your current profession and you are ready for a change, moving rurally can be an excellent excuse to learn skillsets for a new profession. Enroll in night classes in the city before you make the move. If you've already moved, look for adult education classes available at local city colleges or high schools. There are many free and subscription-based online learning tools that can teach you anything from web development to medical assisting. Also, the prevalence and esteem of online universities and certification programs has increased tenfold in recent years—giving you the tools necessary to work towards a career change at your own pace, no matter where you are based. If you have always wanted to work with your hands, this is your opportunity—inquire with local tradesmen about apprenticeships. Apprenticeships are usually paid, unlike internships, and can last anywhere from a few months to several years. If you decide to go this route, make sure you've saved a little nest egg before making the move, as your apprenticeship wages will likely be a fraction of what you made previously.

FOOLPROOF PROFESSIONS

There are some careers that are frequently needed in rural areas that offer a living wage and sometimes even benefit packages. Engineering, construction, health care, finance, IT, legal services and education all are good bets for people looking for work in these industries in the country. Another growing need in rural areas is eldercare as the baby boomer generation is headed towards retirement and rural areas tend to have a higher concentration of older populations. By starting the job search early in the general area that you want to move to, you can gage professional needs by searching local job posts and companies for open positions. Some companies and businesses looking for qualified candidates will be willing to pay your relocation costs or even pay for certification or additional training needed for the job, so securing a job before you move can potentially save you hefty moving fees or continuing education expenses.

LEVERAGE YOUR CITY CONTACTS

Just as you would if you were looking for a new position in the city, leverage your contact list for leads on jobs in your field. Ask colleagues, clients, family and friends if they have any people, company or job leads in the area you are considering. You'd be surprised how small the world can be once you plant the seed of your future move in the ears of others. If there is a company or business you want to get hired at in the community you're moving to, check LinkedIn and see if you share any first or second level contacts with people who work there. Spreading the word about your upcoming move may open up telecommuting or contract opportunities you never expected.

MAKING YOUR OWN WORK
STARTING YOUR OWN BUSINESS

A path many new country arrivals take, either out of desire or necessity, is starting their own thing. Working for yourself can be both rewarding and incredibly disappointing. Running your own business requires you to take the reins and depend on yourself to build the foundation, scale at a steady pace and, above all, make enough of a living to get by. I have seen firsthand many new arrivals start their own business only to fail in the end for numerous reasons. Working for yourself is not easy, but the feeling at the end of a successful day cannot be compared. If you are moving to an area without any job prospects, starting your own business might be the only way you can make this new life in the country work for you. That being said, don't rest on your laurels in the city before you go. Start writing your business plan, begin building a foundation for the future and establish a client/customer/ readership base before you make the leap. Be prepared to work long work hours, weekends, and sacrifice taking vacations during the first five years.

BUILD THE FOUNDATION BEFORE YOU MOVE

Just a few months after Ashley Yousling and her family relocated to the Bay Area, the company she worked for was acquired by Apple. Her three-block commute was now a one and a half hour commute to their headquarters in Silicon Valley. A new mom, Ashley was tired of sacrificing so much time away from her young son. She asked herself a hard question, "What do I want to do with the rest of my life?" She kept coming up with the same answer: leave the city and build a fiber company in Idaho. A self-proclaimed planner, Ashley wasn't one to jump into anything without building a foundation for success. On her weekends, she would take trips outside the city to learn from sheep farmers and fiber experts. In the evenings, she worked diligently to build her future business. Ashley began by starting Woolful, a weekly podcast interviewing knitters, spinners and fiber folk. Woolful's following grew and she launched an online store offering specialty wool and knitting patterns. A year after launching Woolful, Ashley and her husband bought a farm in Northern Idaho. She left Apple and started a job at a San Francisco tech start-up that offered her more flexibility and the option to work remotely part of the time. Most weekends, the young family would make the painful sixteen hour drive from San Francisco to Idaho. They spent their weekends repairing fences, acquiring sheep and building their future yurt home. Ashley's city salary was essential to surmount the compiling expenses associated with constructing their rural dreams. Two and a half years after launching Woolful, Ashley has fiber contacts all over the world, thousands of subscribers and steady yarn sales on her website. These successes allowed her to make the leap and move full-time to Idaho. Ashley still works remotely, but her plan is to leave her design job as soon as her fiber business is generating enough of a profit to feel financially stable. Their new rural locale doesn't have any decent-paying job prospects, so she doesn't feel comfortable leaving the success of her new business up to chance. By chewing off bits at a time and staying the course, she has been able to construct a sturdy foundation for her business, move full-time to her farm and grow a community of people around the world that are cheering her on as her vision for the future comes into focus.

STARTING A BUSINESS AFTER YOU'VE MOVED

If you are already in the country working for others and wanting to start your own thing, never fear, lots of people make the move before they decide they want to build their own business. In many ways, already living in your new rural locale can be a benefit as you are better plugged into your community and have a much better understanding of the public needs and wants.

WHAT'S MISSING?

All community-facing businesses require a dedicated customer base, no matter if you're a farm stand, interior designer, marketing consultant or a shoe shop. The number one reason new businesses fail in rural areas is that they can't quickly establish loyal patrons. Don't start a consignment store or breakfast diner if there are already several within a 25-mile radius. The first thing anyone considering going into business for themselves should do is get a lay of the land and consult the experts. What is your community lacking? What does it desperately need? Put yourself in the shoes of the local consumer, as many ex-urbanites have a different idea of what their new locale is missing. I can't tell you how many restaurants and shops I've seen go under in our tiny community. Even if you live in a seasonal area where city folks come in droves for several months out of the year, you are still going to need the support of your local community to get you through the quieter months. Go visit your business development or planning board, attend a Rotary meeting or plan a mixer with local business owners to brainstorm with them what they think would be a valuable addition to the town.

WHAT DO YOU KNOW? WHAT CAN YOU LEARN?

What do you love doing? What is your passion? What can get you through long tedious days and slim months and still keep a smile on your face? Ok, got it? Great. No? That's okay, take time and work for someone else until you figure this out. Now go find ten people based in rural locations that are doing what you want to do and interview them. How did they build their customer base? Do they make enough money to pay their bills or do they have the help of a second steady income stream? What do they offer that has been the most profitable? What do you still need to learn so you have a diverse enough skillset to build to a strong following? By reaching out to other small business owners, you can set realistic goals and learn from their missteps and mistakes. You can also find friends and mentors to help guide you on your journey. Mentorship isn't just a corporate thing; I know many farmers, artists and tradespeople who rely on the wise guidance of mentors.

GETTING STARTED, ONE CHANCE FOR FIRST IMPRESSIONS

No matter what kind of business you are trying to get off the ground, it is important to put your best foot forward and kick things off with a bang. This requires putting the time in and getting all your ducks in a row before you open your doors. Write a mission statement and business plan, design a logo, website and business cards and get your social media game on point. If you are developing a product(s) for sale, make sure your packaging is well designed, price point established and vendors are lined up. If you are opening a store or restaurant, have a soft open with local press, small business owners and patrons. Make sure your employees are well trained and prepared for a busy opening month. These seemingly small details can make or break new business ventures because in small communities you don't have a second chance to make a good impression. In the city, it is easier to fumble in the beginning and find your stride later because your businesses maintain a relative anonymity with new patrons. In a small town, everyone talks and if you fall flat your first couple of months out of the gate, it is difficult to win back support of potential customers.

DON'T THINK SMALL—IMPORTANCE OF SOCIAL MEDIA

Just because you moved to a small community doesn't mean your new business should only cater to a local audience. Leverage your city contacts, friends, ex-clients, etc. for opportunities, direct sales or press attention. By diversifying your customer base and casting a wide net, you can avoid seasonal slumps and maintain "city" prices for your services and/or wares. Landing a couple of jobs or sales with larger companies can allow flexibility to offer discounts to your local community without struggling to stay in the black. We now live in a time when social media helps a woman living in a tiny town of 200 people develop a loyal following and sales for her soaps and apothecary products all over the world. There is absolutely no reason why small business owners shouldn't learn how to use these free and valuable tools to their benefit—unless of course you are offering professional geographically based services like accounting, legal or the like. Every small town clothing shop, knitter, potter, designer, etc. can expand their client/customer base by following these few simple pieces of advice.

INSTAGRAM

Curation is key: Take nice photos, put them in a thoughtful order and write nice captions. This sounds easier than it is, believe me. Most rural Instagrammers who've built a strong following take photos on a real camera and then transfer them to their phone. Taking nice photos on a smartphone doesn't have the same quality or depth of field options that a regular camera offers. Participation is important: You won't build followers unless you participate in the community built around your area of expertise. If you are a small farmer, follow other small farms and comment, ask questions and build community. Beyond growing your customer base, Instagram can also be helpful for advice, mentorships and building long-lasting friendships. Be quick to answer questions people post on your photos and don't go overboard with self-promotion.

Honesty is the best policy: Show some honest behind-the-scenes from time to time. Overly curated perfection is boring; add some reality to your posts to keep followers interested. Know that it takes time to build a strong group of followers; it won't happen overnight.

Promote others over yourself: FBF (Follow Back Fridays) is a great way to promote other Instagrammers that you appreciate or admire. Share the love and you will receive love in return.

FACEBOOK

Although some might feel Facebook is a dinosaur in the social media game, remember, people are often a bit slower to adapt to new media in rural locales. Having a Facebook page is essential for all small business owners—no matter the service you are offering your community and beyond.

BLOG

A blog is an excellent way to communicate with your audience and build a strong customer base. Be aware though, blogging is no cakewalk—it takes time, dedication and writing/photography/web development skills. If you only think you can carve out the time to write a post every month or so, it might not be a good marketing tool for you. With the advent of Instagram, many people have abandoned their blogs and focused on Instagram as their main engagement tool. The benefit of blogging is some bloggers are able to develop a wide readership base and incorporate paid advertising and sponsorships to offset their expenses. Sometimes a blog can start as a marketing tool for a business and then grow to actually become the business. It is important though to be realistic and ask yourself if you want to devote the time needed to grow an audience, research, write posts, etc.

SLOW AND STEADY

Adjust the instant gratification of your city brain and pace yourself for slow and steady growth. In the country good things take time to flourish; there are very few overnight successes. It can take years to get established and build an unwavering business. The first few years you might barely break even or not turn a profit at all. Rather than get discouraged, set benchmarks for attainable growth each year and work hard to reach those goals. Be practical and smart about your initial start-up costs. Do you really need the latest computer or will your old laptop work until you start turning a profit in year two? Do you need employees right away or can you man the ship for a couple of years before you are able to afford additional help? Can you find local high school or college students interested in interning? Be smart about your bottom line, adjust and adapt when things aren't working, and don't expect to break even in your first year. You can always make improvements as you go, while it is important to make a good first impression, find inexpensive workarounds in the beginning and upgrade as your business grows.

TRADE ECONOMY

Perhaps one of my favorite parts of rural living is the prevalence of a trade economy. Farmers trade with other farmers for items they don't grow or raise themselves. Carpenters trade renovations for orthodontic care for their children. Graphic designers trade web design for credit at local restaurants. Sometimes trade can be better than getting paid. After launching our graphic design and photography business, my husband and I did loads of full and partial trade projects to 1) Help build our portfolio 2) Help get the word out about our business and 3) Get (what felt like) wonderful free things and services from other small businesses. We traded web, logo design and photography services for chickens from a local farm, legal services, acupuncture, restaurant credit and Pilates classes. The benefit of trade is that usually both parties feel like they are getting a wonderful deal. It is important to ensure there is clear communication before any trades are agreed to and that everything is ironed out ahead of time so there isn't any miscommunication along the way. Also, if someone offers to trade for something you wouldn't normally want/need, don't feel obligated to agree, even if you have done lots of trade with others in your area already. It is important that whatever you are trading your services or products for is something that you want, otherwise it won't feel mutually beneficial and can lead to resentment. Our trade projects are some of the work that we are proudest of. Many projects we've taken on for trade are with small businesses that might not be able to afford our design and photography hourly rates. By establishing a trade, we are able to work with great little businesses and help them work towards their own sales and marketing goals. It feels amazing to help other small businesses grow and get free acupuncture to boot! Trade is magic, don't be afraid to explore the trade economy in your new locale.

BRIDGES—DON'T BURN THEM!

Never has "the customer is always right" been such an absolutely-must-follow piece of advice. It is much easier to blacklist difficult customers or clients in the city, as you have a never-ending supply of new patrons you can appeal to. In the country, forget it. One disgruntled person could literally be the catalyst for the failure of your business. Be consistent, be kind and don't show your teeth even if someone is particularly painful to deal with. If you are running your own professional or consulting services, make sure you develop a clear and concise contract where everything is in writing before you start a project. Remember, you might have to play the role of educator, as the people hiring you may have never hired someone to do PR, video production, accounting, etc. for them before. It is important that they clearly understand what your role is, what specifically you are delivering and the cost of your services. You don't want anything to be left to speculation if things take a turn for the worse. If something goes wrong, as painful as it might be, suck it up and make it right, even if that means eating some costs or working beyond what was originally agreed to. If you have a negative experience with a client or customer, make sure that by the end of the project they are happy and feel like you went out of your way to make things right. Never spread your grievances about difficult people or projects to others in town, as word spreads fast and can be open for interpretation. Playing nice doesn't just apply to customers—it goes double for competitors. Even if you have solid competition from other small businesses, you need to make friends and play nice. You are all in this together and one misstep can land you a terrible reputation that will be difficult to shake. Also, you never know when competitors might send business your way if they are too busy or don't have the capabilities in-house to produce something they are hired for.

Okay, there you go, that was a lot of information on one of the most important steps towards developing a fruitful and happy life in the country. There are so many paths one can take when it comes to earning a living rurally but the key advice for success is consistent: be kind, be hard working, be available, be reliable, don't burn bridges and put yourself out there. As easy as that seems, adjusting to a slower pace and fewer options often makes for a difficult transition. Prepare yourself ahead of time, do your homework and, most importantly, be willing to adapt to your new environment.

THE LONG GAME

Enjoying the good life

"I think people automatically assume that life will slow down when you move to the country, but it doesn't. The country offers the framework for a slower life, but slowing down is always a daily discipline."

— Billy Jack Brawner, Photographer and Home Builder

Leaving the city and building a life in the country takes time, patience, creativity and determination. The first couple of years likely won't go as you had planned. You might make some missteps, or run into problems that feel insurmountable. Transitioning to country life is a long game; it is as much about the process as it is about the outcome. Once you've started to feel at home, you will look back fondly on those times where you were scratching your head looking for a solution or shuffling around your house feeling lost and you will laugh at your trials and errors. Take comfort in the fact that you are living in a time when convenience can be found anywhere. You can find work remotely, you can have instant access to free information about nearly anything you want to learn, and in just a few clicks you can buy any supplies you need without leaving home. I'm not saying you should rely entirely on these conveniences, as a majority of people leave the city on a quest to become more self-sufficient, but these conveniences can help you navigate your way and ease the challenges along your journey.

Don't expect to escape your problems and societal issues by moving to the country. People who come thinking they will be able to just change their environment and everything will fall into place inevitably fail. Eventually, you will find a tremendous inner peace with this new life you've built. Of the hundreds of people I've photographed and interviewed for Urban Exodus, over 95 percent of them, when asked if they would ever return to city life, respond with a spirited "No!" Not all of them were having an easy time, most still were in the midst of hitting road blocks and navigating their way through their new life, but they all realized that living rurally was exponentially better than living in the city. Returning to the natural world feeds an innate human desire rarely satisfied in the confines of the concrete jungle. When I asked farmer, activist and Back-to-the-Lander Eliot Coleman why some people stayed in the country while others only lasted a few years, he responded, "It's very simple, the ones who got into it as a reaction against the world they disliked didn't last, while the others who were in pro-action toward the world they wanted to see, did last. The positive action is stronger than the negative reaction. There is an old saying that you should choose your enemies carefully because you become more like them than anyone else. In positive pro-action you have no enemy, rather a goal you want to see realized."

LEARN TO PACE YOURSELF AND
ENJOY THE WORK AS MUCH AS THE REWARDS

Getting into the rhythm of your new country life means going with the flow and not being so task oriented that you never take time to sit on your porch and take in the scenery. Living rurally means that your 'to do' list will never be done—you will cross things off and add things on for the rest of your life. Learning to enjoy the good life means exactly that—you need to enjoy all things, both the hard work and the pay offs. Don't bite off more than you can chew and take it one step at a time. If the weather is amazing but you have lots of things you need to get done, take the morning to go for a hike and spend your afternoon tackling whatever needs your attention. Country living is the "Good Life" as long as you continue to balance work with enjoyment. Over time you might notice that your values have shifted, your overall health and well-being has improved, and your relationships, both with family and friends, have evolved. Living rurally gives you the opportunity to become a part of a community, learn to be more self-sufficient, reconnect with the natural world and allocate more time to pursue your passions.

THE MORE THE MERRIER

When you've settled in and begun enjoying the new life you've created, it is only natural to want to try and entice your city friends and family to make the move. Once you've found your stride, it's hard to imagine how you ever tolerated living in the congestion and chaos of an urban environment. Initially, most of my friends thought I was a crazy person for leaving a good job and life in the city to try my hand at country living. Now, after witnessing all of the positive changes in my attitude, my health and my newfound skills, they have come around and some have even started considering a country move themselves. Several city friends have recently made the leap, while others continue to daydream about going country. The best ways to convince your friends and family to leave the city is to open your home and have them visit. While they are there, take them to all of the outdoor and cultural activities your community has to offer. Leave a real estate booklet on the coffee table when they visit so they can see what housing options are available. Send them homemade or locally made gifts in the mail and keep friends and family updated on your daily triumphs and failures on social media. Heck, buy them this book! Be honest, don't overly sugarcoat your experience and explain both the complexities of the hard work required and the rewards. If a friend shows interest in leaving the city, be there for them and offer them words of wisdom and encouragement. It isn't an easy leap to make, but it's totally worthwhile.

ADDING PERSPECTIVE TO YOUR VALUE SYSTEM

"I speak less and am more contemplative before I do speak. We move more slowly and methodically through projects. I think this is very valuable—slowness. Everything I did in the city was rushed."

– Kate MacLean, Longest Acres Farm

Leaving the rat race and moving rurally adds perspective to what is really important in life. By spending more time alone in the quiet, without the constant distractions of the city, it is impossible to ignore your own inner monologue and you end up getting to know yourself much better than you did before. You can't run away or escape your problems in the country, so you will develop courage to face them head on. Space and quiet to think helps give perspective. Being forced to interact with the same people every day makes people more accepting, more tolerant and more forgiving. In the country, you are also much more intimately connected with life and death. When someone in the community dies, everyone attends their funeral, whether they were close with them or not. Both animals and people are constantly being born and dying in the country and being surrounded by these daily occurrences helps put the journey of life and what is really important in perspective. Money, power and acquiring things suddenly seem much less important than experiences and relationships.

I am the same person I've always been, but what I value and prioritize in my life has shifted. I was kind and considerate in the city, but I didn't go out of my way to make an effort with new people I met. I felt like the insular community I had built for myself was enough and I wasn't motivated to expand it. In the country, I am friends with a wider range of people—of all ages and from all walks of life. Being friends with a broader demographic has also made me much more aware and understanding. When problems arise or I encounter obstacles, I face them head on now instead of hiding from them. Before, I sacrificed my health and relationships to move forward in my career; I was living to work. Now I use my career to stay creative, engaged and support myself; I work to live. I don't feel the need or desire to live beyond my means. There is no longer a feeling of wanting to keep up with the Joneses. Living a life well lived feels more important now than the numbers in my bank account. Being more closely connected to the circle of life and the passing seasons has made me realize that life is short and shouldn't be misspent. The value shift I have experienced has been such a welcome byproduct of leaving the rat race of city life. I couldn't imagine defining myself by my job title anymore. I prefer to measure my worth by my kindness, good deeds, relationships and life experiences.

IMPROVING YOUR HEALTH AND WELL-BEING
"I was very short tempered in the city because I felt like things were eating away at my time that I had no control of. Moving to the country made me learn to be calmer and more patient in all facets of my life. It has eliminated so much stress and really improved my overall health and well-being."

– Richard Blanco, Poet and Writer

Living rurally can greatly improve your quality of life, including health and overall well-being. A country property requires more upkeep and maintenance and thus physical strength and endurance is often a byproduct of living outside of the city. Growing your own food and raising animals is like signing up for CrossFit—it requires a lot of exertion. You might think you are in good "gym" shape in the city, but spending a day hauling brush, raking leaves or digging a trench will immediately make you think otherwise. Eating locally sourced food and preparing meals at home instead of eating at restaurants is better for your waistline, energy levels, wallet and mood. In addition, according to many published studies, living outside of an urban center reduces your risk of anxiety, depression and other mental illnesses. Just being able to spend time outdoors can release natural mood enhancers in your brain. Human beings aren't meant to sit at a desk all day. Our bodies were designed to stay active and spend time outdoors. Living within the confines of a city can stifle your physical and mental health. Road rage, standing in lines, breathing recycled air, eating restaurant food…these are not conducive to a healthy lifestyle. Navigating your way through the woods while hiking is like a puzzle for your

brain—you pay attention to roots and obstructions, leading your way through instead of bumbling along. That is a great metaphor for country living in general—you play an active role in your health and well-being, and you can't rely on the infrastructure of a city to carry you through.

Although I gained ten pounds when I first moved to the country (which I blame on being depressed and wearing sweatpants every day), I now feel much healthier than I was in the city. My muscles are strong from working outside. My mind is clear from spending time exercising in, and exploring, the great outdoors. My body is nourished with food I grew and my friends raised. I cook most meals at home instead of relying on restaurants and pre-packaged Trader Joe's meals to feed me. My stress levels have gone down tremendously. The first thing city friends remark on when they come to visit is how relaxed and happy I am. I was never relaxed in the city. I had the temperament of a squirrel: running around feverishly collecting acorns for the winter. I used to have terrible anxiety and although I still battle with social anxiety, my overall constitution has immeasurably improved. I haven't let go of all of my type-A tendencies but I no longer burn the candle at both ends. At the end of a long, hard day I walk into the field behind our house and breathe deep, letting any stress float away. I just never realized how much I needed space, quiet and the outdoors to heal me and improve my well-being.

STRENGTHENING YOUR RELATIONSHIPS

"I believe people get to know people better in the country. People have more time to devote to relationships and friendships. My friends in New York were all so busy, we had big overheads to maintain and thus we had no time."

— Joyce Tenneson, Photographer

The country allows more time and space to nurture relationships—both with family and friends. Significant others in the country are more than just romantic partners—they are teammates. Beyond sharing love and laughs, you share workloads, navigate through uncharted territory and weather storms together. Over half of the people I've photographed for Urban Exodus work alongside their partners, so they also share the weight of providing for themselves and their families. Most families find that their relationships strengthen and evolve outside of the city as well. Parents are able to loosen their grip and let their children have more independence in rural areas. Letting a child be free and explore the natural world on their own helps instill confidence, curiosity and creativity. Beyond family relationships, friendships also are stronger in the country. People need people in the country, so they make time for friendships to blossom and grow. Although friendships can take time to establish, once you meet your posse, those friendships will stand the test of time. You can't write people off if you get into a disagreement; you have to learn to compromise and work through things because you can't avoid anyone in a small town. Relationships in the country endure; the people that fill your life will remain until you move or die.

Moving rurally has completely transformed my relationship. Before I moved to Maine, I worked 70+ hour weeks and only saw my significant other on weekends. Now my husband and I co-operate a business, teach photography workshops and generally do everything together. While this might not work for some relationships, it has only strengthened ours. Our communication continues to improve and evolve and I've learned when to take the reins and when to sit in the passenger seat. We are teammates. Neither of us could make this life we've built work on our own. We keep laughing and crying our way through the hard lessons we continue to learn. I couldn't imagine moving back to the city and only seeing him after work and on the weekends. This winter we are welcoming our first child and I feel at ease knowing that we already have figured out how to work as a team.

As for friendships, I never thought I would find such witty, thoughtful, smart and fun women to spend my life with. While I had a great group of friends in the city, I never felt the deep connection with some of them that I feel with most of my friends now. Chock it up to being so busy working and only spending time together in loud, dimly lit bars. Now it feels like my friends and I are dialed into one another's wavelengths. The moment I feel stressed or overwhelmed, a text comes in from a friend asking if I want to go for an afternoon walk or come over for a cocktail. I know that my friends here will always be there for me and I never feel nervous about asking for help. When one of my friends is struggling, the group rallies together to get them through it. Whenever there is conflict, it is proactively worked through, instead of being swept under the rug. In the country, friendships are for the long haul; I feel incredibly blessed to have found a group of friends that I can continue to make memories and grow old with.

BECOMING PART OF A SUPPORTIVE COMMUNITY

"Although it's not true that all people in small communities are more caring, the opportunity to care is more present when you are out of the overwhelming scale of a city. When my mother passed away, people we didn't know well left us whole meals on our porch. In a small community you are more tenderly aware of the lives around you, period."

— Kenzie Fields, Artist Rep

Becoming a member of a tight-knit community is a special thing. Communities look out for one another and come together during difficult times. Small communities are not without their drama and dysfunction, but living in a place with fewer people means that people are more in need of one another for camaraderie and support. In a time where the people feel more polarized than ever before, cities could learn a thing or two by observing how small communities function. Even if you don't agree politically, socially or religiously with your neighbors, they are still a member of the community and thus should be treated with the same respect and kindness as everyone else. Being a member of a small community means participating, offering a helping hand and being kind and respectful. You get back from your community what you put in; you can't just rely on others to do all the work and reap all the benefits.

The community I've found here in Maine is incredible. This community looks out for one another, is quick to lend a hand and is slow to judge. I was at first worried that everyone thought we were outsiders, but that was just because we didn't initially make an effort to participate or get involved. As soon as we put ourselves out there, the community welcomed us with open arms. Our neighbors are constantly giving us a hand and offering their guidance as we continue to grow and build our life here. Our baby's room is already filled with hand-me-down clothes, backpacks, a crib and the like, awaiting her arrival in the winter. These items came to us unsolicited, both from close friends and more distant acquaintances; our community is a lending library of love, knowledge and things. I never felt a sense of community living in the city. I had a group of close friends and acquaintances, but there weren't years and generations of history shaping and nurturing those relationships. Even though, at times, the lack of anonymity can be difficult, I can't imagine going back to being a nameless face in the crowd. I love walking through town, waving and greeting everyone I know. It feels good to be a part of something bigger.

LEARNING TO BE SELF-SUFFICIENT

"Everything from our meats, vegetables and breads are harvested, processed and made with our own two hands. We are canning, sewing quilts and clothes, knitting blankets and sweaters and making our own soaps. I feel like while the rest of the world is moving forward, we are taking a step backwards, but it's a good thing. The trades I am learning out here are skills that are vanishing. If we don't teach our children how to connect to the land and the art of self-sufficiency, this rich lifestyle will eventually become extinct."

– DeAnna McCasland, Homesteader and Photographer

As discussed in the previous chapter, great pride comes with learning to be more self-sufficient. Most people living in the city wouldn't last a few weeks without electricity, running water or access to a supermarket. In the country you don't have to be entirely self-sufficient, but mastering certain skills can both enhance your experience and ensure your survival in emergency situations. Nothing feels better than growing and raising your own food, making your own personal care products, chopping wood, building your own furniture and doing your own home and auto repairs. In the city, space and time constraints don't give people the opportunity to become more self-sufficient. Living rurally doesn't necessitate that you develop these skills, but living can be so much richer and more fulfilling when you embark on a journey of being more self-sufficient.

When I lived in the city I could barely keep a houseplant alive. I didn't know how to operate power tools, cook meals, grow food or honestly do much of anything. I outsourced everything I didn't know how to do. I have acquired, by practice, mentorship and osmosis, numerous new skills. I know how to sharpen chainsaw blades and operate a wood chipper. I've learned how to grow, harvest and preserve my own food. I know how to safely forage for wild food. I can dress a wound, perform CPR, and I know what to do should I encounter a bear, cougar or rabid animal (and now you do too!). Does this make me better than I was before? No not really, but it does make me more confident in my abilities and sure of myself. I know that if a natural disaster strikes, we will be able to weather the storm. We can fend for ourselves if we have to and that feels good.

RECONNECTING WITH THE NATURAL WORLD

"I appreciate the quiet here the most—both in terms of sound and distraction. When I am in the fields, I can literally hear the woosh of the wings of a raven as she flies above me. I know that there is an active coyote den in the woods to our east, a bear that lives on our northern hillside and a heron that enjoys our pond in the summertime. I know this all because they are my neighbors, and because we have the luxury to listen and watch as we live alongside them. That sort of attention to the natural world is impossible in the city."

– Nick Zigelbaum, Longest Acres Farm

Leaving the city allows you to reconnect with the natural world. The stars shine bright above you, the wind howls through the trees at night and various wildlife tromps through your yard. The constant hum of sirens, honking and jackhammering in the city is replaced with the symphony of Mother Nature as she crescendos in warmer months and diminuendos when it cools. Reconnecting with the natural world is a healing experience. Human beings were not meant to walk around on even concrete, eat food made in laboratories and sit for hours at a desk in a high rise building, hundreds of feet above street level with the AC cranking. There have been numerous studies conducted by universities and private research groups around the world that have found that reconnecting to the natural world improves health and well-being. Walking through city parks can have a similar effect for short periods of time, but there is nothing quite as healing as living immersed in nature.

Living in Seattle, I spent much of my free time getting lost in city parks. I didn't realize it then, but that was my body telling me how much I needed nature to heal my stress and anxiety. I never tried to cross country ski through a blanket of newly fallen snow, or plunge into icy cold ocean water, or climb mountains without a map handy; now I do all these things. It's not that I couldn't have gone adventuring more on my weekends but I wasn't bold enough or brave enough to navigate "weekender" traffic. It takes a lot of energy (and usually a car) to get out of urban metropolises on the weekend. While it took me a while to reconnect fully with Mother Nature, I now embrace her in all her glory, every season, not just my favorite times of year. The harbingers of each season make me giddy—the first snowflake of winter, the cheerful song of a returning bird in spring, the twinkle of summer's first firefly and the blush of fall's first leaf.

NURTURING YOUR PASSIONS

"In the country we are blossoming and making ten times more art than before…it's incredible."

— Jimmy Aceino, Illustrator and Musician

In the country, there are less structured things to fill your time. There are fewer happy hours, climbing gyms, art classes, shows and restaurants to go to. Shorter commutes and fewer distractions give people more time to nurture their existing and developing passions. Most people also find that moving away from the city gives them more space, both physically and mentally. The space allows creativity to blossom. Sure, you can make beer in your apartment building's basement or sign up for an adult art class, but you can't practice your drums or operate power tools at all hours. In the country, you have relatively free rein of your domain. If you want to stay up all night building a table, you can. The skill share in the country is incredible; people are more than willing to share their talents, skills and tools with you if you are interested.

Before moving rurally, I had completely given up nurturing my passions. I used to sing jazz, paint, draw, take pictures and write. Coming home from a stressful day at work in the city, I felt devoid of all creativity and would either go drinking at a bar with friends or get lost in the mindless activity of watching television. My art supplies were covered in dust in a box in my closet. Creativity is like a muscle; you have to exercise it to keep it in shape. If you let it go unused for too long, it shuts down. When I moved I suddenly had more time, more space and more incentive to explore my long-since-abandoned passions. Each morning before work I decided to do a one-hour art project. It was incredibly frustrating at first, but several months in I could see the progress; my creativity was returning. Starting the Urban Exodus project helped further nurture and reconnect me with my passions for writing, taking pictures and drawing. I would've never had the space, time or courage to nurture my passions in the city to the extent that I do now.

COUNTRY CONFESSIONS

"Life is life, with all its joys and pain, no matter where you live. And that is what's so beautiful about it."

– Melissa Coleman, Writer

No truer words could be spoken, nor could end this book so eloquently than those of best-selling memoirist Melissa Coleman. It doesn't matter where you choose to live. You can live in the country or live in the city and still have a beautiful life. For some, an urban metropolis has everything they want and need to live a full life. For others, cities fall short. You are the master of your universe. You can't escape all of your problems by changing where you live. If you feel stressed, overworked or depressed in the city, you need to get to the root of those issues before making any drastic life changes. Escaping to the country isn't going to cure all that ails you. Going country means committing to build a life for yourself that is different than the life you led in the city. You need to enjoy the hard work, surmount the obstacles you face and open yourself up to new experiences and new people.

This book offers a lot of detailed advice for making the move, adjusting to your new lifestyle and enjoying this new journey you've embarked on. Know that no one is a master. Perfection does not exist. Don't be fooled by *Martha Stewart* or *Country Living* magazine—those spreads are staged, primped and primed before making it into print. After four years I continue to stumble and, at times, fall flat on my face. I still have yet to develop a system to water my garden; I let the weeds get way out of control and by the end of August I somehow always end up gardening in slippers because I get distracted with things that need to be tended to on the way to the compost pile in the morning. The stairs on our back deck are rotting, all our trim needs to be scraped and painted and we have a to do list that feels nearly a mile long. And you know what? I'm totally okay with it.

I didn't choose the country; the country chose me. Looking back on my journey, I feel so lucky that one fateful night, five years ago, I met my partner in New York City (the same day he had signed papers on the farmhouse where we now live). Transitioning to country living was no cakewalk. But as someone who had only bucolic visions of what a post-city life would look like, I'm happy my hand was forced and I made the leap. I was brainwashed by the societal myth that opportunity and advancement only exists in the city. The rural exodus has been steady since the Industrial Revolution. Young people leaving family farms and businesses behind to find success in the city. My hope is that this book helps dispel that myth and reverse the trend. Living rurally, for me, is living the "Good Life." I could never return to city living. I'm happy to visit for a few days, for a taste of the culture and food that I miss and the myriad of other stuff that I really don't. Success can be measured a multitude of different ways. Although there are fewer high-paying steady jobs in most rural areas, opportunity can be found or created anywhere. I would've never been brave enough to start my own business in the city; lack of jobs in our area necessitated that courage. I owe a lot to the country. It healed me and put me on a path to pursue my passions. It made me realize that life is about the journey, not about the end result. It is hard to break the chains of convenience and the safety net of structure that bind you in the city, but I am here to tell you that it's totally worth it. It is time to ditch the city and go country! Join us!

ACKNOWLEDGMENTS

First, an enormous thanks to all of the wonderful folks I've photographed and interviewed for Urban Exodus. Thank you for opening your homes to me and sharing your triumphs and challenges. It has been an absolute honor to meet you, learn from you, commiserate with you, become friends with you and break bread with you. Thank you to my California family—Mom, Dad, Jackie, Claudio, Niko, Jenny, Devon, Michael, Giles, Joe, Sean, Paul, Kim and Colin. My Maine family—Jacob, Dottie, Liv, Ken, Olivia, Ichabod, Marilyn and Ola. To my lovey friends who went on brainstorming walks with me, let me read out loud to you, helped me edit, contributed stories, tasted recipes and modeled for me (you all know who you are—thank you a million times over!). Thank you to Marissa, Will and the amazing team at Page Street Publishing for making this book a reality—I couldn't have done this without you. I also want to acknowledge the incredible community in Midcoast Maine that has welcomed me with open arms. I couldn't ask for a better bunch of folks to call friends or a nicer place to call home.

ABOUT THE AUTHOR

Alissa Hessler is an art director, photographer, writer, illustrator and designer living in Midcoast Maine. She operates the website Urban Exodus, photographing and interviewing former urbanites across North America who left the concrete jungle for greener pastures. Alissa developed Urban Exodus after she moved from Seattle in 2012 because she wanted to create a place where people could learn from and be inspired by those who had left the city and moved rurally. In addition to Urban Exodus, Alissa co-operates Hessler Creative, a boutique branding and photography studio with her husband Jacob Bond Hessler and co-teaches photography at institutions across the country, including Maine Media Workshops and Santa Fe Photographic Workshops. When not working, she keeps herself busy playing with her insane terrier Dottie, singing to herself while working in the garden, thrifting for treasures, experimenting in the kitchen, exploring nature and doing art projects.

INDEX